GUIDE TO THE HISTORY OF MEXICO

GUIDE TO THE HISTORY OF MEXICO

A MODERN INTERPRETATION

ALFONSO TEJA ZABRE

Austin   New York
THE PEMBERTON PRESS
Jenkins Publishing Company
1969

Special Contents
Copyright © 1969
Jenkins Book Publishing Company, Inc.
1 Pemberton Parkway
Austin, Texas

ALFONSO TEJA ZABRE

Born December 23, 1888, at San Luis de la Paz, Guanajuato, Alfonso Teja Zabre was a typical Mexican scholar of the first half of the twentieth century. Although he studied law and received a degree in jurisprudence from the University of Mexico, he became one of Mexico's greatest historiographers, biographers, novelists, poets, sociologists, diplomats, and contributors to the field of jurisprudence. His accomplishments and contributions in each of these fields was more than casual.

Teja Zabre's career as a man of letters began in 1910 with the publication of a book of poetry. Half a century later, he had published twenty-three books on poetry, literature, sociology, jurisprudence, history, three biographies, and three novels. Of his biographies, the ones on Morelos and Cuauhtemoc are outstanding. In historiography, his *History of Mexico* and *Guide to the History of Mexico* are eminent. Like a number of his other works, the *Guide* was translated into several languages, and it served as a textbook from 1935 to 1944.

Thus it was not surprising for the Mexican Ministry of Foreign Affairs to translate and publish Alfonso Teja Zabre's *Guide to the History of Mexico* in 1935. It was the best and most impartial account of Mexican history available at a time when Mexico needed to inform the world of its historical development. Only by understanding the history of Mexico could the world understand the tumultuous revolutionary era it had just witnessed.

Teja Zabre's approach to the history of Mexico is oriented towards economics. Time and again he finds economics to be the cause and effect of Mexican history. The *indianismo,* church and state relations, and foreign interest as well as involvement in Mexican history are related to economic catalyst.

At times, Teja Zabre seems to lean dangerously towards the political left. He speaks of the proletariat and the struggles between the classes, the conflict of centralist versus republican governments, and foreign domination through religious or economic control. Yet, he was merely reporting Mexican history as he could document it. Teja Zabre was the child of parents who participated in the period of reformation by Juarez. He grew up during the regime of Porfirio Diaz, which set aside many of the reformation principles and re-strengthened the role of the wealthy landowners, foreigners, and the Church. Finally, he had lived through and witnessed the Twentieth Century Revolution which was indeed an agrarian, economic, class struggle. A lesser historian would not have written impartially about the Revolution. Yet Alfonso Teja Zabre resisted the temptation to analyse and interpret and chose merely to report the fact.

It is not surprising, therefore, for Teja Zabre's *Guide to the History of Mexico* to have been chosen for classroom as well as for foreign consumption. It came at the peak of his career and was and is one of Mexico's best history books. Reading the book as impartially as it was written will reveal it to be the best account of the historical development and evolution of Mexico, its people, and its Twentieth Century Revolution.

Don Alfonso Teja Zabre, best described as the dean of twentieth century Mexican scholarship and history, also served his country in the diplomatic field. Today, he is still fondly remembered in Honduras, Cuba, and the Dominican Republic. Moreover, many of Mexico's contemporary historians cherish the memory of having taken classes under the *maestro* or having used his textbook.

Having spent his remaining years in journalism, Alfonso Teja Zabre reached the apex of his career in 1960 when he was named to the Mexican Academy of History. His introductory lecture dealt with the Inspector-General Don Jose de Galvez.

Don Alfonso Teja Zabre died in Mexico City on February 28, 1962. His motto had been "While alive, enlighten." Fortunately, his personal and magnanimous contributions were not to follow his motto for even after death Alfonso Teja Zabre continues to educate. Thus it is with great pleasure that the Jenkins Publishing Company presents *The Guide to the History of Mexico* to enlighten a new generation of history readers.

Richard G. Santos
Archivist of Bexar County
Office of the County Clerk

CONTENTS

PART ONE

PRIMITIVE MEXICAN CULTURE

PART TWO

THE COLONIAL PERIOD

FIRST STAGE OF SPANISH COLONIZATION.—EXPANSION OF THE SPANISH POWER

Page

PART THREE

INDEPENDENT MEXICO

NATIONAL INTEGRATION

PART FOUR

THE REVOLUTION

1

The history of Mexico is perhaps, one of the branches of universal history in greatest need of rewriting. The history of our country is the chronicle of a nation stirred by political and social convulsion, with a lengthy historic past crammed with vital events, and abounding in vestiges of a vast original culture, that are yet being disinterred and deciphered, and constitutes a vast field which cries out for investigation.

2

And on studying Mexican history from a modern standpoint, we shall find that the events of most far-reaching importance, hardly even noticed up to now, are inventions, like the reduction of ores by mercury amalgamation, introduced into Mexico by Bartolome de Medina in the middle of the sixteenth century and the cotton gin invented en 1793 by Eli Whitney in the United States. Latter on, came the use of machinery in mining, the treatment of ores by the cyanide process and the Diesel engine. Each one of these advances in the sphere of production set its stamp on a whole era, much more strongly than any number of dynastic or political changes.

And similarly, we shall find that the influence of such things as roads, corn, salt, or domestic animals for food or transport constitute true factors of history, and that industrial processes for irrigation, for sanitation, and the feeding and health of the people, are of primary importance to collective existence or national redemption.

3

Mexico's independence is not merely a political crisis and an economic struggle to eliminate the Spaniard (from the Church and from the State) in order to put the creole in his place. It is the process of disintegration or decline of the Spanish Empire, submitted to multiple pressure from outer cultures overflowing with expansive energy, to inner wearing down from effort made, and above all to the work of adaptation involved by the influence of land on man and vice versa.

Every cause so far put forward to explain the decline of Spain, is almost always a series of symptoms or of joint causes, of consequences or of reflex action and reaction. The fundamental origins of the fact have been glossed over in history and sociology, without ever reaching to the essence of the economic and biological complex. Explanations given are almost always partial and too prone to simplistic restriction.

In the first place, no one should assert that the decline of Spain was the result of a single cause and far less of a single or deliberate and conscious factor. It would be more appropriate to speak of the fall of the Spanish Empire, or of Spanish Imperialism, rather than of Spanish or Iberian decline or the fall or collapse of Spain. And it would be still more accurate to speak of a transformation of the feudal regime which had reached its culmination with the hegemony of Castile.

The fall of the Spanish Empire is the fall of a whole worldwide system of economic production. It may be said that the greatness and power of the Iberian peoples coincided with the western Mediterranean aspects of civilization, while their decline supervened when the geographical position of high European culture shifted and opened its way out over the Atlantic to the New World.

Spain's geographical situation, controlling the exit from the Mediterranean Sea at a meeting-point of the routes of world circulation then known, made the energies of civilization become concentrated in her territory. Those activities that had previously been directed from Italy towards the Asiatic World and which contributed to Venice's rise to power, were driven out of their course by the resistance and power of Islam and were compelled to open for themselves a way across unknown seas. This work of civilization by natural destiny fell to the Iberian peoples and they carried it out on a prodigious scale.

4

The opening of oceanic routes to the Indies and the discovery of America altered the manner and technique of the production of wealth. Hispanic culture was enriched by contributions from the Greek and Latin worlds, by development of its own possibilities, by contact with Oriental culture through the Arabs and later by the enormous material and spiritual influence resulting from conquest and colonization of the New World.

·The Spanish Empire, however, bore within it the germ of its transformation and finish.

"Spain was the axis of Europe, in spite of certain disadvantage of position, and the meeting-place of diverse cultures that on her soil were harmoniously amalgamated... Spain, in spite of her geopraphical aloofness was the spot where a number of races were biologically crossed, the cross-roads of interference with one another of the most diverse currents, but yet assimilated them and impressed upon them an indestructible ethnical element."

Spain's geographical aloofness ceased to exist when the route round the Cape of Good Hope was discovered, which brought about the ruin of Venice and the rise of the Iberian peoples. All the more was Spain able to become a busy center of world economic activity, and consequently of amalgamation and grafting of currents of humanity, when the tide of civilization turned towards the Atlantic.

Those same activities of Spain were the cause of a transformation of universal systems of communications, industries and trade.

Spain herself opened the Atlantic route to the French, the Dutch and the English. And those countries more advantageously situated harvested the fruits of the economic revolution to which the discovery and conquest of the Americas gave rise.

5

From the very moment that Cabot, on behalf of England, discovered the short route from the European world to the American world, and even forestalled Columbus in setting foot on the mainland, the bond between Spain and her future colonies was threatened. And this danger to Spain's colonies, of such remote origin, could not but grow by reason of the manner in which each one of those powers undertook its work of colonization.

Spain launched forth on mighty adventure in tropical lands, defying their invincible torrid climate, while the English proceeded more slowly and succeeded in gaining, inch by inch, possession of cool and temperate lands, wide open and adjacent to each other, and well adapted to the introduction of the processes of that new era that was to substitute the work of machines for that of men's hands. Spain had to face the intricate problems of an aboriginal civilization deeply rooted in the soil, which she could neither evade nor destroy, and which was eventually, in exchange for cheap labor, to give raise to racial and class conflicts exacerbated by deficient production of staples for human consumption.

And that very abundance of gold and silver was the complement of that seductive outward appearance of the tropics, because mining wealth, although useful for bolstering up precarious agriculture, cannot replace that more necessary wealth consisting in abundance of agricultural production.

6

Another example of the way in which history may be rewritten is afforded by the different angle from which the most outstanding event of modern times in Mexico; the Revolution, may be viewed. A fresh outlook upon revolutionary ideology is revealed when we assert that the proximate cause of the Revolution was not a mere political aspiration, something which has been often repeated. But the vision of the economic conception must also be broadened. And so we find in the permanent and renovating tendency of the revolution, in the first place, the unceasing coursing of vital currents, and after that the phenomena of integration and disintegration, of readjustments and want of balance caused by the fact that "in civilized life conventions and institutions arise or persist regardless of the laws of biology, because man makes his laws without adjusting them to his natural convenience." And hence the necessity of that slow, violent or intermittent process of readjusting civilization to nature.

7

And so we must, in the history of Mexico, and in the background of the war of independence, seek a social movement, and deeper down, an impulse emanating from biological causes. We shall not only find the revolt of the oppressed classes, who rise in arms at the magic touch of the principles of the French Revolution, but also the action of a vital necessity. Political separation wrapped up in the ideology and rhetoric of Jacobin clubs and masonic lodges is nothing more than a consequence of the complicated phenomena caused by want of equilibrium in the economic sphere, and more especially of the new industrial era characterized by the fall in the value of silver, the increase in cost of production due to exhaustion of surface deposits, to fires and floods in mines and the victory of English sea power over Spain's to the detriment of the latter's communications with her colonies.

The treatment of silver ores by the Patio Process meant for Mexico the most far-reaching consequences.

Reduction plants were established at mining camps, and towns were founded that later became important centers. Fortunate miners came to constitute a class privileged by its wealth; with sufficient resources at times to contribute to defray the expenses of the Church, of local public institutions of this and other colonies, and even to assist the crown of Spain itself.

But the opulent scale on which mining was carried on in New Spain could not but bring about, at the same time, a slow and yet steady fall in the value of the metal mined, the growth of a proletarian class exploited by the work of mining, transport and treatment of the ore, and the breakdown of mining appliances and methods, as the richest deposits, and those closest to the surface, became exhausted.

8

In the middle of the eighteenth century Mexican pesos were the coin preferred all over the world. But by 1800 the effects of widespread flooding of mines and of inferior operating methods, as compared with European practice which succeeded in lowering cost of production by means of steam pumps and more efficient methods of treating ores, began to be felt. When Baron von Humboldt visited New Spain in 1803, although he greatly admired the underground works and the potential wealth of deposits, he also noticed serious deficiencies consisting in disconnected workings and unwatering appliances operated by mule power.

Among the contributory causes of the war of Independence the depression in the mining industry and its consequent reaction on the mining proletariat, must be noted. Reduction works were destroyed and the workings were in many cases set on fire and burnt out. The booty most sought after, of course, were the silver trains. And Anglo-Saxon pressure, apparently brought to bear in favor of independence, was assuredly not foreign to the fact that about 1820 English syndicates bought up mines at one time famed for bonanzas, for trifling sums.

9

Nevertheless, not even English industry and methods succeeded in putting the Mexican mining industry back on its feet. English engineers encountered enormous difficulties in the way of adapting their technical methods to the traditional ways of working of the Mexican miner and also in getting such things as boilers and steam engines up to the plateau. They likewise had to suffer the consequences of the war of emancipation and of the economic and social crisis that supervened which showed itself in the form of revolution, while years after that a fresh fall in the value of silver due to over-production in the United States after the Civil War, also hit them hard. Eventually, English capital yielded most of the ground to American undertakings when the expansion of the United States became more strongly felt in Mexico due to the railways and to new systems of mining and treating ores, more especially the cyanide process that came into use at the close of the nineteenth century.

And just as we must, in studying the Wars of Independence and Reform, investigate deep-seated factors closely connected with the mining industry, which was in turn connected with agriculture and the general economy, so we must, in modern revolutionary movements, study this action for yet further industrial transformations, in which are included problems arising out of the increased use of machinery, and those connected with crops, fuel and transport. To the mining of silver and gold we must add, in these last times, the political and social influence of Mexico's entry into the ranks of petroleum producing nations, and the harnessing and spread of electric power.

10

To sum up, we shall find it necessary to investigate deepseated and hitherto but superficially studied causes, in the work of national integration, in early governments and in institutions ever gnawed by bankruptcy engendered by civil war and the misery that produces banditry; the mutilation of Mexico's territory and her internal problems as affected by geography and the transformations worked by industry; the wars and social movements of reform as a continuation of the revolutionary impulse, and class-war begun in the conflagration that marked the movement for Independence; onward progress stage by stage, up to the halting introducion of new systems of communications and production by means of mechanical methods introduced in the nineteenth century. Then, came those same influences that contributed to the restoration of the Republic, and to the current of material prosperity that was in turn promoted by the peaceful regime of the Diaz-Limantour epoch. And still the same causes and problems ever working to produce anew the phenomena of the Revolution and industrial transformations of this century, with new formulae and modern ideologies which yet involve similar geopraphical and vital enigmas.

A survey of the history of Mexico thus acquires new aspects deserving study and investigation. This work must be undertaken and carried through by a whole generation. For from its diffusion and knowledge there must follow a more generous and human view of the real state of things in our country, new courses for propounding and solving the vital problems of our political, economic and social life, a clear understanding of the integration of a true Mexican culture and its full justification before the rest of the world and in History.

SYNOPSIS

What we call Spanish culture is a part of the second stage or age of the great Occidental Culture, that is held to have arisen at the end of the Middle Ages, in the Italian Republics of the fifteenth century. After flourishing in Italy, Western or European culture appears in Spain and France, in its highest expression, creative in aspect and overflowing with energy, prior to becoming transformed into an industrial civilization and shifting over to England and the United States, by a movement similar to that realized by the culture of ancient times, from the Hellenic to the Roman World.

At the time when Spanish culture was transplanted to New Spain, it was at its highest point, and from a national feudal organization became imperialistic expansion under the house of Austria. Consequently, it brought to this part of America the elements of modern culture, with traditions and antecedents assimilated from ancient Culture, to wit:

A scientific, philosophic, aesthetic and moral tradition of Greek origin.

A legal and political tradition of Roman origin.

A religious tradition of Hebraic origin.

Certain mechanical inventions, such as the wheel, gunpowder, printing, the mariner's compass.

Changes in methods of production.

Domestic animals for food and transport.

These fundamental features are here represented by the different factors or signs of historical vitality in synoptic form.

THE GEOGRAPHICAL FACTOR

Prehistoric Stage

Geographical position:

·Between the 14th and 32nd parallels. (Crossed midway by the Tropic of Cancer.)
(Same latitude as Sahara Desert, Egypt, Arabia and India.)

Morphology or Relief of the Soil:

Primary or Palaeozoic Era.

(Cambrian.) North America is divided into great land-masses. Cascadia, Columbia, Honduria, Antillia, correspond to what now is Mexico. No land life.

Primary or Palaeozoic Era:

(Permian.) Union of the various continental fragments. Level of land rises.

Secondary or Mesozoic Era.

(Triassic.) Northern Mexico undergoes a subsidence along a belt roughly parallel to degrees of latitude.

Secondary or Mesozoic Era.

(Infra-cretaceous.) Mexico invaded by the seas. In the west the ancient land of Sonora emerges.

Tertiary Period.

(Oligocene.) Mexico begins to assume its present shape. The Gulf of California is a valley. Yucatan has not yet emerged above the surface of the Ocean.

(Miocene.) The peninsula of Lower California breaks away from the main body of the continent. Emergence of Yucatan.

Tertiary Period.

Intense volcanic eruptions. Mountains thrown up and mineral wealth stored.

Quaternary Period.

Four glacial periods.
Three inter-glacial periods.

Man makes his appearance in America, having crossed over from Asia during the third inter-glacial period.
In the 4th glacial period communication between Asia and America is cut off. The American races, during their 100,000 years isolation, develop into the red or bronze race.
After the 4th Glacial Period, Asiatic immigration is renewed, but the physical features of the American race that had grown up on the Continent, are prepotent.
Post-glacial or present Period.

2

A few maps will explain far more clearly than any description, however lengthy, what were and are the geographical features of ancient Mexico, New Spain and Modern Mexico. But we must insists on the importance of data referring to the climate. We shall from the Physical Geography of Professor Pedro C. Sanchez take the data of interest to the student of Mexican history, here condensed as regards the climates prevailing over our present territory, in our lost provinces and in the countries that have exercised most influence on our historical evolution.

Comparison of Mexico's Climates

Equatorial (Guinea) Climate.—Southern Yucatan and Tabasco, part of Chiapas and Quintana Roo.

Tropical (Senegalese.)—Veracruz, Campeche, Tabasco, Yucatán, Pacific Coast from Sinaloa South.

Chinese.—Gulf Coast north of Tampico.

Saharan Desertic, Hot.—"Bolson de Mapimi," portions of Sonora and Lower California.

Mediterranean Steppe.—(Like Syria, Arabia.) Part of Northern Mexico, on the plateau.

High altitude warm climate.

(High sub-tropical. Like climate of Ecuador, Bolivia, Colombia, Abyssinia, Transvaal.) Central Plateau, Valley of Mexico.

Mountain Climates.

Influence of the great Cordilleras.

California.—Mediterranean (like Portugal and Morocco) and Alpine cold in the countains.

Texas, Arizona, New Mexico.—Temperate Steppe Climate.

(Ukrainia and Manchuria.) Cold desert. (Aralian.)

Spanish Climate, Castilian Plateau, transitional temperate. Mediterranean on coasts.

United States.—New England. Temperate (Sub-Mediterranean Danubian.) The West, a temperate steppe climate. (Ukrainian.)

3

THE ETHNIC FACTOR

Race

Primitive inhabitants of America, of Asiatic origin (Polynesian and Mongoloid types.)
Spanish race. Ligurian or Mediterranean family; Etnic, western Pyrenean, Alpine and Armenoid branches.
Early inhabitants of Spain: Iberians, Celts. (Celtiberians.)
Influences: Phoenician, Greek, Carthaginian.
Roman Conquest.—Jewish Migration.
Barbarian and Germanic invasions: Goths, Suevi and Vandals.
Iranians or Aryans; Alani.

Arabs, with mixture of Berbers and Ethiopians.
Outside contributions: Italians, Flemings and wandering Gypsies.
In Mexico: Indians, mestizos, various castes.
Creoles.

4

THE ECONOMIC FACTOR

Forms of Production

Pre-capitalistic spirit of enterprise: The Crown and the Church.

Acquisition and exploitation by force.—Distributions of lands and slaves to the conquistadors. Agriculture and mining carried on by slave labor. Indians as beasts of burden and messengers. Unregulated slavery.

Regulated Slavery.—"Encomiendas" or grants, and "Repartimientos" or allotments.—Personal service.—Tribute *per capita*. Feudal property of great lords.
Monarchical centralization and concentration; paramount ownership by and right of eminent domain of the Crown.
Slavery in virtue of sham contracts; Indians treated as minors.

Caste privileges.—Concentration of wealth in hands of great estate owners and ecclesiastical corporations. Property of heretics and infidels (Jews, Moriscoes and Lutherans) confiscated. The Inquisition as an economic instrument.
Monopoly of lucrative functions by European Spaniards. Rise of a creole, mestizo and Indian proletariat.

Class struggles of the pre-capitalistic period.—Property held in mortmain.—Economic social inequalities and the Revolution for Independence.
Rise of new classes of society; militarism and professional politicians. Tendency to secularize Church property. Usurers and bankers. From clergy to bureaucracy.
Creoles or native whites replace Spaniards in fat official jobs, while military men enjoy the position in society formerly filled by the nobles; the Church keeps her economic privileges.
Indians and mestizos continue to constitute a proletariat and permanent unbalance keeps alive revolutionary agitation under the name of Reform.

An individualistic, liberal and capitalistic system sanctioned by the Constitution of 1857.

Industrial capitalism.—Partial phenomena of concentration of wealth in the hands of privileged groups and fresh revolutionary agitation.

Church property secularized only in part, Indian communities suppressed, and great estates untouched.

French Intervention, and the Empire, as disturbing incidents.

A liberal and individualistic Republic.—The policy of Conciliation (towards the Church.)

The Revolution of 1910, provoked by the same everlasting economic unbalance. Recovery of proletariat rights, the rise of workers' organizations, the regime of labor unions.

State socialism.—Economic policy.—Rationalization of industry. Integral socialism applied to actual Mexican conditions.

Elements in Technique of Production

1521 to 1561.—Trade entirely restricted to certain ports and carried on with Spain exclusively, without regulating fleets nor fixed dates for sailing of ships.

Introduction of process for reduction of metals by amalgamation with mercury. Industrial revolution due to abundance of gold and silver.

Floods in mines.

1561 to 1778.—System of fleets of convoys.

1578 to 1821.—Trade comparatively unrestricted.

1793, invention of the cotton gin, which, with the steam engine (ships and looms) favored the enormous movement of expansion of the United States, with serious reactions on Mexico.

1821 to 1917.—Free trade restricted by fiscal protection.

The public debt and its international consequences.

Economic consequences of French Intervention, and of secularization and nacionalization of the property of the Church.

Railways, and their influence on the national economy.

The economic boom from 1887 to 1910, to which the introduction of the cyanide process for metals and the rise in the price of copper and sisal, contributed materially.

The age of electricity.

The Diesel internal combustion motor and engines consuming petroleum and gasoline as fuel.—Their influence on the economy of the revolutionary period.

5

IDEOLOGY

Doctrines of policy and action.

From the time of the Spanish Conquest:

Feudal ideology.—The knightly spirit. Right of conquest, justified by conversion to Christianity and civilization of the conquered. Religious orthodoxy, Catholic and Papal. Privileges of the nobility. Legal privileges of communities and municipalities.

Absolute monarchy.—Submission to the Crown.—Loyalty and allegiance of vassals. Regalism. Alliance of Church and State as temporal institutions. Royal Patronage.

The conflict in the Middle Ages between the Crown, the Church and the nobility.—The ideas that gave rise to the Reformation and the Renaissance. Missionaries who denounced the abuses of the Conquest.—The rights of the Crown versus the privileges of the nobility. Philosophy versus dogmatism and the Divine right of kings. Humane sentiments versus despotism. The Inquisition as a political instrument.

Precursors of democratic ideology. Rousseau, the encyclopedists, humanitarianism, liberal monarchy. Their influence on Mexico's emancipation.

Democratic ideology.—The rights of man.—Utilitarianism. (Bentham.)—Institutions as public services and neither absolute nor divine in character and origin.—National sovereignty, sole, indivisible, inalienable and imprescriptible. Resistance to oppression.—Natural Law. Division of governmental Powers.—Taxes and parliamentarianism, —Equal rights and equal conditions.—Universal brotherhood.—Individual liberty.—Separation of Church and State.

Evolution of ideology in Mexico by means of wars of Independence and Reform, up to 1857.—Politics and romanticism.

Positive ideology.—Capitalism and classic economy.

Material progress, organic peace, the religion of science, Materialism.

The Revolution.—Political reform.—Economic reform.—Agrarian distribution of lands.—Labor unions.—Functional or corporate democracy.—The technical State.—Class warfare; exaltation of the proletariat.—Managed economy.—Integral socialism.

6

THE INDIVIDUAL FACTOR

Heroes, Representative Men, Leaders

Maya and Toltec era.—Quetzalcoatl. (Kukulcan.)
Primitive Mexico.—Tenoch, Netzahualcoyotl.
Mexico at the height of its splendor, Tenochtitlan. Moctezuma II.
Discovery of America.—Christopher Columbus and their Catholic Majesties. (Anton de Alaminos.)
The Conquest of Mexico.—Cortes and Cuauhtemoc.
The Empire of Spain in its heyday. Charles V and Philip II.
The missionaries.—Fray Pedro de Gante.—The venerable Las Casas.
The Colonizers.—Viceroys Mendoza and Velasco.—Archbishop Zumarraga.—Bartolome de Medina and Juan Pablos.

Philip II and the Count-Duke of Olivares.—Charles the Bewitched. Regency of Ann of Austria, Father Nithard and Valenzuela, the favorite.

The House of Bourbon.—Philip V, the Princess des Ursins and Cardinal Alberoni.—Ferdinand VI and Ensenada, his Minister.—Charles III, and his ministers, Grimaldi, Esquilache and Floridablanca.— Charles IV, Count Aranda, Jovellanos and Godoy.

The Governors: Acuña, Bucareli, Revillagigedo.—The Intendant Jose de Galvez.—(Father Kino and Junipero Serra.)

Precursors of Independence.—Verdad and Talamantes.

The Military Leaders of Independence.—Hidalgo, Morelos and Mina.

The military leaders of the royalist cause.—Calleja and Iturbide.

Political consummation of Independence.—Iturbide and Guerrero.

The fight for national integration.—Liberals: Doctor Mora, Ramos Arizpe, Gomez Farias.—Conservatives: Alaman, Bustamante, Santa Anna.

Reform.—Benito Juarez.

Intervention and Empire.—Napoleon III and Maximilian of Austria.

Restoration of the Republic.—Porfirio Diaz.

The Revolution of 1910.—Francisco I. Madero.—Venustiano Carranza.—Alvaro Obregón.—Plutarco Elias Calles.

7

THE LANGUAGE

The Conquest imposes the Spanish language at the expense of the many and scattered Indian dialects. The Spanish language is:
Mostly Low Latin, of Indo-European and Sanscrit origin, with Hellenic influence.
Remains of Iberian and Celtic dialects and of early Phoenician and Greek contributions.
Gothic or Germanic contributions.
Arabic influences: Arabic words, Morisco dialects, negro, Egyptian and Asiatic dialects.
Greek through Arabic channels.
Alien influences.—Hebraisms, Italianisms, Gallicisms, Anglicisms. Cosmopolitan influences, scientific terms.
Sectional influences: Basque, Catalan, Bable, Andalusian. (Madrid, Gypsy and slang.)
Colonial influences.— Americanisms.— (Malay and Polynesian words.)

Mexicanisms:

Accent,
Music,
Construction,
Local terms,
Native languages.

8

ARCHITECTURE

The best evidence of the strong personality and vital impulse of primitive Mexican culture is to be found in native architecture, as completed by the decorative arts. The following summary sets forth what has been discovered as to the capacity of early builders, judging from progress achieved in the art of building construction.

Esplanades and streets at Teotihuacan.

Buildings astronomically oriented at Copan.

Alto relievo carved on surface of excessively hard rock at Xochicalco.

Truncated pyramids with temples on top, at Tikal and Tixmucuy.

A court of a thousand columns with carved and plainted figures, at Chichen Itza.

Vaulted chambers with double galleries at Uxmal.

Porticoes at Chacmultun and Zayi.

Arcades and triumphal doorways at Labna.

Underground vaults, bridges and aqueducts at Palenque.

A platform built up with thousands of tons of material, at the Governor's House, at Uxmal.

Blocks of hard building stone cut true and square and put together without mortar, by reason of the perfect fit of the faces at the joints, at Mitla.

Cresting, open work and masks at the House of the Nuns, at Uxmal.

Mastery over the hardest materials; panels of sandstone and compact limestone at Palenque.

Hardwood instruments and figures, approaching the perfection of Greek art. (Data from E. J. Palacios.)

And as regards the Spanish period, architecture is of special historical importance because:

I. It is the most visible, solid and permanent condensation and representation of the evolution of culture in New Spain and Mexico.

II. It is the most imposing artistic creation of European culture in the New World.

III. It has the great spiritual value of perpetuating the memory of bygone eras and institutions, with a personality of its own, not without certain aboriginal touches.

Colonial Architecture

First period.—Sixteenth century.

Early Franciscan.—From the time of the Conquest until royal authority was firmly established.

Feudal features: Military posts, missions, churches, plain but massive. (Tuscan order.)

Lack of ornamentation and resources (Church of Regina, Lower and side walls of the Cathedral of Mexico City, West side.)

The tendency towards baroque marks the beginning of transformation into plateresque. (Abundant use of metal; Gold and silversmiths.)

A peculiarly Mexican touch is added to architecture by the labor, mostly Indian, and the raw materials (volcanic rock, white and brown stones from near Pachuca, Puebla and Oaxaca. Also basaltic lava, andesite, tufa.)

Second Period.—Sixteenth to seventeenth centuries.

Greatest splendor of the Monarchy.—Influence of the Renaissance; The Classic, Graeco-Roman or "Herreran" style. Reminiscences' of the Escorial. Domes and bell-towers. (Church of Santo Domingo and main facade of Cathedral, Mexico City.)

The dominant note of Spanish baroque prevails by exaggerating the plateresque style until the fantastic exaggerations of "Churrigueresque" are reached. (Reminiscences of Italian "borrominesque.")

Third Period.—Seventeenth to eighteenth centuries.

Mexican colonial style spreads, preserving all its former features but without creating new forms. *Churrigueresque* prevails, as exemplified by structures like the *Sagrario,* next to the Cathedral in Mexico City, and the Church of La Santima (*Altar de los Reyes* in the Cathedral.)

Fourth Period.—End of eighteenth and beginning of nineteenth centuries.

Neo-classic style.—Tresguerras.—Tolsá.—The domes of the Cathedral.—The School of Mines.

Due to Bourbon influences touches of French Renaissance are imported, and architecture subsequently sinks into a decadence that grafts *rocaille* and even rococo onto neo-classicism and Spanish baroque. (High altar of Cathedral, Mexico City.)

Fifth Period.—Nineteenth century up to restoration of the Republic and industrial era.

Constructive and creative stagnation. Churches and convents turned into barracks and schools.

Sixth Period.—End of nineteenth centry and first decade of twentieth century.

Influence of industrial architectural art and of European bourgeois. (Railway stations, use of brick, plaster, and stucco.)

Seventh Period.—The Revolution.—Imitations of colonial style.— Reminiscences of primitive times.—Maya and Aztec decorative features.—Cosmopolitanism.—Confusion of creative forms and attempts.— Steel and cement.

9

SCIENCE AND ART

Vocabulary and grammars of the missionaries.
Early colleges of San Francisco and Tlaltelolco.
Religious and dogmatic books.
Castilian mysticism.
Scholastic philosophy.—The early Royal and Pontifical University.
Initiation into modern science.
Jesuit schools.
Influence of French encyclopedists.
The forerunners of the movement for independence.
Crisis of independence.—Decline of culture. Closing of the University.
The Bureau of Public Education.
Lancastrian schools.
Alternatives and academic and decorative confusion of the Reform period and of the Empire.
Positivism.—Comte, Barreda, and the Preparatory school.—Laical education and compulsory primary education.
Neo-spiritualism.—Rebirth of the University in 1910.
Socialization of culture.

LETTERS

Literature in Mexico is a branch of Spanish literature transplanted.
Books of religion and knightly romances.
Novels and romances of knighthood fall into discredit.—Cervantes.
Reflections of the Golden Century of Spanish literature; Cervantes de Salazar, Balbuena, Terrazas, Juan Ruiz de Alarcon.
Decadence: Conceptism, euphuism and similar schools.
Picaresque literature.
The poets of the Parthenic Triumph.—Sister Juana Inez de la Cruz.
Neo-classical idealism.—Navarrete, Jesuitic and French influences.
The romantic movement.
The first touches of nationalism: the "Mexican Thinker."
The classic and romantic schools. Literature and Politics. Ignacio Ramirez, Guillermo Prieto, Altamirano.
Modernism.—Gutiérrez Najera, Diaz Miron, Nervo.
Realism.
Revolution and ultraism.—Populism.—Socialization of art.

PAINTING

Mural paintings of the Maya Empire. (Chichen-Itza.)
Decorative frescoes.
Ideographs and hieroglyphics of early Aztecs. (Codices.)
Colonial painting in Mexico, a reflection of the Spanish school of the time.
Early sixteenth century painters.—Sentiment exclusively religious: asceticism and austerity.
Rodrigo de Cifuentes, Alonso Vazquez, Simon Peirens. (Franciscan touches.)

Seventeenth century.—Mexican school; characteristic features: softness, sweetness, mannerisms, affectation.

Echave, Luis Juarez (Jesuitical tendency.)

Eighteenth century.—French influences; mysticism, amiable beginnings of a renaissance and neo-classic tendency.—Miguel Cabrera, Jose Alcibar.

Nineteenth centruy.—Period of Decline.

Diluted romanticism.—Imitation of and confusion with previous formulae.—Academicism.—Salome Piña, Felix Parra, Jose Maria Velasco.

Our own times.—Realism. Saturnino Herran. Modernism, Julio Ruelas, Enciso, Montenegro.

Revolutionary movement.—Rehabilitation of popular art.

Rationalism and social tendency.—Diego Rivera and Jose Clemente Orozco.— Mural paintings.— Primitiveness.— Decorative frescoes, ideographs and symbolical representations.

CHRONOLOGICAL SUMMARY

PRIMITIVE CULTURE

Pre-archaic Period

Prior to the year 5,000 B. C. the first nomad tribes made their appearance in the New World; they were either Asiatic in origin, or aborigines, but with Asiatic characteristics (Mongoloid, Polynesian.) Their abilities seem to have been confined to the lighting of fire, rough stone cutting and primitive hand-weaving.

Archaic Period

Otomis, Tarascos, Huastecs

Rudimentary agriculture, primitive pottery making and weaving on looms; primitive religion and art lacking in symbolical meaning, mostly in the higher and dryer sections of the tropical zone.

Post-archaic

Centers of culture with agricultural life, and development of social institutions, religion and art; spread to lower and more humid levels of the tropical regions and to the temperate zone.

Maya Period

600 B. C. Appearance of Maya peoples.

613 B. C. to 176 A. D.—Prehistoric Maya Period.

176 to 373 A. D. Rise of southern Maya Culture (Guatemala and Honduras.) Cities of Copan, Tikal and Palenque, founded.

373 to 471. Development of southern Maya culture.

471 to 530. Maya emigration from Tabasco, Chiapas, and Peten, to Yucatan. Foundation of Chichen-Itza.

471 to 629. Southern Maya culture reaches its height; then declines and dies.

629 to 964. The Mayas pass through a transition period, decline and migrations. Movement towards the west of the Yucatan Peninsula (Champoton) and recovery of Chichen-Itza.

964 to 1191. Period of the League of Mayapan. Mayan Renaissance. Northern culture. Maximum splendor of Chichen-Itza and Uxmal.

1201. Mayapan League broken. The Toltecs and Aztecs assist Hunac Cel, the Lord of Mayapan, against Chac Zib. (The very red man.)

1448. The Mayas abandon Chichen-Itza.

1010 to 1437. Period of Aztec influence (Hunac Cel. Kukulcan. Quetzalcoatl.) Contact between Mayan and Aztec cultures. New style of architecture. After 1437, the second Maya culture declines and dies out just as the first had done. Cities are deserted and tribes disperse.

The Toltecs

1000 B. C. Migrations from northwestern America towards the south (Casas Grandes, New-Mexican Pueblos. After that, La Quemada or Chicomoztoc, etc., then through Tepic and Jalisco.)

500 B. C. The Toltecs migrate from Jalisco towards the central plateau and establish the older Toltec culture, by subduing the Olmecas and Otomies. (Teotihuacan-Tula.)

200 B. C. Olmec migration from the Lower Mississippi Valley to the Panuco region.

320 to 550. Warfare between Olmecs and Toltecs, a portion of the latter move towards the scuth. (Pipil peoples of Nicaragua.)

670. The Acolhuas leave Jalisco and make their way east, replacing the ancient Toltecs that had moved south.

718. Re-establishment of the Toltec kingdom, or second Toltec period.

Table of the Toltec Dynasty

843-895. Quetzalcoatl.

895-930. Matlaxochitl.

930-933. Mauhyotzin.

933-973. Matlacoatzin.

973-994. Tlicoatzin.

994-1070. Huemac. Migration towards Yucatan.

821. Aztec migrations from northwestern Mexico, towards the central plateau.

1051. Aztec tribes in the Valley of Mexico. (Tecpanecs.)

1142. Xochimilcas.

1272. Triple alliance between Texcoco, Culhuacan and Atzcapotzalco.

Tezcucan Dynasty

1225-1284. Xolotl.
1248-1315. Nopaltzin.
1315-1324. Tlotzin.
1324-1357. Quinatzin.
1357-1409. Techotlala.
1409-1418. Ixtlixochitl.
1418-1431. (Tecpanec usurpation.)
1431-1472. Netzahualcoyotl.
1472-1515. Netzahualpilli.
1515-1520. Cacama.

AZTEC CULTURE

Wanderings of the Aztecs

820. The Aztecs leave Aztlan. They pass through Sinaloa, Jalisco and Michoacan.
908. They reach Culhuacan, near Chalco.
1012. Oztocalco.
1064. Tocolco.
1116. Oztatlan.
1299. Chapultepec.

Mexico-Tenochtitlan

1312-1325. Tenochtitlan founded. Theocracy under Tenoch.
1376-1397. Acamapichtli.
1396-1417. Huitzilihuitl.
1417-1427. Chimalpopoca.
1427-1440. Itzcoatl.
1465. Axayacatl, the grandson of Moctezuma Ilhuicamina, is named king.
1481. Death of Axayacatl. Succeeded by his brother Tizoc.
1482. Work begun on construction of new Great Temple.
1486. Tizoc dies of poisoning and is succeeded by his brother Ahuizotl.
1487. Consecrating of the Great Temple. Human sacrifices on a vast scale.
1497. Ahuizotl carries war as far as Tehuantepec.
1502. Death of Ahuizotl, Moctezuma II succeeds him.

Period of Discovery

1484. Columbus makes his first appeal for a voyage of discovery, to King John II of Portugal.

1492. April 17. Articles stipulated at Santa Fe de la Vega de Granada, between their Catholic Majesties and Columbus, for undertaking voyages of maritime discovery.

1492. August 3. Columbus sails from the Port of Palos with a fleet of three ships, the "Santa Maria," "Pinta" and "Niña." The two latter commanded by Martin Alonso and Vicente Yañez Pinzon respectively.

1492. October 12. Francisco Rodriguez Bermejo (Rodrigo de Triana) sights land, before dawn. At break of day (a Friday) the discoverers land on the island of Guanahani.

1493. September 25. Second voyage of Columbus. Sails from Cadiz with 14 caravels and three caracks. He arrived back in Spain on July 11, 1496.

1493. Bull of Demarcation, of Pope Alexander III awarding the New World to Spain and Portugal.

1497. June 24. Cabot discovers Labrador Peninsula on behalf of Great Britain.

1497. May 10, to October 15, 1498. Voyage of Americo Vespucci, with Vicente Yañez Pinzon and Juan Diaz de Solis, through the Bay of Honduras, and Gulf of Mexico.

1498. May 30. Columbus starts on his third voyage. He reached the mainland for the first time, on August 1st, and sailed past the mouths of the Orinoco.

1502. May 9. Columbus starts on his fourth voyage. On August 14 he reached Honduras. Founded Veragua, abandoned in April, 1503.

1503. January 20. Creation and enactment of ordinances for *Casa de Contratación* (Commercial Exchange) at Seville.

1506. May 20. Death of Christopher Columbus at Valladolid, Spain.

1511-1512. Jeronimo de Aguilar and Gonzalo Guerrero, survivors from the wreck of an expedition that had come up from Darien, succeed in reaching Yucatan.

1517. February 8. The expedition headed by Francisco Fernandez de Cordoba sailed from Ajaruco, Cuba.

1517. March 4. Francisco Hernandez de Cordoba's expedition lanced at Cape Catoche. Attacked by Indians at the place later known as "Bay of the Adverse Fight." Hernandez de Cordoba wounded, returned to Cuba where he died.

1518. May 1. The expedition commanded by Juan de Grijalva sailed from Cuba and reached Cozumel on the 4th of May, Campeche on the 26th and San Juan de Ulua on the 24th June.

The Conquest

1485. Hernan Cortes born at Medellin, Estremadura. The child of Martin Cortes de Monroy and Catalina Pizarro Altamirano.

1494-1496. Cortes pursues his studies at the University of Salamanca.

1504. Cortes left Spain for the West Indies.

1511. Cortes took part in the conquest of Cuba under Diego Velazquez.

1518. October 18. Cortes left the Port of Santiago de Cuba for Macaca, La Trinidad and Havana.

1518. February 10. Cortes leaves Havana and steers a southwest course.

1518. March 4. Cortes sails from Cozumel, after rescuing Jeronimo de Aguilar, who had been wrecked with Gonzalo Guerrero.

1519. March 20. Cortes' expedition sails past the mouth of the River Grijalva.

1519. March 23. Cortes meets and fights the Indians of Tabasco. Donna Marina joins the expedition.

1519. April 21. Cortes arrives at San Juan de Ulua.

1519. July 10. Issues charter founding city of Vera Cruz.

1519. August 16. Cortes leaves for Mexico City at the head of 400 infantry, 16 horses, 6 cannon and 1,500 Indian allies.

1519. September 18. The Spaniards enter Tlaxcala.

1519. October 15 and 16. Massacre at Cholula.

1519. November 1. Cortes leaves Cholula.

1519. November 7. Cortes arrives at Mexico, where Moctezuma welcomes him and assigns him quarters in Axayacatl's palace.

1519. November 14. Cortes seizes Moctezuma's person, overthrows the idols and sets up the Cross in the Great Temple of Mexico City.

1520. April 23. The expedition of Panfilo de Narvaez lands at San Juan de Ulua.

1520. May 20. While Cortes is absent from Mexico whence he has gone to encounter and repulse Narvaez, Pedro de Alvarado in Mexico City massacres a number of Indian priests and noblemen. Alvarado and his men besieged at their headquarters.

1520. May 29. Cortes takes Narvaez by surprise and defeats him, then hastens back to Alvarado's rescue, having arrived in Mexico on the 24th.

1520. June 25. Cuitlahuac heads the rebellion against Cortes.

1520. June 17. Moctezuma attempts to harangue his subjects.

1520. June 28. The Spaniards decide to break through the siege.

1520. June 29. Before leaving Mexico City they slay Moctezuma and several members of his family and persons of high degree.

1520. June 30. Disastrous defeat and flight of the Spanish Army. The "Sad Night."

1520. Julio 7. The Aztecs attack Cortes unsuccessfully at Otumba.

1520. July 12. Cortes reaches Tlaxcala, where he has the opportunity of resting and recruiting his forces.

1520. Cuitlahuac's coronation. He makes preparations for the defense of Mexico City and dies of small-pox on November 23d.

1520. December 31. Cortes on his way back to Mexico reaches Texcoco.

1521. March 1. Cuauhtemoc's coronation. The Aztecs hasten to defend their city.

1521. May 31. Cortes suceeds in damaging the Chapultepec aqueduct, thus cutting off Mexico City's water supply.

1521. June 9. The Spaniards fight their way up to the Great Temple.

1521. June 30. Cortes orders the city to be taken by storm but is repulsed.

1521. July 20. A new attempt to take the city by storm is undertaken, and the destruction of Mexico-Tenochtitlan, house by house, begins.

1521. August 13. Cuauhtemoc attemps to escape, but is taken prisoner and the City of Mexico-Tenochtitlan surrenders.

The Colonial Régime

1522. October 15. Charles the Fifth appoints Hernan Cortes to be Captain General and Governor of New Spain.

1523. August 30. The first Franciscan friars land at Vera Cruz.

1524. March 15. Ordinances for the guild of blacksmiths. Marks first attempt at legislation on workers' guilds in Mexico.   •

1524. Population of Mexico City estimated at 50,000.

1524. Letter from Cortes to Charles V praying that the clergy be made subject to the civil power.

1524. October 12. Hernan Cortes sets forth on his expedition to the Hibueras and leaves Licenciado Alfonso Suazo, Alonso de Estrada and Rodrigo de Albornoz as governors of Mexico.

1524. December 29. Gonzalo de Salazar and Pedro Almindes Chirino present instructions from Cortes to take part in the government of Mexico and bar out Estrada and Albornoz.

1525. February. Shrove Tuesday. Cuauhtemoc executed at Izancanac. (Acala?)

1525. April 19. Rodrigo de Paz, on behalf of Cortes recognizes Salazar and Chirino as sole governors. Anarchy and disputes until return of Cortes, June 20, 1526.

1526. July 2. Arrival in Mexico of Licenciado Luis Ponce de Leon, appointed to be Governor of New Spain *pro tempore*, and judge to investigate Cortes' conduct, with a view to impeachment if necessary.

1526. July 4. Licenciado Ponce de Leon enters upon the discharge of his duties as Governor and Judge. Dies on the 22nd of that same month, and left Marcos de Aguilar as his substitute.

1527. February 28. Death of Marcos de Aguilar who left Alonso de Estrada as his substitute.

1527. Mining Laws. Indians forbidden to make jewelry, cut precious stones, etc., 20% tax on production.

1527. July 14. Work begun on construction of fleet to explore Pacific Ocean, by order of Cortes.

1527. December 13. Royal decree establishing an *audiencia* in Mexico, composed of Nuño de Guzman, Matienzo, Delgadillo, Parada and Maldonado.

1528. Foundation of Oaxaca.

1529. December 20. Nuño de Guzman leaves on an expedition to the west and Parada and Maldonado having died, only Matienzo and Delgadillo are left to govern.

1530. By-laws providing that Indians shall neither ride nor own horses.

1530. July 15. Cortes returns to New Spain and takes up his residence at Texcoco until the arrival of the Second *Audiencia*.

1530. December 10. Arrival of *Oidors* Ceynos and Salmeron, members of the Second Audiencia, together with Ramirez de Fuenleal, Vasco de Quiroga and Maldonado.

1531. April 4. Royal Decree prohibiting "shipment to the Indies of books of history and profane subjects, but only works dealing with the Christian religion and virtue."

1534. February 24. Royal decree establishing the first geographical division of New Spain into four provinces: Mexico, Michoacan, Coatzacoalcos and the Mixtecas, and such vaguely defined territories as Yucatan, Tabasco, etc.

1535. April 17. Don Antonio de Mendoza appointed to be Viceroy.

1535. Foundation of the Port of Santa Cruz, now La Paz, Lower California.

1536. January 7. Opening of the College of San Cruz de Tlaltelolco, with sixty native students and courses in reading, writing, Latin grammar, rhetoric, philosophy, music and medicine.

1536. July 2. Arrival in Mexico of Fray Alonso de la Vera Cruz, Professor of Arts in the University (Scholastic theology, dialectics, philosophy) and founder of the College of San Pablo.

1536. First book printed in Mexico, or in the whole of the Americas; *"Escala Espiritual"* of St. John Climacus, translated by Fray Juan de Estrada. Printed by Juan Pablos.

1538. August 23. Royal decree ordering Viceroy Mendoza to bring expert farmers to New Spain.

1541. October 8. Viceroy Mendoza founds the City of Valladolid, later known as Morelia.

1542. January 6. Foundation of Merida, Yucatan, by Francisco de Montejo.

1542. February 11. Foundation of the City of Guadalajara.

1542. November 20. Charles V enacts the "New Laws of the Indies" at Barcelona, in order to prevent the abuses of the system of *encomiendas* or grants of Indian laborers.

1544. March 8. Arrival of the *visitador* or Inspector Tello de Sandoval for the purpose of enforcing the "New Laws" in favor of the Indians. Protest of the *encomenderos* or grantees of labor, supported by some of the religious.

1547. December 2. Death of Hernan Cortes, at Castilleja de la Cuesta, near Seville.

1548. January 20. Juan de Tolosa, in the company of Oñate, Bañuelos and Ibarra, founds the town of Zacatecas.

1550. Viceroy Mendoza transferred to Peru.

1548-1554. Foundation of Santa Fe de Guanajuato.

1551. September 21. Royal decree ordering creation of the University of Mexico.

1551. November. Luis de Velasco inaugurated as Second Viceroy.

1553. January 25. Viceroy Luis de Velasco opens the University of Mexico.

1555. December 29. Deed executed by Bartolome de Medina with an account of his discovery of the process for reduction of silver by amalgamation with mercury, i. e., the patio process.

1564. Death of the first Don Luis de Velasco, and the *Audiencia*, composed of Ceynos, Villanueva and Orozco, takes over government.

1566. Conspiracy headed by the Marques del Valle, Martin Cortes.

1566. Augusto 3. Alonso and Gil Gonzalez de Avila beheaded for their share in the conspiracy of the Marques del Valle.

1566. September 17. Arrival of the 3d. Viceroy, Gaston de Peralta.

1568. Viceroy Peralta goes back to Spain.

1571. The Tribunal of the Inquisition established.

1573. January 1. Foundation of the College of St. Peter and St. Paul, later College of San Ildefonso and Preparatory School.

1573. November 1. The Jesuits founded the College of Sta. Maria de Todos los Santos, with the assistance of Dr. Francisco Rodriguez Santos.

1573. December 1. Royal Decree bestowing lands, woods, water and common lands on Indian villages.

1573. Work begun on construction of Cathedral at Mexico City.

1577. October 4. Viceroy Enriquez de Almanza leaves for Peru.

1578. June 21. A faculty of Medicine is established at the University of Mexico.

1580. October 4. The Fifth Viceroy, Lorenzo Suarez de Mendoza, Conde de la Coruña, enters upon his office.

1583. June 19. Death of the 5th Viceroy and the *Audiencia*, composed of Licenciados Villanueva and Sanchez Paredes, and Doctors Farfan and De Saude y Robles, takes over the government.

1584. September 25. The 6th Viceroy, Don Pedro de Moya y Contreras, Archbishop of Mexico and Inquisitor, takes over the government.

1585. The 7th Viceroy, Alvaro Manrique de Zuñiga, Marques de Villa Manrique, takes possession.

1590. January 27. The 8th Viceroy, the second Luis de Velasco, enters upon his office.

1595. November. The 9th Viceroy, Gaspar de Zuñiga y Acevedo, Conde de Monterrey, takes possession.

1596. Foundation of Villa de Felipe II (later San Juan Bautista de Tabasco and now Villahermosa.)

1596. The city of Monterrey founded.

1603. October 27. The 10th Viceroy, Juan de Mendoza y Luna, Marques de Montes Claros, takes over the government.

1605. July 12. A fleet sails from Cadiz for New Spain bringing with it the first copies of Don Quixote sent out to the Colony.

1607. July 20. Don Luis de Velasco II, again takes over the government as 11th Viceroy.

1608. September 17. Viceroy Velasco inaugurates the great drainage works of the Valley of Mexico.

1611. June 19. Fray Garcia Guerra, Archbishop of Mexico, takes office as 12th Viecroy.

1612. February 22. Death of Fray Garcia Guerra, whereupon the Audiencia, presided over by the senior *Oidor, Rev.* Licenciado Pedro Otalora, takes over the government.

1612. October 18. Government taken over by Diego Fernandez de Cordova, Marques de Guadalcazar, as 13th Viceroy.

1621. March 14. Departure of Viceroy Fernandez de Cordoba for Peru, and *Audiencia,* presided over by Licenciado Paz de Vallecillo, takes over duties of office.

1621. September 12. Diego Carrillo de Mendoza y Pimentel, Marques de Gelves and Conde de Priego, takes over government as 14th Viceroy.

1621. November 29. First course in surgery at Mexico City university in charge of Mexican-born Doctor Cristobal de Hidalgo y Sandoval.

1624. November 3. Arrival of 15th Viceroy, Rodrigo Pacheco Osorio, Marques de Cerralvo.

1633. Augusto 12. Campeche looted by Dutch pirates led by John de Fors.

1853. September 16. The Marques de Cerralvo hands over reins of government to his successor, Lope Diaz de Armendariz, Marques de Cadereita, as 16th Viceroy.

1640. August 28. Reign of Marques de Cadereita comes to an end and he is succeeded by the 17th Viceroy, Diego Lopez Pacheco Cabrera y Bobadilla, Marques de Villena.

1639. August 15. Foundation of the village of San Felipe de Chihuahua, in the Province of New Biscay.

1642. June 10. Juan de Palafox y Mendoza, Bishop of Puebla, takes over government as 18th Viceroy.

1642. November 23. Palafox's reign comes to an end; he is succeeded by Garcia Sarmiento Sotomayor, Conde de Salvatierra, 19th Viceroy.

1648. May 13. Viceroy Sarmiento sails for Peru and Marcos de Torres y Rueda, Bishop of Yucatan, is entrusted with government of New Spain, as President of the Audiencia; he died on April 22, 1649.

1649. April 11. Auto da fe held by the Inquisition. Tomas Treviño burnt alive.

1650. The Spaniards, commanded by Hernan Martin, penetrate to the country of the Texas Indians, between the Neches and Sabine Rivers, Texas.

1650. June 28. The 20th Viceroy, Luis Enriquez de Guzman, Conde de Alba de Liste, takes the oath of office.

1651. November 12. Juana de Asbaje y Ramirez, later called the Tenth Muse, born at San Miguel Nepantla. She took the veil under the name of Sister Juana Inez de la Cruz.

1653. August 15. Francisco Fernandez de la Cueva, Duque de Albuquerque, enters upon the duties of his office as 21st Viceroy.

1660. September 16. The 22nd Viceroy, Juan de Leyva, Conde de Baños and Marques de Leyva, enters upon the duties of his office.

1664. June 29. Entrance of the 23d Viceroy, Diego Osorio Escobar, Bishop of Puebla.

1664. October 16. Antonio Sebastian de Toledo, Marques de Mancera, takes over the government as 24th Viceroy.

1673. December 8. The 25th Viceroy, Pedro Nuño Colon de Portugal, Duque de Veragua, took the oath of office. He died 5 days afterwards.

1673. December 15. The 26th Viceroy, Friar Payo Enriquez de Rivera entered upon the duties of his office.

1680. November 30. The 27th Viceroy, Tomas Antonio de la Cerda y Aragon, Conde de Paredes, took over the government.

1683. May 17. The pirates Nicolas de Agramonte and Lorencillo (Laurent de Graff) landed at Vera Cruz.

1686. November 30. Arrival of the 28th Viceroy, Melchor Portocarrero Lazo de la Vega, Conde de Monclova. Nicknamed "Silver Arm."

1688. November 20. Gaspar de la Cerda Sandoval Silva y Mendoza, Conde de Galvez, takes over the reins of government; he was the 29th Viceroy and held office until January 21, 1696, having then turned over the government to the *Audiencia.*

1692. June 8. Popular riot on account of scarcity of staple articles of food. Public buildings set on fire. Carlos de Sigüenza y Gongora saves the Archives of the City Council.

1693. Carlos de Sigüenza y Gongora published the "Mercurio Volante," being the first attempt at a newspaper in New Spain.

1696. February 27. Juan Ortega y Montañez, Bishop of Michoacan and 30th Viceroy, takes over the Government, the office having been refused by Manuel Fernandez de Santa Cruz, Bishop of Puebla.

1696. The 31st Viceroy,, Jose Sarmiento Valladares, Conde de Moctezuma, takes possession of his office.

1697. March 12. Riot on account of scarcity of grain in Mexico City.

1701. November 4. Juan Ortega y Montañez, takes over the government for a second time, as 32nd Viceroy.

1702. November 27. Francisco Fernandez de la Cueva, Duke of Albuquerque, enters upon his office as 33d Viceroy.

1711. January 15. Arrival of the 34th Viceroy, Fernando de Alencastre, Duque de Linares.

1716. August 16. Government taken over by Baltazar de Zuñiga, Duque de Arion, as 35th Viceroy.

1722. October 15. Arrival of the 36th Viceroy, Juan de Acuña, Marques de Casafuerte.

1734. March 17. Death of Viceroy Juan de Acuña; he is succeeded by Antonio de Vizarron, Archbishop of Mexico and 37th Viceroy.

1740. Pedro de Castro, Duque de la Conquista, enters upon the duties of his office as 38th Viceroy.

1741. August 22. Death of Pedro de Castro; government exercised by the *Audiencia* until the arrival of the 39th Viceroy, Pedro Cebrian, Conde de Fuenclara, in 1742.

1742. A rough census of New Spain, based on the number of families shows 3.865,529 inhabitants.

1745. May 13. The architect, Francisco Eduardo Tres Guerras, born at Celaya, Guanajuato.

1746. July 9. The 40th Viceroy, Francisco de Güemes y Horcasitas, Conde de Revillagigedo, takes over the reins of government in Mexico City.

1755. November 10. Government taken over by Agustin de Ahumada, Marques de las Amarillas, 41st Viceroy.

1760. February 5. Death of Viceroy Ahumada, government by the *Audiencia* until the 28th April, on which day Francisco Cajigal de la Vega took over the Government, *pro tempore*, as 42nd Viceroy.

1760. October 6. Viceroyalty taken over by Joaquin de Montserrat, Marques de Cruillas, as 43d Viceroy.

1765. August 25. Arrival of *Visitador*, or royal visitor, Jose de Galvez.

1766. August 25. Government taken over by Carlos Francisco de Croix, as 44th Viceroy.

1767. June 27. Expulsion of the Jesuits.

1771. September 23. The 45th Viceroy, Antonio Maria de Bucareli, took possession of his office.

1776. November 15. Jose Joaquin Fernandez de Lizardi, nicknamed the "Mexican Thinker" born in the City of Mexico. Liberal journalist. Author of a novel called "El Periquillo Sarniento." Died June 21, 1827.

1779. April 9. Death of Viceroy Bucareli.

1779. August 29. Martin de Mayorga, the 46th Viceroy, takes over the government.

1783. April 29. Matias de Galvez, as 47th Viceroy takes over the government.

1784. November 3. Death of Viceroy Matias de Galvez; government by the *Audiencia* presided over by Vicente Herreras.

1785. June 17. The 48th Viceroy, Bernardo de Galvez, takes possession of his high office.

1786. November 30. Death of Viceroy Bernardo de Galvez. Government in hands of Regent, Eusebio Beleño.

1787. May 8. The 50th Viceroy, Manuel Antonio Flores, takes over government, with military powers only, administration of the Treasury Department being entrusted to Fernando Mangino.

1789. Juan Vicente de Güemes Pacheco Padilla, 2nd Conde de of Revillagigedo, takes over the reins of government as 5ist Viceroy.

1792. January 1. Opening of the School of Mines.

1793. 4. Population of whole country estimated at 4.483,569 inhabitants, while another estimate places it at 5.200,000.

1793-4. Census of Mexico City by order of Revillagigedo; population 135,000.

1794. July 12. The 52nd Viceroy, Miguel de la Grua Talamanca y Branciforte, brother-in-law of the royal favorite, Godoy, takes possession of his office.

1794. September 8. Appearance of broad sheets celebrating the consequences of the French Revolution.

1795. April 27. First course of Mineralogy started in Mexico with Andres del Rio as professor.

1799. November 10. Meeting of the "conspiracy of the *machetes*" (cutlasses) headed by Pedro de la Portilla, a tax-gatherer, with 2 muskets and 50 sabres as sole weapons.

1798. March 31. The 53d Viceroy, Miguel Jose de Asanza, takes possession of the government.

1800. April 30. Arrival of Felix Berenguer de Marquina, 54th Viceroy.

1801. January 1. Uprising headed by Mariano the Indian, at Tepic.

1803. January 4. The 55th Viceroy, Jose de Iturrigaray, takes possession of his office.

1804. December 26. Royal decree providing for alienation of charitable funds, which meant the collection and remittance to Spain of 44 million pesos.

1804. According to Humboldt's estimate, the population of Mexico at this time was 5.837,100 inhabitants.

1805. October 1. First number of the "Diario de Mexico," published by Don Carlos Maria de Bustamante and Don Jacobo Villaurrutia. This first daily newspaper, dragged out a precarious existence until 1817.

THE MOVEMENT FOR INDEPENDENCE

1808. March 17. Rioting at Aranjuez.

1808. June 23. The events in Spain which gave rise to the abdication of Charles IV and Ferdinand VII, become known in Mexico.

1808. July 19. The City Council of Mexico requests the Viceroy to declare a state of provisional independence, inasmuch as sovereignty has devolved upon the kingdom.

1808. August 9. Meeting of the City Council; an Alderman, Azcarate, and the Clerk, Licenciado Verdad, made speeches insisting on fact of national sovereignty.

1808. September 9. At a meeting of the Mexico City Council Don Jacobo de Villaurrutia moves that a General Meeting of the Kingdom be convened.

1808. September 15. Arrest of Viceroy Iturrigaray by partisans of the *Audiencia*, of the Inquisition, and of the Spanish group, led by

Gabriel Yermo, a large landowner. The same group appointed Marshal Pedro Garibay as Viceroy.

1808. Population of country estimated at 6.500,000. (Humboldt.)

1808. October 4. Licenciado Francisco Primo Verdad dies in prison, having probably been hanged.

1809. July 19. The 57th Viceroy, Francisco de Lizana y Beaumont, Archbishop of Mexico, takes over the office, having been appointed by the Central Junta at Aranjuez. On the 8th May he turned the government over to the *Audiencia,* Don Pedro Catani having acted as Regent.

1809. September 9. Conspiracy at Valladolid, framed by Don Mariano Michelena, Captain Garcia Obeso, Friar Vicente de Santa Maria and others. Failure of the conspiracy due to an informer.

1810. September 13. The 58th Viceroy, Francisco Javier Venegas, takes possession of his office.

1810. September 10. Information lodged in regard to conspiracy at Queretaro, San Miguel and Dolores, schemed by Ignacio Allende, Miguel Hidalgo and others.

1810. September 15 and 16. Cry of independence at village of Dolores.

1810. September 21. The insurgent troops occupy Celaya, after passing through San Miguel. Miguel Hidalgo appointed Captain General.

1810. September 24. Edict by the Archbishop elect of Michoacan, Abad y Queipo, excommunicating Hidalgo and his followers.

1810. September 27. Proclamation by the Viceroy, Venegas, offering ten thousand pesos each for the heads of Hidalgo, Allende and Aldama.

1810. September 28. Guanajuato occupied and the *Albondiga de Granaditas,* or Castle, taken by storm by the insurgents. Defeat and death of Riaño. Hidalgo leaves Guanajuato on October 10 and takes Valladolid on the 17th.

1810. October 10. Hidalgo leaves for Valladolid. He takes it on the 17th.

1810. October 20. Interview between Hidalgo and Morelos at a point between Indaparapeo and Charo. Commission and oral instructions for war of independence.

1810. October 30. Insurgent troops win a victory at the Monte de las Cruces. Hidalgo stays close to the City of Mexico until the 2nd November, when he falls back to Queretaro.

1810. November 1. The troops of Morelos attack Acapulco. On the 9th they take the hill called the Veladero.

1810. November 7. Calleja's army inflicts defeats the insurgents at Aculco.

1810. November 25. Calleja retakes Guanajuato, whence Allende withdraws after being defeated. Reprisals by Calleja on the 26th and 27th.

1810. November 26. Hidalgo enters Guadalajara, that had previously been occupied by an insurgent, Torres.

1810. December 6. Decree issued by Hidalgo, abolishing slavery and tribute. Jose Maria Chico and Ignacio Lopez Rayon form a government as Ministers.

1810. Mexico is estimated to have a population of 5.910,000. (Data furnished by "Semanario Economico.")

1811. January 17. Defeat and dispersion of insurgents, at Puente de Calderon. Calleja enters Guadalajara on the 21st.

1811. March 21. Capture of Hidalgo, Allende and other insurgent chiefs by Ignacio Elizondo, after they had passed through Aguascalientes, El Pabellón, Zacatecas and Saltillo, and when they reached a place called Acatita de Bajan. From there the prisioners were taken to Monclova and after that to Chihuahua.

1811. July 26. Insurgent leaders Allende, Aldama and Jimenez executed at Chihuahua. Thirty more undergo a similar fate a few days later.

1811. July 30. Execution of Miguel Hidalgo.

1811. January 4. Defeat of royalist chief Paris at the hands of Morelos' troops.

1811. May 3. Morelos begins his march on Chilpancingo. He occupied this town on the 24th and Tixtla on the 26th. He repulsed Fuentes, a royalist, on August 15th, occupied Chilapa on the 18th and Chiautla on the 5th December.

1811. June 22. Ignacio Lopez Rayon, appointed chief of the Revolution defeats Emparan before Zitacuaro. On August 19th he organized at this place a Junta of Government together with Liceaga, Verduzco and Yarza.

1811. July 13. Licenciado Rayon proposes to Morelos the formation of a Junta to direct the revolution.

1811. August 1. Congressmen from the Americas at the Cortes of Cadiz insist that the colonies be granted:

1. Political equality with the metropolis.
2. Freeedom of industry and agriculture.
3. Freedom of trade.
4. Suppression of state monopolies and of preference for European Spaniards in public offices and positions.

1812. January 1. Calleja occupies the town of Zitacuaro after defeating Rayon. The Junta moves to Sultepec.

1812. February 9. Morelos enters Cuautla. On the 12th the main body of royalist troops left Mexico City. Attack on Cuautla on the 18th. On March 5th the work of investment was begun and bombardment on the 10th. Matamoros made a sortie on the 21st April in an attempt to bring in provisions. Siege broken on May 2nd.

1812. June 4. Morelos re-appears and his vanguard defeats royalists at Citlala. On July 13th he appears before Huajuapam to assist Valerio Trujano. On August 10th he enters Tehuacan in order to launch his third campaign.

1812. September 13. Leonardo Bravo is executed in Mexico City. His son, Nicolas, subsequently pardoned three hundred Spanish prisioners.

1812. October 5. The decree providing from freedom of the press is proclaimed in Mexico.

1812. October 13. Morelos leaves Tehuacan. On the 29th he takes Orizaba by assault. On November 1st he fights Aguila at Acultzingo. He returns to Tehuacan and then moves on Oaxaca, the 25th November, taking the latter place by storm. On January 9, 1813, he marches on Acapulco.

1813. February 13. Calleja takes over the office of Viceroy.

1813. April 6. Operations of Morelos against Acapulco begin. On the 9th June Galeana occupies Roqueta Island. On the 17th August the Castle is surrounded. The fort surrenders on the 20th August.

1813. September 15. Congress of Chilpancingo installed with Rayon, Bustamante, Quintana Roo, Dr. Cos, etc.

1813. October 13. Morelos this day re-enacts abolition of slavery decreed by Hidalgo, December, 1810.

1813. November 7. Morelos begins his fourth campaign and marches on Valladolid where he arrives December 22nd; attacks it on the 23d. Iturbide defeats Matamoros on the heights of Santa Maria. Defeat and rout of the Insurgents at Puruaran on January 5, 1814. Matamoros executed 3d February.

1813. November 6. Proclamation of independence in decree issued by the "Congress of Anahuac lawfully installed in the City of Chilpancingo in North America."

1814. October 22. Constitution of Apatzingan proclaimed.

1815. September 29. Congress leaves Uruapam for Tehuacan, escorted by Morelos. This military leader is defeated and captured at Texmalaca on the 5th November. Carried as a prisoner to Mexico City, November 22nd.

1815. November 27. Ecclesiastical degradation of Morelos by the Tribunal of the Inquisition.

1815. December 22. Execution of Morelos at San Cristobal Ecatepec.

1817. April 15. Francisco Javier Mina lands on the Mexican coast, near Soto La Marina.

1817. May 24. Mina starts on his march to the interior of the country.

1817. June 8. Mina defeats Villaseñor at Valle del Maiz, and Armiñan at Peotillos, June 15th.

1817. June 28. Mina defeats Ordoñez at Los Arrastres. Attacks the city of Leon without success and falls back on the Fuerte (Fort) del Sombrero, where the insurgent leader Pedro Moreno was in command.

1817. August 4. Liñan attacks the fort and is repulsed.

1817. August 9. Mina succeeds in breaking through the investing cordon round the Fuerte del Sombrero, after three unsuccessful attempts. Pedro Moreno remains in the Fort.

1817. August 29. Liñan takes the Fort.

1817. August 31. Liñan follows Mina to the Fuerte (Fort) of Los Remedios. Mina manages to evade him.

1817. October 10. Orrantia defeats Mina at Las Cajas.

1817. October 26. Mina arrives at the Venadito Ranch after an unsuccessful attack on Guanajuato.

1817. October 27. Orrantia takes Mina by surprise, at dawn.

1817. November 11. Mina executed in front of the Fuerte de Los Remedios.

1818. January 1. Royalist troops occupy the Fuerte de Los Remedios, and on the 6th March they take the Fuerte de Jaujilla.

1821. January 2. Vicente Guerrero attacks Moya at Zapotepec.

1821. January 10. Letter from Iturbide to Guerrero urging the latter to join him.

1821. January 20. Guerrero answers Iturbide in haughty terms.

1821. January 17. Concession granted to Moses Austin for colonizing Texas.

1821. February 4. Iturbide again addresses a letter to Guerrero.

1821. February 15. Interview between the two leaders, at Acatempan.

1821. February 24. The Plan of Iguala proclaimed; Independence, Union, and Religion.

1821. March 2. Iturbide's troops take the oath of allegiance to the Plan of Iguala or of the Three Guaranties.

1821. July 8. Viceroy Apodaca is removed from office by a group of the military, and General Pedro Novella appointed in his stead.

1821. July 30. Arrival of the new Viceroy, Juan O'Donoju, at Vera Cruz.

1821. August 24. Iturbide and O'Donojú, at Cordoba, conclude a treaty confirming the Plan of Iguala with certain modifications.

1821. September 13. Iturbide, O'Donoju and Novella meet at a point near the City of Mexico and conclude an armistice. O'Donoju is recognized as the 62nd Viceroy.

1821. September 27. Triumphal entry of Iturbide into Mexico City with the Army of the Three Guarenties. Independence is looked upon as achieved.

INDEPENDENT MEXICO

INTEGRATION OF THE NATION

1821. February. The Spanish Cortes reject the Treaty of Cordoba and declare O'Donoju a traitor.

1821. September 8. A Provisional Junta of Government for the Mexican Empire is installed. Appointment of five regents, including Iturbide and O'Donoju.

1821. October 8. Death of Juan O'Donoju, the last Viceroy of Mexico.

1822. February 24. A Congress meets to draw up a Constitution.

1822. May 18. Iturbide is proclaimed Emperor, under the title of Agustin I.

1822. October 22. Iturbide dissolves the Constituent Congress and attempts to create an "Instituting Junta."

1822. December 2. Insurrection of Santa Anna at Jalapa on behalf of Congress and a Republic. Joined by Guadalupe Victoria. Plan of Casa Mata, February 1, 1823.

1823. March 7. Iturbide reinstates Congress. He abdicates on the 19th of the same month and sails for Europe on the 11th April.

1823. April. Congress appoints an Executive Triumvirate composed of Pedro Celestino Negrete, Nicolas Bravo and Guadalupe Victoria, the last two last having, due to their absence, been replaced by Mariano Michelena and Miguel Dominguez.

1823. May 16. Decree ordering the sale of the property of the Inquisition.

1823. November 7. The new Congress assembles for the purpose of drawing up a constitution.

1824. February 7. A loan of £3.200,000 sterling contracted with S. Goldsmith and Co., of London, bearing interest at 5% and at a discount of 55%.

1824. April 3. Congress outlaws Iturbide. The latter lands at Soto La Marina on July 14th, is captured and tried by the local Congress, and executed on July 19th, at a place called Padilla.

1824. October 4. The Constitution of the Republic of Mexico, establishing a federal regimen, proclaimed.

1824. October 10. The President, General Guadalupe Victoria, and the Vice-President, General Nicolas Bravo, inaugurated.

1824. Population of Mexico at this time: 5.500,000. (Poinsett's figures.)

1825. November 18. Surrender of the last Spanish garrison in Mexico, at San Juan de Ulua.

1826. July 17. Spanish-American treaty concluded at Panama between Mexico, Colombia, Central America and Peru, with clauses providing for an alliance between these countries.

1826. December 29. The "Seven Constitutional Laws" establish a Central Government and power along conservative lines.

1827. December 20. Decree providing for expulsion of Spaniards.

1828. November 3. Riot at the Acordada, prison in Mexico City.

1828. December 4. Looting of the Parian, or Bazaar, at Mexico City.

1828. Electoral contest between Gomez Pedraza and Guerrero. The *Yorkinos* (York rite party), ultra-radical liberals, support Guerrero. The *Escoceses* (Scottish rite party) consisting of moderates, conservatives and former partisans of Iturbide and of the Crown support Gomez Pedraza.

1829. January 12. Congress declares Gomez Pedraza's election null and void and recognizes Guerrero as President and General Anastasio Bustamante as Vice-President. Both are inaugurated April 1st.

1829. July 26. The Spanish expedition commanded by Brigadier General Isidro Barradas lands near Tampico. It reaches this place on the 15th August. On being attacked by Santa Anna, it surrenders on September 11th.

1829. December 4. Insurrection of Vice-President Bustamante at Jalapa, his tendencies being conservative. President Guerrero leaves Jose Maria Bocanegra in power as Provisional President and sallies forth to combat the insurrectionists.

1830. January 14. Congress disqualifies Guerrero from governing and recognizes Bustamante as President.

1830. Population of Mexico: 7.796,000. (Figures from Burkardt.)

1831. January 25. One Picaluga betrays General Vicente Guerrero, and delivers him into the hands of his enemies.

1831. February 14. Execution of General Vicente Guerrero.

1832. December 23. Treaty of Zavaleta recognizing Gomez Pedraza as President and restoring the federal system of government.

1833. April 1. The Texas Convention moves for separation from Coahuila.

1833. April 1. Valentin Gómez Farias inaugurated as Vice-President in charge, due to absence of President elect, Antonio Lopez de Santa Anna.

1833. May 26. Insurrection of Escalada in Morelos, his battle cry being "Religion and Privileges" and dictatorship of Santa Anna.

1833. August 17. Law for secularization of property belonging to the California Missions.

1833. October 14. Closing of the Pious College of Santa Maria de los Santos.

1833. October 21. Suppression of the Royal and Pontifical University of Mexico.

1833. October 23. Law-for the Organization of Public Education in the Federal District.

1833. October 27. Civil executive procedure for collection of tithes, done away with.

1833. October 31. Circular from the Ministry of Justice prohibiting sermons on political subjects.

1833. November 6. Law doing away with civil action for compelling performance of monastic vows.

1833. November 7. Motion by Zavala in Congress for payment of public debt by secularization of ecclesiastical property.

1834. May 25. Revolutionary Plan of Cuernavaca, contrary to liberal reform.

1834. Restoration of University with amended by-laws.

1834. Population of country: 7.734,292 inhabitants. Source of information: Galvan's Almanac.

1835. January 28. Santa Anna turns presidency over to General Miguel Barragan and leaves on an expedition to fight the rebels at Zacatecas, where he is victorious on May 11th.

1835. October 23. Constitutional Bases providing for centralization of power, proclaimed.

1835. November 7. Texas Convention decides on separation from Mexico, alleging Santa Anna's centralist despotism.

1835. December 4. Hostilities with Texas break out, at Bexar.

1835. December 5-11. Attack on and taking of San Antonio by Texan separatists.

1836. March. Texas Convention declares independence.

1836. March 6. Santa Anna attacks and takes the Alamo by storm.

1836. April 21. Houston defeats Santa Anna at San Jacinto.

1836. May 14. Treaty of Velasco and withdrawal of Mexican troops from Texas.

1836. December 28. The "Seven Constitutional Laws" finally establishing centralization of power, and extending the presidential term of office to eight years, proclaimed on this day.

1836. Approximate figures for population, 7.843,132 inhabitants.

1837. February 6. President Jackson of the United States, in his message to Congress speaks of the necessity of resorting to arms against Mexico.

1837. March 1. U. S. Senate recognizes independence of Texas.

1837. April 12. General Anastasio Bustamante inaugurated as President.

1838. March 21. Ultimatum presented by the French Minister in connection with claims of his nationals.

1838. April 16. Relations with France broken off.

1838. November 27. French fleet bombards San Juan de Ulua and this fortress and Port of Vera Cruz surrender to the French.

1838. December 5. French troops land at Vera Cruz. Fight in which Santa Anna is wounded in the leg.

1838. Population of country: 7.500,000 inhabitants, according to Almonte's abridged geography.

1839. March 9. Treaty of peace with France recognizing claims amounting to $600,000.00.

1839. March 18. President Bustamante leaves to fight the anti-centralist insurrection at Tampico and leaves Santa Anna in power.

1839. Population of the country: 7.044,000 inhabitants. Figures from Geographical and Statistical Institute.

1839. May 29. Uprising headed by Santiago Iman, at Tizimin, Yucatan. He takes Valladolid and proclaims federalism on February 8, 1840.

1840. July 15. Coup d'Etat of Urrea with the assistance of Gomez Farias, in favor of the Constitution of 1824.

1841. March 31. Congress of Yucatan declares its independence and establishes a liberal regime.

1841. September 28. Plan of Tacubaya, and subsequent covenant of La Estanzuela under which Santa Anna returned to the presidency, on the 11th October.

1842. June 10. A Congress meets to draw up a constitution, of moderately liberal tendency, but an insurrection provokes its dissolution.

1843. January 6. A Junta of Notables meets, and draws up Organic Bases for Centralization, issued July 12th.

1844. April 12. Treaty of annexation of Texas to the United States.

1845. March 1. U. S. Congress approves annexation of Texas.

1845. May 27. Santa Anna exiled to Venezuela after imprisonment at Perote.

1845. December 14. Insurrection of Paredes Arrillaga at San Luis Potosi, at the head of troops intended for war with Texas.

THE AMERICAN INVASION

1846. March 25. General Zachary Taylor occupies Fronton de Santa Isabel and advances on Matamoros. Mexican troops attack in April and capture an American detachment. U. S. Congress declares war.

1846. May 8. Battle of Palo Alto and Mexican troops fall back on Matamoros, May 9. Battle of Resaca de Guerrero or La Palma. May 18. Matamoros evacuated.

1846. May 20. Federalist insurrection of Gomez Farias at Guadala-ara. Paredes Arrillaga leaves Mexico City to put it down but General Mariano Salas revolts in the capital. Congress meets December 6th and appoints Santa Anna as President.

1846. May 20. Vera Cruz blockaded by the American fleet.

1846. September 18. Taylor's troops appear before Monterrey.

1846. September 20. Attack on Monterrey begins.

1846. September 24. Surrender of Monterrey and suspension of hostilities until November 13th.

1846. December 27. Colonel Doniphan takes Paso del Norte (El Paso) and on March 1, 1847, reaches Chihuahua.

1847. January 11. Law authorizing disposal of property held in mortmain to raise 15 million pesos for prosecution of war with the United States.

1847. February 8. American fleet off Vera Cruz. March 5th. 8th and 9th, reconnoitering and landing. March 15th, investment of Vera Cruz complete.

1847. February 22 and 23. Battle of La Angostura, near Saltillo and Hacienda de Buena Vista.

1847. February 22. Revolt of the "Polkos," until March 20, when Santa Anna returns.

1847. March 22 and 29. Bombardment and seizure of Vera Cruz.

1847. April 17. Battle of Cerro Gordo or Telegraph Hill.

1847. May 15. General Worth enters Puebla.

1847. August 19 and 20. Battle of Padierna. Military operations at Churubusco, Portales and Garita de San Antonio. Armistice. September 8. Battle of Molino del Rey. September 13, attack on Chapultepec. September 14 and 15, American troops march into City of Mexico.

1847. November 12. General Anaya inaugurated as Provisional President, but almost immediately replaced by Manuel Peña y Peña.

1848. February 2. Treaty of Guadalupe between Mexico and the United States, approved by Mexican Congress May 13th of same year.

ANARCHY AND DICTATORSHIP

1848. June 12. President General Jose Joaquin Herrera inaugurated as President, at Queretaro.

1851. January 15. General Mariano Arista inaugurated as Presiden-

1852. July 26. Local uprising at Guadalajara.

1852. September 13. Revolutionary plan against Arista on behalf of Santa Anna.

1852. December 14. Insurrection of Moret at Durango.

1852. Population of country: 7.661,919 inhabitants. (From Almonte's Guide.)

1852. September 13. A new plan proclaimed at Guadalajara. Articles: upholding of the Federal Constitution, refusal to acknowledge the Public Power and invitation to General Antonio Lopez de Santa Anna to return to the country to assist in upholding the federal system and to re-establish peace and order.

1853. January 4. President Arista resigns, due to opposition in Congress. Provisional presidents, Juan B. Ceballos from January 4 to February 7th and General Manuel Maria Lombardini up to April 20th.

1853. January 6. The President, Mariano Arista left the capital at dawn on this day, after turning the government over to the President of the High Court of Justice, Juan B. Ceballos.

1853. February 7. Ceballos resigns the presidency and his resignation is accepted by Lombardini, Uraga and Robles, the leaders of the revolting divisions. The former is appointed as depositary of the Executive Power.

1853. April 20. General Santa Anna arrives in Capital and takes office as President of the Republic.

1853. Treaty approving the Gadsden Purchase.

1853. December 16. Santa Anna becomes Dictator and the title of Most Serene Highness is conferred upon him.

1853. November 5. The first section of electric telegraph, promoted by Juan de la Granja, is inaugurated between Mexico City and Nopalucan.

LIBERAL REFORM

1854. March 1. Plan of Ayutla.

1855. August 9. General Santa Anna leaves Mexico City at three in the morning on his way to Vera Cruz; General Martin Carrera takes over the reins of government and appoints Romulo Diaz de la Vega as Commander in Chief and Governor of the District.

1855. August 13. At one o'clock in the morning, the garrison of the Capital revolts in favor of the Plan of Ayutla, making a few changes and appointing General Romulo Diaz de la Vega as its leader.

1855. September 12. General Carrera resigns the Presidency leaving General Romulo Diaz de la Vega as Governor of the District.

1855. October 4. General Alvarez is appointed provisional President *pro tem* of the Republic of Mexico, by the Junta of representatives of the States.

1855. ovember 23. Law suspending ecclesiastical and military jurisdiction and privileges.

1855. December 8. The President *pro tem* of the Republic appoints General Comonfort as his substitute.

1855. December 11. General Comonfort takes over the office of President of the Republic.

1856. February 18. Installation of the Constituent Congress or Assembly.

1856. March 31. Decree providing for secularization of Church property to compensate the Government for the expenses incurred in the campaign against the Puebla reactionaries.

1856. June 5. Suspension of the Society of Jesus.

1856. June 24. Secularization of church property.

1856. May 15. Statutory Ordinance legalizing the liberal régime

1856. June 28. The decree signed on the 25th of the same month, providing for expropriation of property belonging to civil and ecclesiastical corporations, published in Mexico City.

1856. October 20. Insurrection of Orihuela and Miramon, suppressed December 3d.

1856. December 10. Revolt of Rosas Landa at San Luis, ending in Osollo's defeat, February 7, 1857.

1857. January 1. General Mejia seizes $240,000 that had been deposited at the British Consulate at San Luis Potosi.

1857. January 27. Proclamation of Law establishing Civil Register.

1857. January 30. Secularization of cemeteries.

1857. February 5. Proclamation of Federal Constitution.

1857. February 26. Circular from the ecclesiastical authorities, at Puebla, prohibiting the faithful from taking the oath of allegiance to Mexico's new Constitution.

1857. April 11. Civil executive action for collection of parochial dues, suppressed. (Iglesias Law.)

1857. July 4. Opening of railway from Mexico City to Guadalupe.

1857. Population of country: 8.283,088. (Garcia Cubas.)

1857. December 1. Inauguration of General Ignacio Comonfort as President.

1857. December 17. Zuloaga revolts proclaiming the abrogation of the Constitution of 1857, the presidency of Comonfort and calling a new congress to frame a constitution for the Republic. (Plan of Tacubaya.)

1858. January 11. Uprising in Mexico City proclaiming General Zuloaga President.

1858. January 18. Benito Juarez establishes his constitutional government at Guanajuato and moves to Guadalajara.

1858. March 8. Defeat of liberals at Salamanca.

1858. March 13. Military uprising against Juarez at Guadalajara.

1858. January 22. The Junta of Representatives, according to plan, proceeds to appoint a president *pro tempore*, General Felix Zuloaga having been elected to the post.

1858. January 28. The following five decrees published: (1) Decree annulling law of June 25, 1856 on secularization of property of ecclesiastical corporations, (2) Decree abrogating law on parochial dues, April 11, 1857: (3) Decree restoring ecclesiastical jurisdiction and privileges to the same status as in 1833; (4) Decree restoring the Court of Justice and everything relating to the law courts, to the status as of November 22, 1855, when the called Juarez Law was proclaimed, now abrogated by this decree; and (5) Decree reinstating the persons who had lost their positions on account of refusal to take the oath of allegiance to the Constitution.

1858. April 7. Juarez appoints Degollado Commander in Chief and leaves Colima for Manzanillo. Board ship for Panama April 11th, reaching this place on the 22nd and New Orleans on May 8th.

1858. May 4. Benito Juarez arrives at Vera Cruz and establishes his government there.

1859. January 1. General Miramon is elected President of the Republic by the Junta of Notables, by fifty votes.

1859. January 23. The decree issued by Miramon as Commander in Chief, restoring Zuloaga to the Presidency, published in Mexico City.

1859. February 2. General Miguel Miramon takes over the Presidency.

1859. March 18. Miramon makes his appearance before Vera Cruz, but leaves on the 30th.

1859. March 22. Degollado threatens the City of Mexico.

1859. April 11. Degollado defeated at Tacubaya, by Marquez. Execution of liberal prisoners.

1859. July 12. Law enacted by Juarez, established freedom of worship, and secularizing the property of the Church, and closing monasteries and novitiates of nuns.

1859. July 23. Juarez enacts law on civil marriage.

1860. March 6. Mexican S. S. "Marques de la Habana" and "General Miramon" commanded by fleet captain Tomas Marin, anchored of Anton Lizardo; attacked and captured that same night with the assistance of the American sloop of war "Saratoga" and two American steamers.

1860. August 10. Gonzalez Ortega and Zaragoza defeat Miramon at Silao.

1860. December 28. Laws of Reform proclaimed. Said laws were enacted at Vera Cruz on July 12, 13 and 23 by the Constitutional Government, and provide for freedom of worship, closing of monasteries, conditions for existence of nuns, secularization of Church property and solemnization of civil marriages.

1861. January 1. The Constitutionalist army enters the City of Mexico.

1861. January 6. Laws enacted at Vera Cruz on the 4th December preceding, and ratified by Minister Juan Antonio de la Fuente, proclaimed in Mexico City. Said laws provides for separation of Church and State; freedom of worship, forbid all outward manifestations of same, the right of sanctuary, official recognition of clergymen, attendance by civil officials at ceremonies of worship in an official capacity, or any official courtesies such as drawing up of troops, etc. The taking of oaths, being a religious act, is done away with when entering upon any offices, or making any contracts, certificates and other public documents and acts of civil life.

1861. January 11. President Juarez returns to the Capital.

1861. January 12. The Government deports the following persons from the Republic: The Spanish Minister, Francisco Pacheco, the Ministers of Guatemala and Ecuador, Felipe Neri del Barrio and Francisco Pastor, and the Apostolic Delegate, Monsignor Luis Clementi.

1861. June 3. Execution of Melchor Ocampo.

1861. June 16. Santos Degollado dies on the Toluca road.

1861. Defeat and death of Leandro Valle at the Monte de las Cruces.

1861. July 17. Congress suspends payments on the Foreign Debt.

FRENCH INTERVENTION AND THE EMPIRE OF MAXIMILIAN

1861. October 31. A Convention concluded between England, France and Spain for intervention in Mexico, is signed at London.

1861. December 17. Spanish troops land at Vera Cruz.

1862. January. The French and British fleets arrive at Vera Cruz.

1862. February 19. Treaty or agreement of La Soledad.

1862. April 9. The triple alliance between England, France and Spain broken off.

1862. April 28. Victories of French and reactionary troops at the heights of Acultzingo.

1862. May 5. Defeat of French troops, under the command of General Lorencez, before Puebla.

1862. Population of country: 8.396,524 inhabitants.

1863. March 16. Forey begins the siege of Puebla, defended by Gonzalez Ortega.

1863. April 13. The Mexican cavalry breaks through the siege.

1863. May 17. Puebla surrenders unconditionally.

1863. May 31. Juarez leaves the capital for San Luis Potosi.

1863. June 7. The French Army enters the City of Mexico.

1863. July 10. The "Junta of Notables" offers the Imperial Crown of Mexico to Archduke Maximilian of Austria.

1863. December 23. President Juarez leaves San Luis Potosí for Saltillo.

1864. March 28 to 31. The French warship "La Cordelière" makes an unsuccessful attack on Mazatlan.

1864. April 10. Maximilian accepts the crown and signs the Treaty of Miramar, concluded with Napoleon III.

1864. May 28. Arrival at Vera Cruz of Maximilian and Carlotta.

1864. June 12. Maximilian and Carlotta make their entry into Mexico City.

1865. October 3. Law enacted by the Imperial Government providing the death penalty for all persons forming part of armed bands.

1866. July 8. The Empress Carlotta leaves for Europe.

1866. August 10. Interview between the Empress Carlotta and Napoleon III, at St. Cloud.

1866. September 27. The Empress Carlotta visits His Holiness Pius IX and shows first symptoms of insanity.

1866. November 20. Maximilian discusses the matter of his abdication with his ministers and counsellors, and the majority decide against it.

1866. December 18. French troops begin to leave Mexico.

1867. January 14. A meeting of the "Junta de Notables" decides against Maximilian's abdication.

1867. January 22. Juarez establishes his government at Zacatecas, but is compelled to leave this place on the 28th by Miramon.

1867. February 1. Escobedo defeats Miramon at San Jacinto.

1867. February 19. Maximilian establishes his headquarters at Queretaro.

1867. March 10. Queretaro besieged by the liberals.

1867. March 11. Th last French troops leave Mexican soil.

1867. May. 15. Fall of Queretaro and capture of Maximilian.

1867. June 14. A court-martial meets and sentences Maximilian, Miramon and Mejia to death.

1867. June 19. Execution of Maximilian, Miramon and Mejia on the *Cerro de las Campanas,* or Hill of the Bells."

RESTORATION OF THE REPUBLIC

1867. July 21. Benito Juarez re-establishes his government in the City of Mexico.

1867. December. Congress declares Benito Juarez President and Sebastian Lerdo de Tejada President of the Supreme Court.

1869. September 16. Opening of the railway line between Mexico City and Puebla.

1869. Population of the country 8.743,614 inhabitants. (Garcia Cubas.)

1870. October 13. Law of amnesty for political offenses, three persons, Leonardo Marquez, Archbishop Labastida and General Uraga being excluded.

1871. May. 2. Insurrection at Tampico.

1871. October 1. Revolt at the Ciudadela in Mexico City.

1871. November 8. Revolt of General Porfirio Diaz proclaiming the *Plan de la Noria*.

1871. December 1. Juarez constitutional President.

1872. July 18. Death of Benito Juarez.

1872. July 19. The President of the Supreme Court of Justice, Sebastian Lerdo de Tejada, inaugurated as President of the Republic.

1872. Population of Mexico: 9.097,056.

1872. November 17. Congress declares Sebastian Lerdo de Tejada President by popular election.

1872. November 21. Porfirio Diaz, who had arrived in the City two days before, visits the President, Lerdo, at the latter's home.

1873. January 1. The Mexican railway opened to Vera Cruz.

1873. September 25. The Laws of reform declared constitutional.

1874. Population of Mexico: 9.343,740.

1876. January. Plan of Tuxtepec opposing Lerdo's re-election.

1876. March 21. General Porfirio Diaz amends Plan of Tuxtepec at Palo Blanco.

1876. October 26. Congress declares Lerdo re-elected.

1876. October 30. Manifesto of the President of the Supreme Court of Justice, declaring the elections for President of the Republic illegal.

1876. November 16. The troops of General Porfirio Diaz obtain a victory at Tecoac.

1876. November 20. President Lerdo leaves the City.

1876. Gen November 26. General Porfirio Diaz takes office as President of the Republic.

1877. January 2. Manifesto of Jose M. Iglesias, dated at Guadalajara, setting forth his reasons for considering himself entitled to the presidency, *pro tempore*, of the Republic.

1877. May 5. General Porfirio Diaz inaugurated as constitutional President.

1878. April 9. John W. Foster, Minister from the United States to Mexico, informs General Diaz that he has received orders from his Government to recognize him as President of Mexico.

1878. May 5. Constitution amended to prohibit re-election.

1878. June 25. General Escobedo fails in an attempt to restore the Lerdo régime.

1878. Population of Mexico: 9.384,183.

1878. October 12. Exhibition, for the first time, of some of Edison's inventions in Mexico.

1879. June 24. General Mier y Teran orders the execution, at Vera Cruz, of a number of persons involved in the uprising on the warship "Libertad."

1880. Population of Mexico: 9.577,279.

1881. December 1. Inauguration of General Manuel Gonzalez as President.

1880. Population of country: 10.001,884.

1882. February 23. The National Bank of Mexico begins operations.

1883. December 15. Law on Survey and Colonization of Lands, authorizing the formation of companies to develop public lands by surveying, delimiting, subdividing them, etc., and settling colonists thereon, such companies to be entitled to one third of lands by way of .compensation.

1885. June 22. Enactment of a law for consolidation and conversion of the national debt. Among the credits admitted to conversion, are the bonds of the English debt, amounting to fifty one million pesos ($51.000,000.00.)

1886. Population of country: 10.971,685.

1886. October 4. A conspiracy against the Government discovered at Zacatecas.

1886. October 31. General Garcia de la Cadena, the leader of the revolutionary movement that very nearly broke out on the 4th, captured. He was executed in the morning of the following day.

1887. October. Constitutional amendment to allow of re-election.

1888. December 1. Second re-election of General Porfirio Diaz.

1888. First General Census: 11.490,830.

1889. December 1. The First National Congress of Public Education, presided over by Justo Sierra, assembles.

1890. The Minister of *Fomento* grants concessions for ironworks at Monterrey and San Luis Potosí. Operations began in 1893. Silver production jumps from 39 to 47 million pesos.

1891. Patents taken out by MacArthur and Forrest, the inventors of the cyanide process for reduction of metals. The process first applied in 1893. Gold production gradually rises from 3 million pesos, to 50 million pesos in 1906.

1892. May 15. Students and workers demonstrate in Mexico City against the re-election of the President of the Republic.

1892. December 1. Third re-election of General Diaz.

1893. February 23. Jose I. Limantour becomes Minister of Finance.

1894. January 1. From statistics recently published, it appeared that at the beginning of the year 1894 there were in the Republic the following schools for higher education:

Sixteen high schools, nireteen schools of law, nine medical schools, eight engineering schools, twenty six theological seminaries, one school of practical Mining, eighty-one lyceums, four schools of Fine Arts, two agricultural colleges, two commercial academies, seven schools of arts and crafts, four *conservatoires* of music, one school for the blind, one for deaf-mutes, one Military College, two naval colleges and a great number of primary normal schools.

The appropriations for the support of these schools amounted to Ps. 3.512,000.00.

1895. General census: 12.632,427.

1896. December 1. Fourth re-election of General Diaz.

1898. February 14. New electric light service inaugurated in Mexico City, supplied by the German firm of Siemens and Halske.

1899. July 1. During the fiscal year 1898-1899 Federal income amounted to Ps. 60.023,349.23, a figure never theretofore reached by the public annual revenue.

1899. December 1. Fifth re-election of General Diaz.

1900. General census: 13.545,462 inhabitants.

1900. Railway mileage this year, 9,286 as compared with 325 miles in 1881.

1900. Revenue from Customs houses. Ps. 27.696,970.

1904. Sixth re-election of General Diaz, the office of Vice-President created and presidential term lengthened to six years.

1906. Establishment of one of the chief workers' unions, called the "Great Center of Free Workers" of the Puebla and Vera Cruz cotton mills.

1907. January 5. Award rendered by the President of the Republic, General Diaz, unfavorable to the interests of the Puebla and Vera Cruz mill hands.

1907. January 7. The workers of the Rio Blanco Vera Cruz cotton spinning district are attacked by Federal troops.

1907. July 6. The Government reorganizes and acquires control of the greater part of the railways of the country.

1908. Creelman, an American newspaper man, interviews President Diaz. Francisco I. Madero publishes his book entitled "The Presidential Succession in 1910."

1909. April 1. Manifesto of the "Democratic Party," drawn up by Calero, Urueta, Batalla and Zubaran.

1909. June 20. A group of revolutionaries headed by Ricardo and Enrique Flores Magon, and Antonio Villarreal, attacks Casas Grandes, in the State of Chihuahua, and four days later there was an uprising at Viesca, Coahuila. On the following day 100 men crossed the border and seized a place called Las Vacas, while on the 30th of the same month the Palomas, Chihuahua, customs house was taken by another rebel band.

1909. September 28. Several of the editors of a newspaper called "El Antirreeleccionista" were arrested, due to publication of an article on the subject of Magdalena Bay.

1910. General census: 15.160,369.

1910. October 4. Decree proclaimed declaring General Porfirio Diaz and Ramon Corral to have been elected President and Vice-President of the Republic, respectively, for the six year term 1910 to 1916.

THE REVOLUTION OF 1910

1910. October 6. Francisco I. Madero escapes from San Luis Potosí.

1910. October 25. Francisco Madero appoints a committee.

1910. November 20. Revolution breaks out in Puebla and Chihuahua.

1911. Establishment of the Confederation of the Gráphic Arts and other organizations, like the Quarrymen's Union of the Federal District. First revolutionary workmens' unions.

1911. January 30. Revolt in Lower California, headed by Ricardo Flores Magon and other exiled socialists. One hundred men seized and held Mexicali for a short time.

1911. March 5. Madero defeated at Casas Grandes.

1911. March 6. President Taft of the United States, orders twenty thousand soldiers, being 30 per cent of the regular U. S. Army, to mobilize on the Mexican border, and that fleets be stationed in Mexican waters on both the Gulf and Pacific sides.

1911. March 24. General Diaz' cabinet resigns, and Limantour is entrusted with the task of forming a new cabinet.

1911. March 28. A new cabinet is formed with Licenciado Francisco Leon de la Barra as Secretary of Foreign Affairs.

1911. April 1. General Diaz and his cabinet appear before Congress to read his message containing a declaration to the effect that he would be pleased to see Congress adopt a constitutional amendment providing for non-reelection of the President and Vice-President of the Republic.

1911. May 10. Ciudad Juarez taken by the revolutionaries, General Navarro having surrendered with his Staff and 400 soldiers with arms and ammunition.

1911. May 21. Treaty of Ciudad Juarez signed at half past ten p. m. General Diaz to resign before the end of the month and also Ramon Corral. Francisco Leon de la Barra, Secretary of Foreign Relations, to become President of the Republic *pro tempore,* and to issue a call for elections.

1911. May 25. General Diaz signs his resignation at half past two o'oclock in the afternoon. At midnight he left Mexico City for Vera Cruz on a special train, over the Interoceanic Railway.

1911. May 26. Francisco Leon de la Barra takes office as President of the Republic.

1911. July 7. Madero enters the City of Mexico in triumph.

1911. June 14. Dick Ferris, the first (and låst) President of the Socialist Republic of Lower California, arrested at Los Angeles, California. He is charged with violation of the neutrality laws.

1911. August 23. Andres Molina Enriquez proclaims a plan of Agrarian Revolution at Texcoco, State of Mexico.

1911. October 15. Francisco Madero elected Constitutional President.

1911. November 6. Madero inaugurated as President.

1911. November 27. Decree prohibiting re-election of Presidents and Vice-Presidents of the Republic, and State Governors, published.

1911. November 28. Zapata draws up and publishes his "Plan de Ayala."

1911. December 13. Decree of Congress establishing the Department of Labor.

1911. December 16. General Bernardo Reyes crosses the border from the United States into Mexico, to start a rebellion against Madero.

1911. December 25. General Reyes surrenders to the authorities of the town of Linares.

1912. March 3. Revolt of Pascual Orozco in Chihuahua.

1912. July 3. Orozco defeated at Bachimba.

1912. July 15. The *Casa del Obrero Mundial* or Industrial Workers of the World, founded in Mexico.

1912. October 16. Revolt of General Felix Diaz at Vera Cruz with a portion of the 19th Battalion.

1912. October 23. Attack on Vera Cruz. The city recovered by Government troops. Felix Diaz taken prisoner.

1913. February 9. *Coup d'Etat* of the *Ciudadela,* or Mexico City arms depot. General Reyes killed. The "tragic ten days" begins.

1913. February 22. President Madero and Vice-President Pino Suarez murdered. Pedro Lascurain President *pro tem* and General Victoriano Huerta raised to the Presidency.

1913. March 5. Ignacio L. Pesqueira this day proclaims a decree by which the State Congress and Executive of Sonora disavow Huerta's government.

1913. March 26. Venustiano Carranza, draws up the Plan of Guadalupe, disavowing Huerta and assuming the title of First Chief of the Constitutionalist Revolution.

1913. October 10. Huerta dissolves the Federal Congress.

1914. April 2. Torreon taken by Constitutionalist troops under the command of Francisco Villa.

1914. April 21. American troops land at Vera Cruz.

1914. July 15. Huerta's resignation and departure. Francisco Carbajal Provisional President.

1914. August 16. Venustiano Carranza enters the Capital as First Chief of the Constitutionalist Army.

1914. November 1. The Aguascalientes Convention resolves that Carranza on this day be removed from the post of First Chief, and Villa from that of Commander in Chief of the Division of the North and that General Eulalio Gutierrez be Provisional President of the Republic for a term of twenty days, his appointment to be either ratified or a substitute appointed at the end of said period.

1914. November 14. American troops leave Vera Cruz.

1914. November 21. Carranza abandons the Capital and proceeds to Vera Cruz.

1915. January 6. Law enacted at Vera Cruz providing for restoration and grants of common lands to villages.

1915. February 17. Agreement made between the Constitutionalist party and the Industrial Workers of the World in virtue of which the former undertook to assist the cause of the workers.

1915. March 11. Government by the "Convention" (Villa party) in Mexico until July 10.

1915. April 16. Battle of Celaya and defeat of Francisco Villa.

1917. February 5. Proclamation of Queretaro Constitution to take effect as from May 1st of the same year.

1917. May 1. Carranza inaugurated as Constitutional President of Mexico.

1920. April 23. Plan of Agua Prieta aiming at Carranza's overthrow.

1920. May 21. Venustiano Carranza killed at Tlaxcalantongo, Puebla.

1920. May 25. Congress appoints Adolfo de la Huerta as President pro tem.

1920. December 1. General Alvaro Obregón inaugurated as Constitutional President of the Republic.

1921. General census: 14.234,780 inhabitants.

1923. December 7. A revolt headed by Adolfo de la Huerta breaks out.

1924. December 1. General Plutarco Elias Calles inaugurated as President of the Republic.

1928. June 17. General Alvaro Obregon killed.

1928. November 30. Lic. Emilio Portes Gil appointed Provisional President.

1930. February 5. Pascual Ortiz Rubio inaugurated as President of the Republic.

1932. September 1. Ortiz Rubio resigns and General Abelardo Rodríguez takes office as President.

1934. November 30. General Lazaro Cardenas inaugurated as President of the Republic.

PERIODS INTO WHICH THE HISTORY OF MEXICO IS DIVIDED

The History of Mexico may be divided into four fundamental periods.

The first or Primitive Period, is the one preceding the Conquest of Mexico, and is marked by so-called Mexican (Aztec, Native, American) culture, and that of their predecessors, and should extend from the remotest times up to 1521.

The second period or Period of Ancient History, is that of New Spain, or Colonial Mexico, and includes the transmission period or period of transplantation of Spanish or European culture and the work of exploration, discovery and colonization, that is from 1521 to the end of the Eighteenth Century.

The third period is that following Independence, when the Republic of Mexico, after breaking loose from the Spanish Empire and entering upon and living its own life, continued in steady effort for growth and social organization, that is, from Independence up to the Revolution of 1910.

The fourth period is that of the Revolution that began in 1910 and extends down to our day, marking a new era, being as it is a vast movement for social and national renovation.

PART ONE
PRIMITIVE MEXICAN CULTURE

THE EARLIEST INHABITANTS OF MEXICO

1

The time when the first men made their appearance in Mexico is an enigma still wrapped in deep obscurity.

Early historians noted traditions relating to the "quinames" or giants. The dominant note is belief in origin from the earth itself. The Mixtec and Zapotec thought themselves descended from rocks, trees or animals. Nevertheless, the most credible data would seem to show that the first inhabitants of the Americas came from Asia, and belonged to races of Mongoloid and Polynesian origin.

2

Aside from this, such culture as arose on the New Continent may be considered as having been born of the soil itself.

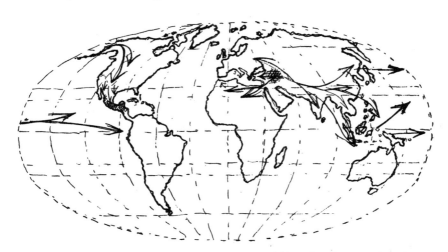

Geographical position of Mexico.—Arrows show probable early migratory movements.

The American Indian, up to the arrival of the Spaniards, was cut off from the rest of the world. And the crops, cities and cultures that arose and had their being on the American Continent, involved a conquest of the soil, and constant struggle with great obstacles consisting in isolation, wild animals and other natural difficulties.

This is why it is generally asserted that Aztec civilization was one of most important of the New World, so that a study of its rise and different phases is essential to an understanding of the evolution of humanity.

3

The earliest inhabitants of America had hardly reached the stage of being able to light a fire, roughly hew stone and support themselves by hunting and fishing. Very gradually, perhaps over thousands of years they improved their domestic utensils and realized the advantage of keeping domestic animals and of settled agriculture. The main food resources of that primitive epoch, besides the products of hunting and fishing, were corn and beans. Now, it seems to be an accepted fact that corn, or maize, is a cultivated grain evolved from *teozintle* or wild maize, a plant still found in certain parts of Mexico. From this fact it is inferred that the earliest civilizations of the Americas arose in Mexico and were founded on permanent agriculture.

4

The making of post and other utensils of burnt clay, weaving and agriculture were also discoveries or arts independently made or evolved in the Americas.

The migrations of the different tribes as they were driven hither and thither by other and stronger tribes; the struggles between nomad tribes and farming communities settled in places with more favorable rainfall (also attracted undoubtedly, by military advantages, such as ease of communication, good water, *maguey* plants, reeds, salt, prickly pears, etc.), finally brought about, by action and reaction, the organization of what was eventually to constitute Mexican culture in the aggregate.

5

The great migrations of the various groups, tribes and peoples, seem to have taken place in three different directions; from north to south, from south to north and radiating from a common center on the Mexican high plateau.

The most important movement, however, is from north to south; from the northwest came the Olmecs, from the country round the lower Mississippi, following the curve of the Gulf of Mexico, through Tamaulipas, Vera Cruz and Tabasco, to Yucatan, where they had a share in the formation of Mayan culture. From the northeast came the Nahoas, from the River Colorado country, in California and thence through Sonora, Sinaloa, Jalisco and Michoacan, to far southern coasts, and to the Valley of Mexico. And the blending of Olmec with Nahoa and with other more ancient or less known tribes, gave rise to the formation of cultural centers at Oaxaca, Tula, Michoacan, Teotihuacan, Texcoco and Mexico-Tenochtitlan.

II

MAYAN CULTURE

1

Among the most ancient of the peoples who later succeeded in establishing centers of high culture, precursors of Mexican nationality, are the Mayas.

Ruins of Chichen Itza.

Panel from Palenque.

At a period so remote that no date can, even approximately, be fixed, the earliest settlers, known as the Itzaes, led by their Chief or High Priest Zamná, settled in what is today the State of Yucatan and spread far to the south, even to Guatemala and Honduras. They were followed by other tribes, probably of the same Olmec origin; who likewise made their way down along the Gulf Coast skirting the foothills of the Eastern Sierras.

2

It is now known that there were two periods of Mayan civilization, one in the south, in what is now Guatemala and Honduras, and other farther north, where the cities of Chichen Itza and Uxmal still stand, as well as a number of others, of which ruins are all that survive. From the remains of palaces, temples, and monuments, we can realize the fact that those peoples had reached a high stage of civilization. Inscriptions and images that have been preserved show proof of the progress achieved by the Mayas in astronomy, in the measurement of time and in artistic production. The ruins of Chichen Itza, with its Court of a thousand Columns and its ruins of palaces, pyramids and towers, are famous all over the world.

3

The outstanding events of the history of the Maya people are: first, its geographical situation, in a country with an excessively hot and damp climate, with neither rivers nor mountains, where man had to contend with great natural difficulties for bare existence and much more so in founding and keeping up centers of population. Secondly: the Mayas never succeeded in welding together the various tribes and cities so as to form them into one powerful nation. Every group had its own chiefs or headmen, its government and even its own dialect, the consequences of which were isolation and warfare.

4

In addition to Olmec and Toltec immigration, the land of the Mayas was settled by certain elements from the West Indies, of the so-called Carib tribes. The influence of the Aztecs was later felt, when their power and consequent expansion reached its height. But the Mayan cities had already, when the Spaniards came, been destroyed and almost entirely overgrown by luxuriant forest.

Stucco work on Palenque Palace.

5

To sum up, the growth of Mayan culture in the south continued up to the year 629, and extended from central Honduras and the hig the high plateau of Guatemala as far as northern Yucatan. Wars, revolution, epidemics, climatic disturbances or difficulties of production brought about the downfall and ruin of those great cities. The forest now reaches up to the tops of the pyramids and monuments. The decline is complete until the year 964.

The renaissance of Mayan civilization is evidenced by the conclusion of an alliance or league between Chichen Itza, Uxmal and Mayapan. This political unification took place in 1004, but was later broken by wars and commotions in which Aztec influence had by then made itself felt, as when the latter aided Hunac-Cel, the Lord of Mayapan, against Chac-Xib, the "Very Red Man."

6

After the year 1437, the northern Mayan culture died out just as the earlier had done. As cities were abandoned and the encroaching vegetation covered the ruins, the people dispersed and become nomad tribes.

Maya Temple at Uxmal.

7

The data available for the history of the Mayas are but scanty, and sister sciences continue their work in the endeavor to solve the secrets of those great lost cultures.

We may not, however, in view of the vast importance of Maya-Quiche culture, omit to seek other explanations of obscure points, more especially to ascertain the real reason for its downfall.

We have above pointed out the most likely causes, such as climatic disturbances, wars and revolutions. Another suggestion is the occurrence of a period of excessively heavy rainfall which, joined to the torrid climate, enabled nature to triumph over human culture. Torrential rains, fever, epidemics, the ever-encroaching jungle, finally brought about ruin and dispersion.

8

Yet other studies of the question point to a social factor, this theory being based on the erection and subsequent ruin of temples, like that at Chichen Itza. Such great works could only be carried out by the labor of great numbers of men; slaves, serfs or proletarians, and only so long as the caste of the oppressors were strong enough. But due to the wearing down process inseparable from every regime of injust exploitation, disturbances arose, alien powers made invasions, the oppressed rose in revolt, war ensued and final ruin supervened.

III

THE TOLTECS

1

It is generally supposed that the tribes known by the name of Olmecs came down along the coast of the Gulf of Mexico, and after leaving traces of their passage and stay in northern Vera Cruz dispersed in different directions.

The Olmec-Nonohualcas followed the coast in a southeasterly direction and finally reached the Isthmian Region, where they contributed to the foundation and development of primitive Mayan culture. The Olmec-Vixtoti emigrated to Oaxaca, where they gave rise to the Mixtec-Zapotec nucleus. And the Olmec-Toltecs settled in the Valley of Mexico.

According to other versions, the Toltecs may be considered as the first recorded comers of the great Nahoa or Nahuatl family. They seem to have appeared about 500 B. C., and worked their way to the higher Mexican table-land along the Pacific coast and the mountain ranges parallel to it, until they reached the central plateau where they subdued the Otomies, earlier comers in the land.

2

This would be the first Toltec Era, also designated the Older Toltec Era, and would be coeval with the foundation of the city of Tollan, or Tula. The Toltecs, however, seem in turn to have been attacked and conquered by fresh currents of tribes who came down from the north, known as the Chichimecas.

Being the conquerors, they took to themselves the name of Toltecs, and thus became entitled to be considered, in ancient history, as the strongest people and the most advanced in the arts of civilization, as they tilled the soil, knew how to melt down and cast certain metals,

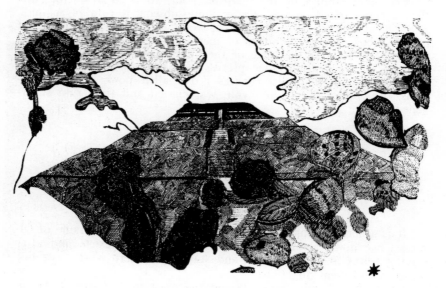

Teotihuacan.—Pyramid of the Sun.

cut precious stones, build roads, and erect temples, monuments and cities. After the earlier Toltec culture was subdued or destroyed, about the year 700, another center with villages under stable government, was again established at Tollan.

3

Then the second or later Toltec Era, about which more is known, began. The cycle of the efforts for culture was then enacted over again; nomad wanderings under the leadership of a Chief or High Priest, Hueman, who guided the people in their journeyings hither and thither; the fight for control of the region, the achievement of supremacy over the earlier inhabitants, who are then oppressed or driven off; the erection of great temples and monuments, the establishment of military or priestly governments, the rise of castes and classes, and disorder which eventually causes civil war, yielding to outside pressure and final decline or dissolution.

Teotihuacan.—Detail of Pyramid of Quetzalcoatl.

Among the legends that have come down to us from the Toltec Empire, there is the story of Xochitl, a princess or lady of high degree associated with the discovery of fermented *maguey*, juice, or *pulque*. The use of this beverage seems to have coincided with the downfall of the Toltec Empire.

4

To sum up, it may taken as a fact beyond dispute that in the valleys through which the River Tula flows there were large towns that not only constituted a nucleus of civilization, but marked one or more cultural epochs. On the basis of regular crops of corn and beans, and of utilization of the *maguey* plants, reed thickets and salt deposits, towns were established under a primitive form of government. Advances in industry and trade began on the scale allowed by local resources. The great truncated pyramid of several stories at Teotihuacan was erected to bear witness to Toltec power and building ability.

As among all peoples similarly circumstanced, an unreliable food supply and only recent emergence from barbarism afford an explanation of human sacrifices, the practice of eating human flesh as a religious ceremony, and their religion itself, in which the Sun, Moon and Stars were the principal deities.

IV

QUETZALCOATL

1

From Toltec chronicles we may take one representative name, of really extraordinary interest. It is that of Quetzalcoatl, who assumes the character almost of a divinity and who is also an historical personage.

The word Quetzalcoatl means "Plumed Serpent." He was likewise the God of the Winds and the Evening Star. He also appears in Maya legends under the name of Kukulcan.

His character is that of a high priest or wise man. He taught men how to till the soil, preached against human sacrifices, was assailed and persecuted on account of his attempts at reform and left his counry departing towards the east, after promising some day to return.

2

Other capacities are also however, ascribed to him: "Quetzalcoatl was a king-priest at Tula and was driven out by the followers of Tezcatlipoca."

Among the Toltecs there were also great bodies of Chichimecs who constituted an inferior social class. The builders, architects and artists, chiefs and priests, were the higher classes of the State and enjoyed a number of privileges while their position was in every way better. Supreme government over the Empire was in the hands of the

priestly class, in turn ruled by the high priest of the worship of Quetzalcoatl.

3

Tezcatlipoca was the favorite deity of the great masses of low rank.
And thus Quetzalcoatl is not only the plumed serpent and the evening
star, but the representative of a privileged class and of an entire social system already declining.

In course of time the functions, privileges and even the insignia of
Quetzalcoatl became causes of discord and strife. Kings, leaders and

Quetzalcoatl's prophesy (After J. Clemente Orozco.)

priests no longer performed their mission. City life and the advance of trade, agriculture and industry brought about the concentration of wealth in the hands of the few. The increase of such wealth and of confort and ease begat indulgence in luxury and all manner of pleasures. The harm worked by sloth and vice became more and more noticeable.

Until at last rebellion broke out, and enemies within and without brought about the downfall of that power which had seemed unshakeable, and marked the rise of other periods of culture and civilization.

V

INTERMEDIATE CULTURE

1

Mexican or Aztec culture is usually considered as including the people who founded the City of Mexico and spread their influence over the regions that later became New Spain, and after that the Republic of Mexico. Mayas and Toltecs were the predecessors of the Mexicans.

Other centers of culture and civilization arose in divers regions. Some of them succeeded in developing to such an extent as to live a life of their own over long periods. Others were poorer and more limited as to possibilities, while yet other and still less favored groups continued to be wanderers and nomads.

Thus we see how the various tribes that were known as Olmecs, Toltecs, Chichimecs and Acolhuas founded centers of population and cultivation. But side by side with these nations that had reached a comparatively high stage of development, other tribes also managed to found permanent settlements. The more remarkable of these were the Mixtecs and Zapotecs in Oaxaca and the Tarascos in Michoacan.

2

Oaxaca is a región highly favored by nature for development of a powerful nucleus of civilization. Those great mountains ranges that come together and coalesce at the Isthmus, abound in table lands and valleys with a pleasant climate and a fertile soil. The immigrant Olmecs came there, after the Nahoas, and on mingling with the aboriginal inhabitants they formed the Mixtec and Zapotec nations.

The peoples thus constituted showed a capacity sufficient to develop a personality of their own. The ruins of Mitla are just as world-famous as those of Chichen Itza, and an unremitting work of exploration and excavation makes it daily more certain that Oaxaca was the seat of an important cultural center.

The decorative work on the walls of Mitla and the gold jewels of Monte Alban are evidences of the building ability, artistic gifts and wealth attained by the ancient peoples of Oaxaca.

3

The Mixtecs and Zapotecs resisted the pressure brought to bear on them by Aztecs, when the latter extended their military sway, and

Mitla.

were never wholly defeated. And such wars usually ended in a kind of alliance or truce, by the marriage of the Zapotec King with the daughter of his Aztec colleague.

The primitive inhabitants of Michoacan are also entitled to be looked upon as the creators of a center with a culture of its own. The tribes that lived in Michoacan, in a country rich in great natural attractions, dotted with smiling and fertile valleys and pleasant lakes, founded a number of villages and supported themselves by fishing and agriculture. They also showed themselves to be skilful craftsmen, apt at pottery-making and decorative work.

4

In the valleys on the high plateau, where the Federal District now is, the tribes of Nahoa origin succeeded in establishing permanent settlements. More especially round those great lakes that have subsequently dried up and become so greatly reduced in area, did a number of tribes choose to settle.

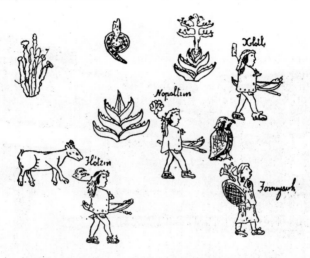

Early Chichimec Kings out hunting. (From so-called Tlotzin Map.)

The frequent fighting engaged between the inhabitants of Tenayuca, Cuautepec, Acolhuacan, Atzcapotzalco, Texcoco and Tacuba has come down to us in chronicles purporting to present that petty warfare as the history of great lords or nobles, marked by the shedding of blood and such events as conquest, regicide, princely marriages and adventures of all kinds. Such happenings in part fall within the historical period, but the facts in regard to them have not yet been made sufficiently clear.

5

Aztecs leaders were warriors like Xolotl or Tezozomoc. From 900 to 1300 A. D. they seem to have been engaged in never-ending domestic strife, without organizing anything in the way of a higher culture, until at last an era of brilliant civilization had its rise at Texcoco.

Tezozomoc and Maxtla are looked upon as usurpers and despotic military leaders. Lastly, Netzahualcoyotl is the outstanding figure of that era and represents the culmination of that aggregation of secondary cultures, forerunners of Aztec supremacy.

VI

NETZAHUALCOYOTL

1

Netzahualcoyotl is not, like Quetzalcoatl, a shadowy personage. He belongs to the type of the primitive heroes. Legends tell us about him from his infancy, how he was the child of a king dethroned by the tyrant Maxtla, and was persecuted, hiding in the mountains, ever fleeing like a "starving coyote."

After that, by turning to account wars and alliances, he reieved help from the Aztecs and was restored to the throne of his ancestors. He was a poet and astronomer. He sensed the fact of Divine Unity.

Netzahualcoyotl.

His court at Texcoco became a center of material and spiritual wealth. He was peaceful and fond of luxury. He had palaces, gardens and baths. He collected tribute of corn and beans, cocoa and turkeys.

2

In the alliance entered into by Netzahualcoyotl with the Aztecs, he reserved for himself the exercise of priestly and spiritual functions. Texcoco had by then eclipsed Tenayuca and Atzcapotzalco, and Tenochtitlan was still nothing more than a collection of huts. But the Aztecs (Tenochcas) had on their side retained military control of the confederation, and the scepter of domination gradually shifted from Texcoco to Mexico or Tenochtitlan.

VII

THE AZTECS

1

The Tenochcas or Aztecs, so their traditions related, had come from Aztlan, from which place the name Aztecs was later formed.

Some authorities hold that Aztlan means "land of herons," or place where the sun rose. But it is more likely that it is merely a modification of "Aztatlan."

A great deal of argument has taken place on the subject of the exact situation of the land of Aztlan; some place it north of Sonora and Sinaloa, others on an island in the Gulf of California or on the Peninsula itself, while yet others favor an island in lake Chapala. Modern authorities point to Aztatlan Creek, in Sinaloa, as the place from where the Aztecs started on their wanderings.

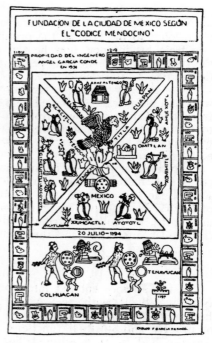

Foundation of City of Mexico, according to Mendocino Codex.

2

At some date between the years 800 and 1200 A. D. the Aztec families or tribes started on their trip south. They had to make their way ever seeking favorable climates, trails, fording-places at rivers, and points of least resistance, as regards other tribes that had preceded them. They had to stop on their way, to procure food, by fishing or letting themselves out as soldiers to other tribes.

They came down the northwestern coast, through Jalisco, Michoacan and more southerly regions almost as far as the Isthmus; thence they ascended to the high plateau.

Foundation of Mexico, after Duran's hieroglyphics.

3

The influence of some great leader (Tenoch); their language, the rise of priestly and warrior castes; a united front in the face of danger and need; military discipline and an organization that began by division of labor and tasks, all this was so to speak, the foundation of their nationality. Their primitive god called Opochtli was the tutelary deity of fishermen. Later on the God of War, under the name of Huitzilopochtli, was exalted to higher rank. And he it was who prevailed as a symbol of the rudest and most savage times, and was honored by religious rites and cannibal feasts. Another form of the same deity, Mexitli, seems in some way to have been connected with the beginnings of regular agriculture (Metl, *maguey* plant) and with the name Mexico.

Acamapichtli.

4

At last they reached the appointed and foreordained spot. On an islet in a lake they discovered an eagle perched on a *nopal* or prickly pear plant.

When did this event occur? Historians do not agree on this point, but a majority are in favor of 1325 A. D., as the most likely year.

They proceeded to erect a small temple, and settled around it; they called the town thus founded Meshico-Tenochtitlan, in honor of their god, Huitzilopochtli, and of Tenoch, the priest who had led them on their wanderings.

5

The first houses built by them were very modest indeed.

They had to live very meanly. However, their need made them discover means of support on their islands. "Chinampas" or floating gardens, so-called, grew in area and were added to by

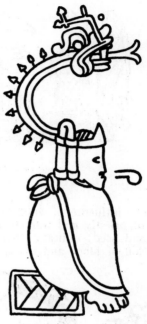

Itzcoatl.

soil brought in for the purpose, thus increasing the area of tillable land. The chain of lakes afforded in area and were added to by easy communication by canoe.

6

The city once founded, the activities derived from an impetuous currrent of culture began to be applied to growth, expansion, and rise in power. We have already mentioned the period of nomad existence and wanderings that preceded the foundation of Tenochtitlan.

Tizoc.

Then came the period of contest and organization; a government of warriors and priests, (Mexitli, Tenoch); a few families scattered on a small island, in the midst of moderate sized lakes, compelled to pay tribute to stronger neighbors, by pressure of threats and persecution.

7

Then, the endeavor to win control of the land, vigorous action in war and in work, ability to turn to good account the advantages of climate and site, and the influence of other cultures.

The huts found by their first leader, headman or king, Acama-

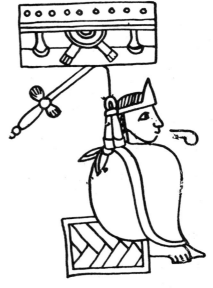

Moctezuma Ilhuicamina.

Chimalpopoca.

pichtli, eventually became houses built of stone, in the reign of Huitzilihuitl.

Chimalpopoca laid the fundations of a temple dedicated to the God of War.

Itzcoatl shook off subjection to neighboring chiefs and his troops ceased to be hired out as mercenaries.

Under Axayacatl Tenochtitlan became more powerful, and extended the area of its lands. In the confederation of the most powerful tribes of the Valley and other regions, the Aztecs took part on an equal footing.

8

Under Moctezuma I, known as Ilhuicamina (The Archer of the Skies) the period of expansion began. The city grew in size and was improved by streets and canals that intersected one another and established communication between the various lakes. Ilhuicamina's troops set out on conquering expeditions.

In Ahuizotl's reign, the Aztecs extended their rule to Chiapas, by means of military expeditions and the force of arms.

Axayacatl.

Ahuizotl.

The dedication of the Great Temple, with much shedding of blood, in a kind of ferocious and religious frenzy, evidences the power attained by the Aztecs.

The soldiers of Moctezuma II carry his standards to Tehuantepec, and his traders and messengers penetrate to far-off Yucatan and Nicaragua, perhaps even further still.

In the Acolhua confederation, or alliance between Tenochtitlan, Texcoco and Tlacopan, the Aztecs occupy a predominant position.

VIII

A SURVEY OF AZTEC CULTURE

TERRITORY COVERED BY IT

The regions to the southeast of them not brought under their sway by the Mexicans, like Tabasco and Yucatan, they called Onohualco; and the country to the north, beyond their dominions, they called the land of the Chichimecs.

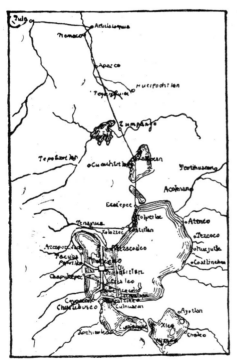

Map of Valley of Mexico before arrival of Spaniards.

They also applied the name Anahuac-Ayotlan to the Pacific Coast between Acapulco and Guatemala; and Anahuac-Xicalango (place where *jicaras* or gourds abound) to the Atlantic coast, and lastly, Anahuac was their name for the Valley or central plateau, in the center of which Tenochtitlan was situated.

POLITICAL INSTITUTIONS

1

The power of the Aztec kings was for from being the same at all times. In the early days of the monarchy it was limited and their authority was patriarchal. As the area of the territory subject to them increased they grew in wealth accordingly and their authority became harsher and even despotic.

The various tribes were not united by bonds that were at all firm. Each town was ruled by its chief, and the various provinces were still disunited.

The ruling class weighed heavily on the lower ranks of the population. The position of the former was based on ownership of the land

and sources of production, on scientific lore, on knowledge of the in-
tricacies of law and religion, and on the strength of their military
and religious organization.

2

Chiefs or "kings" were elected, but it was always a relative of the
king that was chosen.

The center of Aztec domination was the city of Tenochtitlan, which
grew to be a city of close on a hundred thousand inhabitants.

No career was more highly esteemed than the military. The God
of War (Huitzilopochtli, shortened to Huichilobos by the Spaniards)

Huitzilopochtli.

Huitzilopochtli.

was the deity most deeply venerated, and was looked upon as the special protector of the nation. No prince was chosen for the kingship
until he had shown proof of valor and military skill in a number of
battles, and that he deserved the rank of General in the Army.

Away from the city, the population was very irregularly distributed.

The Indians lived in small villages composed of five, ten or fifteen
families, each one in a separate house.

REGIME OF PROPERTY

1

When the Aztecs settled at Tenochtitlan, every family or tribe received a piece of land. Ownership was not vested in the head of the family, but in the *calpulli* or community. When a family died out its parcel of land was distributed among the other residents most in need.

Ownership of land was vested in the individual, only in the case of land belonging to the nobility.

The *calpullis* were subdivided; under each were one hundred heads of families, and under these again, chiefs of twenty families.

Outsiders were not admitted to the use of community lands.

2

Right of possession carried with it the obligation to till the land; any one failing to do so for two years was cautioned and should he fail to till his lot a third year he forfeited his right to it.

A portion of the land was set aside for the State and the fruits thereof went to the King's palace.

The temple lands were in a similar position; the fruits were devoted to keeping up religious worship; each great temple had its own property.

As time passed the system of property underwent changes, until great estates were formed and the land lost its communal character.

AGRICULTURAL PRODUCTION

1

Among the staple crops, besides corn, the chief were beans, coca, *magueyes*, chillies, seeds of various kinds, and cotton.

The *maguey* in itself furnished a number of products essential to the existence of the humbler classes. Besides fencing in their fields, the trunk was used for rafters in roofing their huts, and the leaves instead of shingles. From the leaves they made paper, thread, needles, clothing, footwear and ropes; and the juice gave them wine, sugar, honey and vinegar. From the fleshy portion of the leaf a kind of food could be made, and lastly, the plant supplied them with medicine for several ailments.

They expressed the juice from cornstalks, for the manufacture of sugar.

2

As they had no plows, nor oxen nor other draught animals suitable for use in tilling the soil, they supplied the deficiency by their own labor and a few simple implements. In order to dig or throw up the earth, they used the *coatl*, a kind of hoe made of copper, with a wooden handle, something like a pick, and small shovels.

They were very clever at vegetable gardening and tending fruit orchards, in which they planted with great regularity and neatness a number of fruit trees, medicinal plants and flowers.

Register of Tribute.

UTENSILS AND WEAPONS

They made use of stone and bronze axes, wooden swords inlaid with blades of obsidian along the edge, called *macanas*, lances with flint and obsidian points, and shot their arrows from bows or a throwing stick or *atlatl*. And to ward off blows they had shields.

DIVISION OF LABOR

Every Indian was acquainted with the trades not requiring great skill, nor tools that were scarce.

There were a number of men trained in sundry crafts, more especially stone-cutters, carpenters, goldsmiths and silversmiths, painters who copied birds, animals, trees, flowers, etc., wood carvers, potters, gourd makers, weavers of cloth and tailors, more especially for the robes worn by kings, nobles and priests, and for the worship and adornment of their idols; rush weavers, tanners, shoemakers, and artists in featherwork and makers of obsidian knives.

FOOD

1

The Aztecs were not as great meat eaters as Europeans, but quite often at banquets, and daily, in the case of the nobles, they served up game of various kinds, such as venison, rabbits, wild boar, moles and turkeys and even iguanas and other creatures; but the most usual forma of flesh food consisted in turkeys and quails.

To drink they had sundry wines or beverages made from the *maguey* plant, from palms, cornstalks and also distilled from grain.

As regards the great mass of the people, as they had for many years following the foundation of Mexico led a very miserable existence on the little islands in the lake, they had been compelled to feed on anything they could find. At that time they not only learned to eat the roots of marsh plants, and snakes, but also such vermin as ants, swamp flies and even the eggs of the latter.

They likewise ate a certain earthy substance called *tequesquite* that floated on the surface of the lake, which they sun-dried and then ate as if it were cheese. Having become used to these articles of food, they were not able to give them up even in periods of greatest prosperity, so that their markets were always full of all kinds of animals, reptiles and insects, boiled, fried and roasted, mostly disposed of to the very poor.

TEMPLES AND DWELLING HOUSES

1

Houses were one story only; and but few of them opened on the street.

Temples were provided with an altar for their idols; facing the altar was the incense-burner, in which they burnt *copal* or incense, and flower vases.

The huts of the poor were made of cane and reeds, adobe or stones bound together with earth, and roofs consisted of a kind of long bearded moss or *maguey* leaves.

Huey Teocalli or Great Temple.—Tennis court on south; Calmecac, on the west; God of Fire on the north; Pyramid of Tlaloc and Huitzilopochtli, in center.—Covered four city blocks.

2

Most of these houses had only a single room for the whole of the family and their livestock, and for the hearth and furniture. If the family were not very poor, they might have other rooms, such as an oratory, a *temazcalli* or vapor bath and a small granary.

3

The dwellings of their great lords were built of stone and mortar; they had halls, courts and bedrooms; the roofs were flat, and the walls were whitewashed, smooth and shining.

Wooden doors to houses were unknown, reed curtains being used instead. For lighting purposes they had *ocote,* or fat-pine, torches.

CLOTHING

The poor wore clothing made of *maguey* or wild palm thread; those higher in position wore heavy cotton clothing; but the very highest ranks donned robes of cotton cloth, adorned with different colors and designs worked in animals or flowers, or interwoven with feathers or rabbit's hair, or even ornamented with gold emblems and cotton fringes hanging from their belt or *maxtlatl.*

Warriors wore showy ornaments and plumes, etc.

TRADE

1

Trade played an important part in the life of the Aztecs, and was greatly helped by the fact that the Aztec language was used and understood in many remote regions.

Trade was not only carried on by means of barter, but by actual buying and selling; they had five different kinds of money; the first was a certain kind of cocoa bean, but not the kind used for making chocolate; the second consisted in certain small pieces of cotton cloth used only for the purchase of food stuffs; the third was gold-dust; the fourth that looked rather like real coin, consisted of T-shaped pieces of copper, and was used for small purchases, while the fifth consisted of thin pieces of tin.

2

Mexico was well supplied with market places (tianquistli.)
Fish caught in the lakes and mats woven from the rushes that grew
in their shallower reaches, were bartered for corn, cotton, stone, lime
and lumber. And as the community grew in power, its trade increased
accordingly.

The textile industries, especially the spinning and weaving of cotton, sisal and *maguey* fiber, acquired considerable importance.

3

The city of Tenochtitlan had the chief market of Anahuac, where
bird's feathers and cocoa from Soconusco, the gold and cochineal of
the Zapotecs, emeralds and amber from the Gulf Coast, honey, ochre,
and copper from Olinallan, paper and vases wrought by the Tlahuicas,
the mats of Cuautitlan, the grain and firewood of the "cold country"
and india-rubber, tobacco and aromatic gums were exposed for sale.

EDUCATION

1

The bringing up of boys was entrusted to their father, and of
girls to their mother.

Boys were bathed in cold water and slept on the floor with but
scanty bedclothes. The sons of rich men were also accustomed to this
hard life, in order to make them strong and healthy, and to accustom
boys from early youth to the life of a fighting man.

At the age of four boys began to do light work at their father's
behest, such as fetching water in small vessels; at five they were made
to carry light articles, so that they should, from this age, become used
to what they would have to do their whole life long; because whether
they grew up to be soldiers or merchants or *tamemes* (porters) they
would have to walk with some sort of a load on their backs most of
the time.

2

At the age of six a boy would be sent to the *tianquiztli* or market, there to earn some trifle. When he was seven, his father would

show him how to repair a matlatl or fishing net, if a fisherman, or the rudiments of his own trade, whatever this might be.

At the age of eight, by threats of punishment, he was taught how to remove thorns from *maguey* leaves.

At nine lazy and inattentive boys were punished by being tied hand and foot, while their fathers pricked them with *maguey* thorns.

When boys reached the age of ten, punishment became more severe; incorrigible and disobedient boys were punished by being beaten with sticks by their father. If that did no good, they were made to breathe the smoke from chillies dried and burnt.

At thirteen a boy was looked upon as a young man, and no longer a child, and went to the woods and lakes for firewood and rushes. Lastly, when he reached the age of fourteen he was taught his father's trade.

3

When a little girl was four years old, her mother taught her to seed cotton, and when she was five, how to spin.

When she reached the age of twelve, her mother, in order to accustom her to household work and management would make her get up at midnight to sweep out the house and the street; little girls always slept with their clothes on, both in order to be able to rise quickly at their mother's call, and for modesty.

At thirteen they were accomplished in household tasks; spinning, grinding, corn, making *tortillas,* cooking, etc. At fourteen their mother could teach them the art of weaving.

4

Education in the home was looked upon as complete at the age of fourteen or fifteen, attempts having been made to inspire young people with reverence and fear of the gods, affection and respect for their parents, consideration for the elderly, poor and destitute, love of duty and hatred of vice; as means of avoiding the last mentioned, continuous occupation, truthfulness, obedience and subjection to reason and justice in their actions, were always aimed at.

5

Young women were very quiet and modest; the only place they went to was the temple, to which they repaired with a companion and in silence. Women were not allowed to talk at meals until after marriage; they had to be busy at something all the time and virtue and modesty were instilled into them.

At fifteen public education began. The sons of the nobles who had been consecrated to Quetzalcoatl, went to the *Calmecac* (row of houses) and those who had been consecrated to Tezcatlipoca went to the Tepochcalli (house of the young men.)

THE CALMECAC

Just after the birth of the child, his parents offered him to Quetzalcoatl and presented him to the priests, who accepted him on behalf of the god, although he stayed at home until he reached the proper age.

Education was imparted for the purpose of preparing warriors or priests. So that life in the *Calmecac* was hard and laborious and at the same time a life of prayer and penitence.

Dress consisted of the *maxtlatl* or sash, and a cotton cloak, white in color. They slept on hard beds and entirely apart. Food was scanty, and only what the school supplied, as if parents sent anything from home, it had to be distributed among all the boys. They rose very early.

At dawn they were already busy sweeping out, cleaning, and making ready the articles for worship and sacrifices. They accompanied the priests to war, and therefore had to be trained in the usual military exercises.

Adjoining the temple there was a school for girls, the curriculum of which was unfolded simultaneously with that of the young men at the *Calmecac*. Some of them were devoted to the care of the sanctuary for all time, but a majority left it to be married.

THE TELPOCHCALLI

Life at the Telpochcalli, as regards work, and the ascetic existence of self-denial and prayer, was rather like that at the *Calmecac*. The difference consisted in the fact that the pupils at the *Telpochcalli* were mostly trained for war.

At fifteen the tests for the pupils began. They had to show their ability to undergo hardships that prepared them for warlike exercises. and if found satisfactory, they went with grown men to war to gain experience of actual fighting. They accompanied a soldier whose arms they had to carry and whom they had to serve during a campaign, and if he distinguished himself in any way, by taking a prisioner, say, they were awarded a prize at their school.

RELIGION

1

The chief gods of the Aztecs were Huitzilopochtli, the God of War, to whom human sacrifices were offered up, by tearing the hearts out of prisioners captured on the field of battle; Quetzalcoatl, in his outward aspect of a plumed serpent, was a beneficent deity; Tezcatlipoca, whose name means "Mirror-smoke;" Tonatiuh, the Sun and Meztli, the Moon.

But above their idols, the ancient Mexicans believed in the oneness of God. They ascribed everything to the gods, but explained them by a Single Cause, of which they were all nothing more than manifestations.

The God of Cause was by them called Ometeuhtli, literally the Lord God.

Restoration of Great Temple, by I. Marquina, architect.

2

In order to symbolize the fact that man was unable to understand God, they represented him without showing his face. They concealed it behind a mask or a scepter, called *tlachitoni,* which means "lookout" because he hid his face behind it and looked through a hole in the middle of a golden plate.

They believed in an invisible, impalpable God, who was everywhere, incorporeal, sole, who was at one and the same time male and female. They believed that man had a body "our flesh and our bones," and a soul, and that he was endowed with free will; that his acts entitled him to reward or punishment; that expiation was possible once only, and that virtue was the natural mission of the life of humanity. Religious ceremonies were cruel and bloody, and in some cases involved the eating of human flesh and the tearing of their hearts out of the bosoms of prisioners.

SCIENTIFIC KNOWLEDGE

1

The Stone of the Sun.

It is hardly possible to speak of an Aztec science properly so-called, on account of the loss of most of such data as could have been turned to account for study of the subject, and the lack of a key for interpretation. However, there is no doubt that astronomy and the measurement of time had been carried to a high degree of perfection.

The Aztec Calendar or Stone of the Sun is one of the wonders of the world, and is a notable effort of man's intelligence to express in concrete form the laws of Nature. Measurement of time, something essential to the work of permanent and regular agriculture and of stable institutions, is the first symptom of civilization.

2

Botanical knowledge comprised 1,200 plants, all with their own Aztec names, and Natural History also included a number of animals, reptiles, birds, fishes, insects and minerals. Their physicians made use of such gums as copal, liquidamber, sarsaparilla, jalap, barley, pine seeds and many other healing plants and herbs. And treatment was accompanied by ceremonies and "invocations to their gods and imprecations on disease," by way of surrounding their art with mystery and making it more highly esteemed.

Arithmetic

Their system of numerals was very simple. The hieroglyphic for 5 was a man's hand. This was the starting- point of their whole system; the little finger was 1, the ring finger 2, the middle finger 3, the forefinger 4, the whole hand 5, 6 was 5 plus 1. There were special names for ten, fifteen and twenty. This was the numerical basis, as twenty was expressed by the word *cempohuali* which is the sum of all fingers and toes. After that came twice twenty, three times twenty and so on. Seven twenties plus ten is 150. The number 400 also had a name. The number 800 was expressed by as many grains of cocoa.

Language

The Nahoa language is soft-sounding and simple in structure. Its wealth of w o r d s and development were in accord with the degree of culture and the material resources of the Aztecs. But it has besides

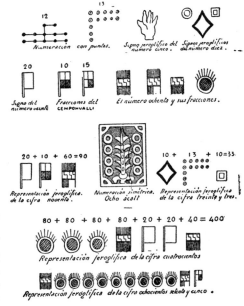

Nahoa system of hieroglyphic numeration.

certain qualities peculiar to it and a study of this language is highly interesting.

The consonants b, d, f, g, the sounds expressed by y in English, and the sounds of ny, r, s, v, w, and l at the beginning of a word do not exist in the Aztec language; its phonetic character is exemplified by the existence of certain other sounds, especially tl (and ca, hua, or hue and t.)

Writing was in the form of hieroglyphics. It was not in the form of sounds and letters. Whenever they had to write down proper names, they represented the subject by a picture.

For example, a king, a shield and a sheaf of arrows and a city, all on one line, meant the conquest by force of arms of the city represented. Nevertheless, an alphabet was already in process of formation by means of letters of a representative character.

History

They were very careful and thorough in their way of measuring time. They depicted warlike exploits and the succession of their great lords, memorable storms and notable phenomena of the heavens, and plagues. The book in which they set down the chronicle of these happenings was by them called "The Book of the Account of the Years."

In addition to recording in pictures notable happenings and especially the history and genealogy of the families of their great lords and prominent men, and notable happenings as they took place, by means of pictures and signs, they also had persons with good memories who remembered these things and could narrate them when called upon.

Art

The Aztecs had an art which answered, as regards its material resources, to the transition stage of a civilization passing from the age of carved stone to that of bronze, but with features of a great and original

  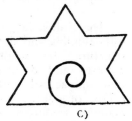

Artistic adaptation of snail shell; (A) Cross section; (B) Artistic adaptation; (C) Plan.

beauty of its own. We shall point out some of its characteristics in the following excerpts:

Painting

"Among the paintings of the ancient Mexicans there were certain almanacs by them called *tonalamatl*, in which they set down their weather reports. Others contained prophesies or auguries for the childrens in which were set down the name, day or birth and sign under which they were born."

They did their painting on cartoons or skins, or on cloth woven from *maguey* thread, or from the fiber of a yucca called iczotl.

The sheets were large-sized and were rolled up rolled up when not in use. The colors employed were of vegetable origin.

The Mayas of Yucatan and the early inhabitants of Teotihuacan executed true mural paintings. Scenes from Maya life have been discovered in the Palace of the Tigers at Chichen-Itza. At Teotihuacan, in addition to several decorative frescoes, one was discovered depicting religious ceremonies. At Chichen Itza the colors employed were green yellow, red, blue and a reddish tint for flesh. The Teotihuacan frescoes were done in bluish green yellow, red and sepia.

Mexican ceramic art.

Poetry

Aztec poetry is known from the ancient Mexican Songs. They are poems in rhymed verse and of popular origin.

It is generally believed that they were sung at feasts.

The subjects of these poems are simple, almost childishly so; they sing the beauties of the fields, mountains and skies and the existence of God, in language as pure and simple as that of a child.

There are other poems in which the legendary exploits of their ancestors, their warlike achievements and deeds of heroism are sung.

Music

In the National Museum at Mexico City are five kinds of pre-Hispanic musical instruments; the *huehuetl* (a kind of drum), the *Teponaztli* (a kind of xylophone), the *atecocolli* or conch, the *tlapitzalli* (a kind of flute.) The *ayacachtli* resembled the rattle used by Indian dancers at this day, a gourd with small stones inside. The *huehuetl* was a hollow cylinder, set up on end, cut away in zig-zag form at the bottom, and closed at the top by a tightly stretched skin so as to produce a drum-like sound when struck with the palms of the hands.

The *atecocolli* or conch had a hole in the sharp top of the spiral. By tightly pressing the lips, as in blowing a trumpet, it emitted a hoarse sound.

The *tzicahuaztli* was an instrument made out of a bone with transverse incisions along its length, over which a small conch was passed producing a sound like that of the Cuban *"guiro."*

The *tlapitzalli* was a flute of burnt clay.

There were also simple instruments of ordinary clay, known as "Whistling jars."

As to their music itself we have no definite information. Songs were intoned and not recited.

Players on the Panhuehuetl, Teponaztli, Ayacachtli and Chicahuatzili.

The dance

Dancing was one of the ways of paying homage to their gods, and also spiritual and physical enjoyment, as evidence of good health and joyousness.

One of the most popular Aztec feasts was that devoted to Macuilxochitl, the god of music, of the dance, of festivals and flowers.

Major dances were held in courtyards. Two or more concentric circles were formed by lords and priests of mature age, and after leaving a space there were several rings of young people; as each ring had to turn in time to the music, the dancers in the inner rings moved slowly and solemnly, while the outer rings had to do so faster and faster, until the outermost whirled round at a dizzy pace.

Dancing was compulsory for young people. The youths of each *calpulli* took the maidens of their own quarter by the hand and began to dance around the musicians.

On very solemn occasions great lords intoned songs gravely and deliberately, danced to in a leisurely

Xochi-Ilhuitl.—Dance of the Flower Month

manner, while in the dancing of the young the time was faster and the songs livelier.

Dress suited the songs sung. Dancing and singing took place in honor of the deity to whom the feast was dedicated so the participants donned different kinds of cloaks, plumes, head-dresses and masks, and at times dressed up as eagles or tigers, at others as warriors, and yet again as savages, monkeys, dogs and a number of other disguises.

When the feast of Quetzalcoatl came round, merchants resorted to the temple, and comedies, dances and other forms of rejoicing went on the great courtyard. They dressed up as birds, butterflies, frogs and beetles; and others pretended to be lame, armless and cripples, the feast coming to an end with dancing.

Serpent's Head.

D e c o r a t i v e a r t s

1

The opinions of authorities on the subject tell us what a high state of development was reached by primitive Mexican art.

Both in the case of their highest development, and in that of their coarser manifestations, the arts of the New World were obviously developed on the spot, and the style of their ornamentation is essentially peculiar and unique; there are pieces that can challenge a comparison with some of the best speciments of classic European art. In them a gracefulness and beauty of line is combined which fully shows the ability of the artists to carry out more important works.

"Only the monuments of the best periods of Greece and Rome are equal in beauty... to this great edifice (the main palace at Mitla.) The stones of the facade are dressed with perfect regularity, the joints well cut, foundations faultless, corners wonderfully exact, and show proof of great knowledge and lengthy experience. In this monuments lintels are no longer wood, but consist of great stones, as in the Greek and Egyptian buildings."

2

Among the presents received by Cortez from Moctezuma was a fish which Charles the Fifth sent to the Pope. Benvenuto Cellini saw and described it as a magnificent work of art, because the silver body with golden scales had been cast in a mold by a process which seemed to defy explanation.

"Even though almost all the gold and silver wrought in Mexico has long since gone into the melting-pot, there are still a few specimens left that show that Spanish conquerors did not exaggerate when they told wonderful stories about the skill of the native workers in gold. I have seen a pair of gold ornaments in the shape of an eagle, at the Berlin Museum, which may almost be compared with Etruscan work, due to the delicacy of the work and of the design." (Tylor.)

Head of Eagle Knight.

3

Paul Morand says: "They were wonderful sculptors, hard and realistic in Aztec and pre-Aztec periods, more graceful and decorative in the Maya epoch. They achieved that simplicity of plane and volume sought by modern artists. They had at their disposal the finest materials on earth, hard and difficult to cut; but they knew nothing of metals, except bronze, until the coming of the Spaniards, and this compelled them to execute delicate tasks, by patient labor of manual polishing and rubbing down with pieces of granite which bestowed on their work the softnes of natural erosion, without the brusque strokes of the chisel or the harsh impact of iron tools. "The Death's head" and the head of the "Tiger Knight" are of such power that they actually, so it is said, surprised the great sculptor Rodin himself.

The Aztecs, with only primitive tools at their command, succeeded in working that hard and brittle material, obsidian, with great skill.

Ancient Mexican mirrors of iron pyrites are executed with such carefully calculated convex surfaces that they reduce the human face to its natural size without distorting it.

IX

CHARACTER OF MEXICAN CULTURE

1

Indigenous or primitive Aztec culture was subject to the influence of certain fundamental circumstances. In the first place, the scanty resources in the way of food, the lack of wheat, rice, barley, rye and other cereals, which constitute the main food staples of the greater part of the countries of the world, confined them to corn or maize. Corn as an almost exclusive basis of food supply, and furthermore grown on non-irrigated lands, with irregular rains, or else under t r o p i c a l conditions, means an insufficiently nourished people.

Moreover, the want of horses, oxen, sheep and goats must also be taken into account. The lack of meat and milk, and other produce of flocks and herds, meant an enormous void in the possibilities of social development and the feeding of the people.

Great Cuatlicue. (Goddess of Death.)

2

One of the primitive customs of the ancient Mexicans, that has attracted most attention, and has drawn down upon them with horror, often to an exaggerated degree, the names of barbarians, cannibals and man-eaters, was their custom of eating human flesh.

It cannot be denied that among the Aztecs bloody sacrifices and the eating of human flesh were a custom. This fact must not, however, be taken as proof of special or hopeless and unprecedented ferocity.

It has been shown beyond all doubt that the Aztecs did not eat human flesh as food, but only with religious, ritual or traditional intent. They ate no human flesh but that of their enemies, as was fully evidenced in the siege of Mexico, in spite of the tremendous ravages of starvation.

3

We merely seek to explain the above facts, and not to excuse them. They are symptoms that reveal the internal condition, character and epoch of development of a culture. A people persecuted, isolated, errant, compelled to live for long periods like wild beasts, in uninhabited and

Moctezuma Xocoyotzin.

unproductive regions, in deserts, in valleys without permanent agriculture, or on the muddy margins of lakes, could not but yield to the
temptation to consume human flesh, and preserve traces of that habit
for a long time afterward.

It is hard to say whether the meanness of their agriculture was due
to lack of communications or to the climate, to their ignorance of the
uses of iron or the lack of beasts of burden.

The fact is that the Aztecs had no animals for transport, no proper
tools or other equipment, and no easy means of communications
(neither roads, nor navigable rivers, nor sea-borne trade.)

4

For that and perhaps other reasons, neither were they able to
extend the cultivation of maize, nor to diversify their crops, nor could
the food resources of one district be made available for others.

This division into isolated regions and enemy tribes and the conditions of poverty and warfare that necessarily ensued, to a great
extent account for the weakness of the Aztecs against the invasion of
the white men. The existence of certain forms of slavery; the patriarchal regime in the family; the excessive harshness of public pu-
nishments, everything was in proportion to the standards of their
primitive economy, engaged as they were in a never-ending struggle
with the enormous handicaps laid upon them by the land itself.

The Aztecs, like the Mayas, the Toltecs, the Tarascos or the
Mixtecs, had sufficient capacity for progress like all other groups
of humanity, within the limits set by Nature and time.

X

DISCOVERY OF AMERICA

THE ROUTE TO THE INDIES

1

What is called the discovery of America, is the meeting of two
great currents of races and peoples, who after a separation extending
over many centuries, were again joined after going right round the
earth.

Humanity, which seems to have originated in Asia, was scattered
by movements of expansion, on the one side towards the west (Asia

Minor, Egypt), to create there western culture, Graeco-Latin or European; and on the other, towards the east, to India, China, Japan and the islands of the South Seas. And those who first arrived on the continent later to be known as America, were groups of men driven by that mighty current that sets out from Asia towards the east. (See maps.)

A time came when the world of Europe was wholly cut off from the world of Asia, due to lack of communications, and to war or hostility among the peoples. The natives of the Americas, in turn

The Santa Maria Caravel.

sundered from Asia by century after century of complete isolation, in a condition of incomplete development, were hardly becoming conscious even of their own personality. They had no conception of the existence of an outside world.

Europe, however, had need of Asia. Trade had contributed to the rise to power of the Arab peoples and of the Italian Republics, which served as a connecting ling between east and west. The movement of Arab and Mahometan expansion eventually became a hindrance to commerce. Rivalries assumed a religious aspect and collisions took place between the Christians of the west and the Mahometans of the east. Europe, weakened by internecine wars, lost ground before the Turks, who controlled a great portion of the Mediterranean, while the Arab peoples succeeded in building up a powerful and brilliant culture, which spread all along the north African coast, and also to Spain.

2

Spain and Portugal, due to a number of favourable circumstances, enjoyed a privileged geographical position, and this was why the task fell to them of achieving the mighty undertakings demanded by the needs of their time.

Among the latter perhaps the most pressing was the opening up of a new route to the East Indies, to the great Asiatic trading centers, overflowing with merchandise not produced in Europe (silks, spices, pearls) and especially in gold and silver, needed for coinage, and enhanced in value by reason of scarcity and increased demand. No overland route could be broken open, not even by war, as in the Crusades. A passage had to be sought by sea and Portuguese sailors succeeded in rounding the Cape of Good Hope and finding the route to the Indies.

EVENTS THAT LED UP TO THE DISCOVERY OF AMERICA

1

The discovery of America is the work of Christopher Columbus. Any voyages made prior to 1492, which may have disclosed to Christianity and Europe the existence of a New World, were the result of accident, led to nothing, nor did they open up routes unknown. This is why they are only mentioned as doubtful occurrences, or of academic interest only.

Among them we may note the voyages of certain Chinese priests to a land by them called Fu-Sang, supposed to have been America. And the voyage of the Norsemen led by Leif Ericsson, who are believed to have reached the eastern coast of North America, or the doubtful discoveries of Portuguese sailors who touched at, or dreamt of a fabled land they called Antillia. All these reported discoveries are even now wrapped in obscurity and haze, like the Egyptian myth of Atlantis, which may be a mere fable or the dim memory of some past convulsion of nature.

2

Christopher Columbus was born at Genoa, on the Italian coast. But little is known with any certainty about his early life.

His bent was geography, especially the making of maps. His keen imagination and ardent ambition, fired by reading books of travel, which recounted all manner of wonders in regard to the countries of the East, led him to conceive the plan of reaching India from the west, by circling the earth. His knowledge was of course far from complete, but his will was strong. And after seeking support in vain

Map showing voyages of Columbus, according to M. F. de Navarrete.

for his plan at the Portuguese Court, he went on the same mission to Spain, where their Catholic Majesties, Ferdinand of Aragon and Isabella of Castile, occupied the throne.

3

A Spanish port was the obvious one from which to fit out an expedition intended to discover the way to the Indies. Spain had both ships and sailors.

The Spanish Court did not at the beginning have much faith in the plans of that unknown sailor.

Still, they decided to hold a council to examine and report on Columbus' plans, while to relieve his pecuniary distress, he was granted a modest allowance.

The council was held at Salamanca late in 1486. Columbus was called upon to appear and to lay his plans before it. The report of the council was adverse.

The Queen referred the plan to the Council of State and it also reported unfavorably on the Genoese geographer's scheme. Besides, Columbus' own ambition was perhaps a greater obstacle even than the very boldness of his plans.

He asked nothing less than to be made Viceroy and Governor of any land that he might discover; the rank of Admiral; one tenth of any treasure, pearls, precious stones, gold, silver, spices, or merchandise gained by the expedition and a grant in fee of one eighth of any lands discovered.

The Queen was desirous of embarking on the adventure on behalf of the Crown of Castile, and to raise the money she was willing to pawn her jewels.

Finally, after all obstacles were overcome, on August 3, 1492 the three vessels called the "Santa Maria," the "Pinta" and the "Niña" sailed from the port of Palos. They were three ships that today seem to us hopelessly diminutive for such a venture as the crossing of an unknown sea, with a crew of scant one hundred men.

Queen Isabella.

THE GREAT ADVENTURE

1

The "Santa Maria" was commanded by Columbus himself, Martin Alonzo Pinzon was the captain of the "Pinta" and his brother Vicente Yañez of the "Niña."

On the 17th September, so Columbus wrote down in his log-book, the air grew ever softer, and a sea bird was seen, of a kind that sleeps not on the sea. The sea was calm, like the river at Seville. On the

19th, the fleet had sailed a distance of four hundred leagues from the Canary Islands. On the 20th they caught with their hands a bird that looked like a tern, but which on closer examination was identified as a river bird.

2

On the 24th the sea was calm, and as the sun rose they saw that the sea was like a seaweed covered plain. On the 22nd, they ran into head winds, and Columbus wrote down: "This wind served me in great stead, because my crew was much excited, thinking that on these seas no winds blew could take them back to Spain."

All the incidents of the voyage are important, each in its own way; birds and fishes, floating seaweed, fog and the position of the stars.

On the 10th October, Columbus wrote in his log-book: "They grumbled at the length of the voyage; the Admiral heartened them as much as possible, holding out to them great hopes of profit." And he added: "aside from this, such complaints were of no avail, as he had set out to find the Indies and would not give up the search until he found them."

3

Lastly, "on the night from Thursday to Friday, the 11th to the 12th October, there was a moon. One Rodriguez Bermejo, or Rodrigo de Triana, saw a white sandhill, gazed intently and finally sighted land. He thereupon ran up to one of the guns and fired it off, shouting out: Land ahead! Land ahead! The crew hushed up to the deck and stayed there until dawn."

It is not known for certain whether that land was a part of San Salvador, or Guanahani, or the Watling Islands.

4

Columbus lived to make three voyages more. But he was unable to carry through his great adventure, as it was too vast an undertaking.

His ambition was to be the ruler and owner of any lands discovered; even as a great lord, superior to the King of Spain himself in wealth and power; but he encountered opposition on the part of the sovereign. The King failed to keep written promises to the Admiral, refused to acknowledge the latter's rights and even went so far as to persecute him, a judge having thrown Columbus into prison and bound him in chains.

Columbus was never able to realize the actual geographical importance of his discoveries, nor did he succeed in founding prosperous colonies. He wasted his presttige on unsuccessful explorations and operations, and died almost forgotten.

COLUMBUS IN HISTORY

1

Even after his death his fate in history has been as troubled and unquiet as his life itself. His merits were denied and belittled in the days when he was engaged on his voyages of discovery. For long years his fame was ignored. After that the pendulum swung to the opposite extreme, and not only were merits as a sailor and savant ascribed to him, but attempts were made to exalt him almost to the rank of a saint.

Finally, his fame in our time has again been threatened, as his weaknesses have come to light from the study of new documents.

2

The part played by Columbus in the discovery of America and his merits as a sailor and as a man are also depreciated so that other persons also entitled to honor from the adventure may not remain in obscurity. There is no need, however, to detract from the honor due to the Discoverer, in order to give their share to the brothers Pinzon, true sailors, navigators and pilots. The universal importance and the exploit of the great discovery are in themselves more than sufficient to give each one his or her part of fame; to Queen Isabella, to Spain, to Martin Alonzo Pinzon, to Genoa and to the Admiral.

Instead of dragging down the historical personality of Columbus, he now appears in a new light. Tradition will continue to live and fame will not cease to honor the poor map-maker, who brought renown to the names of his parents, Dominic Colombo and Susanna Fontana Rosa.

XI

EXPLORATIONS AND DISCOVERIES IN MEXICO

1

After the voyages of Christopher Columbus expedition after expedition was organized and set out. Americo Vespucci touched the mainland to the south, and the whole Continent received his name.

John and Sebastian Cabot in 1497 reached the shores of that land which was later to become an English colony, and eventually the United States of America. Cabot's discoveries were not made under the patronage of either Spain or Portugal, but of England, and through them one more channel for the introduction of European civilization into the New World was opened.

2

In addition to what we may term official voyages of exploration, on behalf of the King of Spain or by his direct representatives, and by Columbus himself or by his heirs, other voyages of adventure or contraband were undertaken.

Trade with the natives, begun by Columbus, and carried on by exchange and barter of European goods for the products of the Americas, exercised a powerful attraction. Colonization was likewise begun, thus combining the work of civilization with that of exploitation.

The Indians were forced to render personal service, and as what was most keenly sought were the precious metals, work in the mines brought with it slavery. Men had to be taken from one place to another and from one island to another to work, and thus the slave trade arose. As the population of the West Indian Islands was but scanty, the slave trade was carried on with negroes brought from Africa.

3

Spain attempted to transplant her own institutions to the New World, by creating organs of government.

Permits and concessions for voyages of exploration and for trading purposes, and for establishing factories and colonies marked the setting up of government in the countries discovered.

Conquerors and colonizers were an extension of the nobility, or the aristocratic class of feudal lords; the crown stood for the centralizing force or concentration of power. And the third class of the feudal period, the Church, also took part in the work of conquest and colonization. From the very first, missionaries, priests and monks arrived in the New World in the company of sailors, traders and royal delegates or officials.

The agents of the Crown bestowed upon such colonization its official character, and its civil organization; to the representatives of the Church fell the task of spreading the Christian faith, and at the same time of performing as auxiliaries of the Government, those tasks which came within the province of the Church as a part of the State, more especially as regards education and charitable work.

4

Columbus reached the entrance to the route leading to the coasts of Mexico. On his fourth and last voyage, still in search of the famous straits that were to afford a passage to India over the South Seas, he came upon a canoe filled with Indians and their merchandise; copper hatchets, cotton cloth, cocoa, and rush or palm leaf mats. And by signs they told him something about their country, which was rich in foodstuffs and gold.

That country they called Ciguare or Ciamba; perhaps what they told the Admiral was vaguely about some portion of Mexico, and the Admiral construing their information in accordance with his own ideas, ascribed it to the Great Can, Cipango, that is India.

5

Columbus refused to take the route thus pointed out to him, because his ships were not in good enough condition, or because of his firm determination to make for the south. But among his crew was a ship-boy called Anton de Alaminos. And he, years afterwards, was destined to be the real discoverer of what is now Mexico, the guide of the expeditions of Hernandez de Cordoba, Grijalva and Cortez.

The official formula authorizing the first voyages of discovery that reached Mexico, was also an inheritance from Columbus. Diego Velazquez attained the governorship of Cuba, after beginning his career as the agent of Diego Columbus, the Admiral's son. And Velazquez himself was the promoter or backer of the exploring expeditions that sallied forth to discover, ransom, trade and colonize among the West India Islands.

DISCOVERY OF YUCATAN

1

Thus was the expedition of Francisco Hernandez de Cordoba fitted out. Anton de Alaminos was pilot to the expedition, which was composed of three ships manned by one hundred men. Something was vaguely known about a "Land of Culua" (on account of the Acolhuas, Mexico being included in the so-called Acolhua confederation), or

Santa Maria de las Nieves. The ships of Hernandez de Cordoba followed the route disdained by Columbus, and thus reached the coasts of Yucatan. Information about the peoples of "Culua," of the far-off Acolhuas, and of kingdoms and cities abounding in gold, became fuller and more precise.

2

They reached an island called *Punta de Mujeres,* Women's Point, on account of the images there found with feminine features.

They were astounded on beholding a stone building and men wearing shirts and cloaks of cotton, feather ornaments and jewels of gold and silver.

The coast of the main land lies close to Mujeres Island. Following this coast towards the north, they came to a cape. From their ships they could see a village. The Indians paddled their canoes up to the Spaniards' ships, and were made presents of necklaces of green glass beads. They invited the Spaniards to land in these words: *Canes Catoche* which means "Come to our houses." The Spaniards accepted the invitation and landed. And suddenly serried ranks of warriors made their appearance and "the first volley of arrows shot by them wounded fifteen soldiers." The Indians were armed with bows and arrows, slings and lances; they wore plumes, and cotton doublets, and carried shields.

3

In the fight that followed the sword of course triumphed, and also crossbows and muskets. The Indians fled and the Spaniards managed to get to some temples where they found clay idols and gold ornaments.

From Cape Catoche they sailed west, feeling their way carefully. After two weeks on this course, their water gave out, and they landed at a spot called by the Indians Campeche. They again found an enemy more than willing to fight.

The warriors were lined up ready for the fray. The Indian priests by dumb show suggested to the Spaniards that they leave the village before certain bonfires they had lit were burned out. Hernandez de Cordoba understood and took the hint and decided to retreat.

4

Foul weather and contrary winds made navigation difficult, their water gave out once more and the explorers found themselves compelled to land in a small haven which was, latter on, to be known as the Bay of the Adverse Fight.

On this occasion, and in spite of swords, muskets and crossbows, the Indians succeeded in overpowering the Spaniards by sheer force of numbers. Forty-eight Spanish soldiers were slain, and two were carried off alive by the Indians. Hernandez de Cordoba was ten times wounded by arrows and made his way back to Cuba in evil plight.

THE VOYAGE OF GRIJALVA

1

Hernandez de Cordoba's expedition revealed the existence of Yucatan, but no clear idea of Mexico has had as yet been gained. It was only dimly surmised that farther away, more to the west, and more to the north, there might be found a country, island or land, where gold was abundant, and inhabited by numerous peoples.

Hernandez de Cordoba died as a result of the wounds sustained by him at Campeche.

2

Diego Velazquez fitted out another exploring expedition, this time under the orders of Juan de Grijalva. As on former occasions, the adventure purported to be for trading purposes only, no powers being granted for conquering any peoples or founding any settlements.

Grijalva went farther afield than Hernandez de Cordoba, but had not at his disposal men, nor arms, nor genius, nor good fortune to open his way into the heart of Anahuac.

Grijalva, with a fleet of four ships, with two hundred men, with Anton de Alaminos as pilot, sailed from Cuba on April 5, 1518. Among the members of the expedition there were several men who were later destined to become celebrated; Pedro de Alvarado, Francisco de Montejo, Bernal Diaz del Castillo.

3

They followed the route previously traversed by Hernandez. They avoided landing where warlike Indians might be a menace. As always, they took with them ship's biscuit, flour, dried peas, cassava bread and salt beef. For trade and barter they took along a cargo of glass beads, caps, canvas shoes, scissors, mirrors and cloth. And they likewise laid in a store of wine. They were better protected against arrows by cotton quilted doublets or cloaks.

They touched at the Island of Cozumel, and then hugged the coasts of Yucatan, Tabasco and Veracruz.

4

Juan de Grijalva.

The pilot Alaminos, who led them, and recognized the coasts, still thought that Yucatan was an island and hoped to find the longed-for passage to the South Seas and the shortest route to the East Indies.

At a spot on the coast of Vera Cruz the Indians made signals indicating friendly overtures. The Spaniards landed and in addition to the customary exchange of goods for provisions they obtained more exact information in regard to the famous land of "Culua," the home of the Acolhuas, that is Acolhuacan or Culhuacan. Grijalva carried on his conversation with the Indians by dumb show, laboriously and imperfectly.

5

On the 24th of June he arrived at that part of the coast where Vera Cruz now is. Alaminos marked on his charts the islands called "Blanca," "Verde" and "Sacrificios," and the islet of San Juan de Ulua.

They landed opposite the latter. The Indians walked about on the beach bearing white flags, and beckoned to the captain to approach. They brought green branches to ward off the rays of the sun, and perfumes, *pinole* (ground corn) *tortillas* (corn cakes) and *tamales* (a kind of pudding made of maize and fowl.)

The Captain, however, soon let them know that all he wanted was gold, and they promised to bring him some on the following day. Surely enough, they came back with a few bars of the yellow metal. The Captain asked for more. Again they came, this time with a little statuette, a mask and a few beads of gold, some stone and other articles of jewelry. They volunteered the information that gold was won from river beds at the foot of the high mountains.

6

Alvarado was ordered to return to Cuba, to quieten the fears of the merchant adventurer, Velazquez, with satisfactory reports and gold. Grijalva continued his journey of discovery. No passage to the Indies was found, and Alaminos knew full well that by following the coast he would again swing round to the east, in the direction of Florida.

7

They passed in front of Nautla, and discovered the Tuxpan Sierra. They reached a cape now supposed to have been Cape Rojo.

The bad state of the ships and the poor condition of the crew, did not allow conquest and far less founding any settlements. Grijalva found himself compelled to turn back and set sail for Cuba. The return journey was long and difficult; they took forty-five days to sail from Tabasco to Cuba. The commercial success of the venture did not satisfy Velazquez. Grijalva's expedition, however, from the standpoint of discovery and pioneer work for other and more fortunate adventurers, was of extraordinary importance.

THE FIRST COLONIZERS

1

An event which happened some time before official explorations brought Europeans into contact with the natives of Mexico, and which had great historical significance, must not here be passed over.

About the year 1512 a Spanish expedition on its way from the Gulf of Darien to Cuba, was wrecked somewhere near the coast of Yucatan. Only six survivors succeeded in reaching land, two or three women among them. Hardships and Indian arrows accounted for four of them, leaving only two survivors, Gonzalo Guerrero, a soldier, and Jeronimo de Aguilar, a priest.

2

These two men managed to escape death and to live among the Mayas. The Indians made slaves of them, but they in turn made themselves useful and learnt the language of their captors. Gonzalo Guerrero rendered military service and was rewarded with an Indian maiden for his wife. He had to have his ears pierced and his face tattooed, and when the members of Hernandez de Cordoba's exploring expedition landed on the coast at the place later known as the Bay of the Adverse Fight, it seems that he contributed to the defeat of his own countrymen. Jeronimo de Aguilar kept the remains of his Spanish garments and his breviary.

3

In spite of the faiture of his expedition, Hernandez de Cordoba succeeded in capturing, as prisioners of war or slaves, two Yucatecan Indians who were christened and given the names of Julian and Melchor. They learnt some Spanish and became the first links in the chain of events of the conquest. From them the Spaniards learnt that Guerrero and Aguilar were living among the Mayas, and this was the first step taken on the way to Tenochtitlan.

XII

THE CONQUEST OF MEXICO

THE EXPEDITION OF HERNAN CORTES

PRELIMINARIES

1

The delay in returning of the expedition commanded by Grijalva made Velazquez uneasy and induced him to send a ship to the assistance of the former, with Cristobal de Olid as captain. But the latter hardly even suceeded in reaching Yucatan, where he was all but wrecked, and found himself compelled to sail back to Cuba. On the other hand, Pedro de Alvarado returned with messages from Grijalva, and above all with actual samples of what they had managed to recover. He also brought news of the rich land of "Culua," also called by the Spaniards "Santa Maria de los Remedios" or Santa Maria de las Nieves" (Our Lady of the Snows.)

And while Grijalva painfully undertook his return voyage. Velazquez was furnishing forth a fresh expedition, and looked round for a new commander, inasmuch as fortune seemed to be adverse to those previously selected. When Grijalva arrived in Cuba, Cortes had already begun to organize his expedition.

2

On this occasion a trading and military adventure on a larger scale was contemplated. That was why Velazquez this time hesitated more than before, in choosing a leader.

A conquering captain had above all to be a "business man." He further had to possess the essential qualities of a fighting man: personal courage, decision, a disposition to risk other men's lives and his own, energy, cruelty, harshness, ability to command and good fortune.

3

Portrait of Hernan Cortes, after an oil painting now in the Hospital de Jesus

The conquest of Mexico could not be undertaken either by Charles V, who was too far away, nor by his Captains engaged in warlike operations in Europe, nor by Velazquez, who wished to discover and win lands without risking his own person, and by furnishing only a part of the funds; nor even by Hernandez or Grijalva, who had neither the qualities nor even the defects that were required.

The conquest of Mexico called for a man and an hour. It had to be carried out by Spanish resources, but organized and adapted for action in America. The pilot would have to be an Antono de Alaminos, well versed in ocean trails. The soldiers had to be white men, yet accustomed to tropical climates and acquainted with the ways of the Indian, both as an ally and as an enemy. Goods for barter, provisions and arms had to be selected taking all these circumstances into account. This work of adaptation was just what Cortes knew how to do and succeeded in carrying out.

As a matter of fact Cortes's record was not, at first sight, such as to recommend him, without discussion, for the position. He was thirty six years of age and was then nothing more than a farmer with a moderate estate. He was born at Medellin, in Estremadura, in 1485, and had left Spain at the age of nineteen.

"He seemed to be a calm and deliberate person of sound judgment, and considerable talent, but boundless ambition."

His studies had gained for him, besides some Latin, "clerkly wiles and abilities." He had at one time thought of serving as a soldier in Italy, and had shown himself to be of a restless and adventurous disposition; he accompanied Nicolas de Ovando to Hispaniola and later assisted Velazquez in the conquest of Cuba, an enterprise sadly lacking in military glory. He was then a village Mayor and a planter who lived by looking after his crops and the work of his slaves.

5

Velazquez wished to find a man for his service who would join sufficient ability to absolute subserviency, and was not satisfied either with Hernandez or Grijalva. Cortes, however, was too big a man to act merely as an agent. He was more ambitious, more fiery in temper than his predecessors, and as soon as the opportunity was afforded him of commanding an expedition, he devoted himself to the enterprise with all his might.

When Velazquez thought of drawing back, Cortes had already engaged his estate and his person in the adventure, and was not disposed

Spanish conquistadors and Indian maidens.

to allow Velazquez to put any one else in his place. Thus began a tremendous game of mutual distrust, tricks and betrayals.

Cortes donned velvet clothing, plumed helmets and decked his person with golden medals and chains. Some traders let him have money and goods on credit, and he drew to himself volunteers by means of proclamations summoning the adventurous to the conquest and settlement of unknown lands. And then he resolved to hasten his departure, even if he had to do without Velazquez' consent.

6

When Cortes at last sailed from Santiago de Cuba, his fleet consisted of six vessels. But at La Trinidad and Havana, openly disobeying Velazquez' orders, a number of volunteers joined the expedition.

The commercial part of the venture consisted in a cargo of rattles, mirrors, glass beads, needles, pins, purses, ribbons, buckles, knives, scissors, hammers, tongs, axes and cheap clothing. They took with them two hundred Indians as servants, Indian women to grind corn and make bread, and a few negro slaves.

The fleet with these later additions reached a total of eleven ships.

Cortes' military forces consisted of 518 soldiers, 32 crossbowmen, 13 musketeers, 16 horsemen and 110 mariners, with ten brass cannon, 4 falconets, and several bulldogs. The chief pilot was again Anton de Alaminos.

The whole of the experience gathered on former voyages was thus at Cortes' disposal. Many of his captains and soldiers had already seen service in Cuba or other islands, under Hernandez de Cordoba or Grijalva. Two Indians from Yucatan, Melchorejo and Julianillo, were the first men to act as interpreters on such an expedition.

FIRST STAGE OF THE CONQUEST

1

Alaminos steered the fleet by following the course by then well known to him. The first piece of luck was the ransom of Jeronimo de Aguilar, who joined the expedition and rendered valuable service as an interpreter.

The other Spaniard who had lived among the Mayas, and whose name was Gonzalo Guerrero, did not dare to come into Cortes' presence. When the expedition was in Tabasco, the Indian chiefs or *caciques* presented the Spaniards with a number of slaves, among them Malinche or Donna Marina, who was destined to become of the greatest use to them as guide and interpreter.

2

The first rumors in regard to the approach of white men reached Mexico about 1515.

Moctezuma's Terror.

According to the story, Netzahualpilli, the *cacique* or king of Texcoco, a son of Netzahualcoyotl, spoke thus to Moctezuma: "Great
and Powerful Lord: I do not wish to disquieten thee, but my duty is
to serve thee. I have discovered as a great truth that but a few years
hence our cities will be destroyed. Ere many days have passed, thou
shalt see in the sky portents that shall bear out my warning to thee."

In fact, a priest one night saw a comet in the eastern sky. The
king wished to see for himself, and the next night mounted to his tower,
where he prolonged his vigil until he saw the comet appear in the sky.

And one day a man who had come up from the coast sought
audience of the king and told him that he had seen hills moving on the
surface of the waters. These were probably Grijalva's ships.

3

Moctezuma dispatched men to the coast in search of fuller information and with instructions to send up pictures of the "houses that
moved upon the waters." He likewise sent messengers bearing presents.
But Grijalva had already sailed on his voyage back to Cuba. The king
of Mexico kept watchmen and messengers on or near the coast. And
when Cortes arrived at the Bay of San Juan, on April 21, 1519, he
found Indians who seemed to be awaiting him.

Cortes told these Indians that he came as a friend, in the name
of the mightiest monarch of the earth. He sent to Moctezuma presents
consisting of a chair, glass beads and a red hat. One of the Indians,
when he saw a soldier wearing a helmet, wished to take it to his king,
and Cortes let him have it with the request that it be brought back
filled with gold.

4

On his side, Moctezuma sent more valuable presents; cotton
doublets, featherwork, mosaic masks, and fowls, dogs, tigers, monkeys
and other animals, made of gold. And "a golden Sun, of fine gold, as
big as a cartwheel, a silver moon and the soldier's helmet, full of small
golden nuggets."

But the adventurers were even better pleased at the arrival of
certain other Indians, who came as ambassadors or messengers. They
were Totonacs from Cempoala. Donna Marina asked whether any of
them knew the land of Mexico, to which they answered affirmatively.
They stated that their lord had sent them to find out who the strangers
were, and to offer their services, something they had not dared to do
before, so long as their enemies, the Culuas, were there.

Thus Cortes learnt that he could on occasion, count on other Indians, the enemies or rivals of the Aztecs, as his allies.

THE ASTUTENESS OF THE CONQUISTADOR

1

All the same, the position of Cortes was fraught with danger. Moctezuma sent him rich presents, yet exhorted him to withdraw. The partisans of Velazquez in the expedition were anxious to return to Cuba.

So that, Cortes was faced by enemies in front of him, within his own army, and in his rear. A series of acts that were at the same time crafty, bold and attended by luck, enabled him to continue his onward march in triumph.

In order to cow and win over the partisans of Velazquez, he captured and punished the more dangerous among them, finally and definitely broke off all his engagments, declared the City of Vera

The Conquistador. (After J. C. Orozco.)

Cruz founded, installed a city council as a Spanish institution, and had himself appointed Captain.

He despatched to Spain emissaries with presents and pleas for the approval of the royal and religious authorities, or a least, to prevent them from being prejudiced against him. He began to investigate the domestic politics of the Indians, and with the *caciques* of Cempoala as his allies, he embarked upon his manoeuvers to turn to good account the wars and rivalries between the Indians.

2

Moreover, he imprinted upon his acts an aspect of grandeur, by deciding to destroy his ships.

As seem to be apparent from the most trustworthy authorities, Cortes' idea was to cut off the retreat of Velazquez' friends, and to strengthen his own position. He did not act on his own initiative alone, but with the support and consent of a large portion of his army.

And so he gave orders that his ships be stripped of all anchors, ropes, cordage, sails, nails and everything else of use, and that holes be drilled in the hulls to render them useless for navigation.

3

Rivalries and mutual hatred between the Indians contributed directly to Cortes' success. He set out on the way from Vera Cruz to Mexico, with the support of the Cempoaltecs and assuring himself of similar support from other enemies of the Aztecs.

The main body of his army thus began to be composed of Indian allies, to whom fell the severest tasks; they acted as guides, vanguard, shock troops, and more than this, as carriers and providers. And even as the brains and leadership of the Conquest had to be the work of the European element, material execution, especially in the conquest of Anáhuac, could not but be carried out with the participation of the Indians.

4

The conquest of Mexico astounds us because it was a gigantic adventure accomplished with elements whose numbers were unbelievably insignificant.

Reasons have been sought for what seems almost a miracle. At first sight the explanation would seem to lie in Cortes' genius, his abilities as a conqueror, adventurer, politician and soldier. But to this must added great good fortune. Cortes seems to have been led, throughout the Conquest of Mexico, by an invisible hand that saved him when in danger and directed him into the proper path. His qualities are very obvious and well-known, and were offset by his faults; he was brave but cruel, crafty but of ill-faith; active but harsh; ambitious, yet greedy; energetic, yet unscrupulous.

5

But if in military enterprises good fortune is largely responsible for victorious leaders and for individual success, there is, on the other hand, much less connection between permanent results and sheer luck. Cortes' defeat or death would merely have put a stop to his own career, but the conquest would have been carried through to its end, because it was a consequence of the drive of a whole people, of a whole civilization, in its advance upon another Continent.

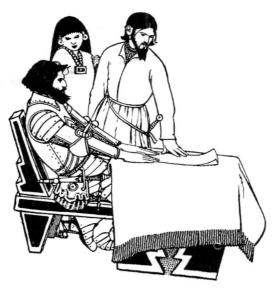

Cortes, Donna Marina and Jeronimo de Aguilar.

6

The triumph of the Spaniards over the Indians may not be explained by isolated factors. Fear of the supernatural and the unknown, the myth of Quetzalcoatl, who was destined to return from the east to restore his rule, Moctezuma's weakness, warfare between Indian peoples and tribes, all these circumstances united to further development of the main cause.

This is discernible in the superiority of European weapons; swords of steel, firearms, horses and other equipment. And above all, organization, military technique, auxiliary services, reserves of food and other supplies, cooperation: the force of a mighty culture in full development launching a powerful stream onto a new world, where the resources of nature and of the times had not permitted the rise of an organization of similar Power.

THE MARCH ON TO MEXICO

1

When Cortes' soldiers began their ascent from the coast to the temperate lands, a new world really began to open out before them.

Messengers from Moctezuma ceased not to bring messages and presents to the Spaniards, thus disclosing the monarch's weakness. Both in Mexico and also in Tlaxcala two opposing tendencies were discernible; a wish to resist the invaders, and fear of the white men, who had steel, fire and horses at their disposal.

With the assistance of his Cempoaltec allies, Cortes easily vanquished the uncertain and wavering resistance of the Tlaxcaltecs. The latter, convinced by their defeat, leant once for all to the side of the Castilian Captain.

After his victory at Tlaxcala, and when he reached Cholula, Cortes found himself compelled to resort to sterner methods, and without fighting, engaged in wholesale slaughter.

We cannot but mention these events, which show the worst side of the Conquistador's character, and enable us to understand, once for all, the nature of these exploits which imprinted upon the Conquest its destructive character.

"In a courtyard in the barracks a great number of Cholula and Aztec Indians were crowded together.

"A musket shot, the signal agreed upon with the Tlaxcaltec and Cempoaltec warriors who thronged the streets, marked the beginning of the slaughter. The courtyard had only three doorways, which were guarded by the Spaniards so that the Indians should not escape;

when they saw there was no way out, and that were being attacked, they vainly attempted to scale the lofty walls."

The slaughter in the courtyard once over, the Spaniards and their allies went about the streets hacking away, burning, destroying and robbing.

The courtyard and streets ran with the blood of three thousand victims, when the order was given to stop the fighting.

"Quetzalcoatl was overthrown from the lofty temple where he was enthroned."

3

The massacre at Cholula, and after that several other mass murders, were a strong reason why the mingling of the cultures was not effected

An aspect of the Conquest. (After Diego Rivera.)

by peaceful methods and an abyss of ill feeling was opened between
the races which lasted for centuries.

And yet, in spite of all this, the Aztec envoys continued to make
overtures to Cortes, furnished him with provisions and rendered him
services, even vying in these attentions with his Cempoalan and Tlaxcaltec allies.

On November 7, 1519, Cortes reached the gates of the City of
Mexico, and was at once received by Moctezuma.

CORTES AND MOCTEZUMA

1

Cortes was lodged like a guest of honor. The Spaniards devoted
themselves to visiting the City.

The streets, the houses, the markets, the canals, the temples, the
crowds with their peculiar dress, all was to them new and strange.

Moctezuma called on his guest, who had come bearing messages of
friendship from another king, then described as the most powerful
monarch of the earth, and continued to bestow on him jewels, clothing
and provisions.

Cortes found out all that might serve his aims of conquest. But
what must have interested the Spaniard above everything was the
discovery of treasure, accidentally hit upon on beginning the erection
of an altar. A secret door was then found and through it the Spaniards

The Spaniards discover treasure.

made their way into a chamber where Moctezuma had the jewels of his ancestors concealed.

2

And while all this was going on, Cortes, by availing himself of the services of his Totonac and Tlaxcalan friends, and with the assistance of his interpreters, Jeronimo de Aguilar and La Malinche, succeeded in acquiring valuable information in regard to the situation prevailing in the land to which he had succeeded in gaining an entrance.

The Spanish soldiers left to garrison Vera Cruz had interfered with collection of tribute by the Aztecs from the Indians of that district, and in the clash which followed several Spaniards had been killed and wounded.

Vainly did Moctezuma promise to punish those guilty of violence against the Spaniards, even though it was more than likely that he himself had given the order for the attack. The Lord of Mexico was borne off a prisoner to Axayacatl's palace, but at the same time assured the nobles and his other vassals that he went thither of his own free will. Cortes seized the person of Moctezuma and was enabled to use him as a tool for his own ends.

3

Even so Cortes' position was far from being clearly defined. In order to clear up the situation, he attempted to bring matters to a head. He exacted from Montezuma submission to the King of Spain; after that he forced him to allow Cuauhpopoca, the Aztec captain who had attacked the Spaniards at Vera Cruz, to be punished; he made Moctezuma deliver to him the treasure of Axayacatl, by way of a first payment of tribute, and as a mark of submission; he elicited from him permission and assistance to send scouts throughout the land, in search of ports on the South Sea, of gold mines and of undiscovered countries.

Moctezuma assented to everything in the hope that he would thus be able to induce Cortes to depart. Cuauhpopoca was burnt alive, and the treasure was divided up between the Spanish captains and soldiers, after prior deduction of one fifth portion for Charles V and another fifth for Cortes.

4

Moctezuma, however, continued to harp upon the subject of the departure of the Spaniards, inasmuch as every request of Cortes had been granted. The latter found it necessary to provoke him further, by insisting on the conversión of the King of Mexico to Christianity, and forcing him to deny his old gods and to allow the idols to be destroyed.

To this Moctezuma demurred and Cortes with his own hands tore the gold masks from the images of Tezcatlipoca and Huitzilopochtli, and planted the Cross at the very top of the great temple in Mexico City.

Moctezuma receives Cortes

THE EXPEDITION OF NARVAEZ

1

The special messengers who ran by relays between Mexico and Vera Cruz, reported that a fleet had approached the coast.

The ships thus sighted brought a new army equipped by Velazquez, under the command of Panfilo de Narvaez, for the purpose, not of conquering the land discovered by Grijalva, but of punishing Cortes.

Narvaez sailed from Cuba with a fleet of nineteen ships, fourteen hundred soldiers, eighty horses and twenty guns, besides Indian and negro servants, etc.

So that Cortes began to find himself in a position growing daily more awkward. He held Moctezuma prisoner, but was in turn surrounded by enemies. His allies followed him largely out of fear and hatred of the Aztecs, but could not be relied upon absolutely. His own troops were disseminated on expeditions or doing garrison duty in different places. Moctezuma, from his prison, made constant attempts

Cortes gazes down at the City of Mexico-Tenochtitlan.

to throw off the yoke. The Aztecs resented the slights put upon their King and their gods. And the partisans of Velazquez awaited their opportunity to attack Cortes.

2

It looked as though Cortes were in a hopeless situation. But he carried out his plan of campaign most cleverly. He left Pedro de Alvarado in command at Mexico, and marched out at the head of two hundred men to meet Narvaez. When he got down to the coast Cortes succeeded in buying over most of Narvaez' officers and men, by presents of gold.

There was only a poor pretense at a fight. Narvaez was taken by surprise at his camp, and but few shots were fired from his cannon which, by an unintentional mischance, killed four of Cortes' soldiers. And even the military band that Narvaez had brought along with him, served to celebrate the Conquistador's victory.

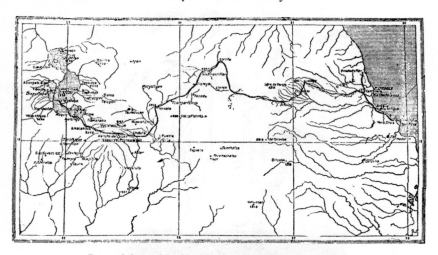

Route of Cortes from Vera Cruz to the interior of the country.

3

When taken prisoner and brought before Cortes, Narvaez, said:

"Thou must be grateful to fortune, in that thou hast captured me at such slight cost."

"I have much to thank fortune for," answered Cortes: "but the least of my exploits in this land is my capture of thee."

He should rather have said that his victory over the sorry Narvaez was the least, in comparison with what he still had to do.

For he was yet to triumph over far greater dangers and adversaries.

UPRISINGS AMONG THE AZTECS

1

Pedro de Alvarado, whom the Indians called *Tonatiuh,* which means the "Sun" had been left in command of the garrison at Mexico City. Pretending that he was menaced by the Aztecs, he jumped to the conclusion that an uprising was imminent, and attempted to follow the procedure of his Captain.

And when a religious ceremony was going on the Great Temple, with dancing, singing, and offerings of flowers, Alvarado with his troops fell upon a multitude of unarmed Indians, and in cold blood carried out a massacre bloodier than that at Cholula.

The nobles danced, unsuspecting and unarmed. There were about four hundred of them, but thousands more were there as spectators.

Suddenly and without warning, the soldiers rushel at the Indians and began to butcher them ruthlessly.

Pedro de Alvarado.

2

After a while the Aztec war cry was heard, uttered by one of their leaders. The Spaniards, vigorously attacked and with one of their captains wounded, fell back towards their quarters, where they were besieged.

Moctezuma intervened as a peacemaker, and went up on to the palace roof to beseech the people to discontinue the attack. The monarch was obeyed, and the attack ceased for the time being.

The Aztecs soon attacked the Spaniards at the latter's headquarters, besieged them and shut off food supplies. Alvarado would have succumbed had not Cortes defeated Narvaez and been able to return to Mexico with reinforcements.

3

On the 24th June Cortes came to the rescue of his lieutenant, and found that the Aztecs received him with hostility. His presence did not allay the excitement, and although the Conqueror was able to rejoin Alvarado, the Indians continued to surround the Spanish headquarters and to attack by throwing stones, burning canes and darts.

On this occasion the rebellion of the Aztecs seems to have been led by Cuitlahuac, Moctezuma's brother and his successor as a "chief of men" and leader of Tenochtitlan.

Cuitlahuac.

CUAUHTEMOC

1

We have, up to this point of our narrative of the conquest, followed the main figure, which is Cortes, who dominates the theater of events. In comparison Moctezuma is but a defeated and inglorious weakling But we must, in order to depict the last stage of the existence of the primitive nationality, bring in another personage, worthier to symbolize the exploits of a people which defended its freedom with an energy born of desperation. We must now turn our attention more particularly to the hero of the defense of Mexico.

2

Cuauhtemoc represents the notion of a geographical fatherland and of the races rooted in the very soil of Anahuac, as having been settled there for centuries. Among the chiefs and leaders of the Aztec people on its wanderings, in its struggles with Nature and man, from Tenoch down to Moctezuma, there is not one worthy to figure in history and legend by the side of the "Falling Eagle."

3

Cuauhtemoc was the son of King Ahuizotl and of Princess Tlilalcapatl, a grand-daughter of King Netzahualcoyotl, and was about eighteen years old in 1520.

He makes his first appearance on the stage of history on June 27, 1520. Moctezuma was compelled to go up into the roof so that his presence might calm down the excitement of the Aztecs. Several Spanish soldiers covered Moctezuma with their shields. And one of the *caciques* who was a prisoner in the hands of the Spaniards spoke on behalf on the king. Hardly had he finished when Cuauhtemoc spoke:

Cuauhtemoc.

"We shall not obey Moctezuma, for he is our king no longer! And since he is so despicable a man, we shall give to him punishment and just payment."

And suddenly, suiting the action to the word, "he raised his arm and aiming at Moctezuma, began to shoot a number of arrows; the rest of the army followed suit."

THE SAD NIGHT

1

Cortes ordered several attempted sallies. But the Aztecs had by then made up their minds to throw away a thousand lives for one, and with their serried bodies cut off all avenues of retreat. Cortes made overtures for peace, and offered to return the gold and jewels and to leave

the city. But these promises were of no avail. The besiegers yielded
not a single inch. Finally, the Spaniards decided on flight at any cost.

Several historians assert that the Spaniards killed Montezuma, although Cortes himself avers that the Aztecs slew their king.

In any event, flight was inevitable. The march was begun as noise-
lessly as possible, and just as the Spaniards thought that they would
be able to get by unnoticed, the darkness was broken by the shouts and
whistling of the Aztecs. They cried out in their own language "The
Teules are going!" "Quick, to the canoes! Let us cut them off at the
bridges!"

This was on the night of the 30th June, 1520, ever afterwards known
as the "Sad Night."

2

In order to facilitate the retreat, a portable bridge had been con-
trived, but before the whole army, with its Indian allies, horses, ar-

The Sad Night.

tillery and baggage, succeeded in crossing it, the Aztecs fell upon them. Only the vanguard was able to pass without mishap, and in the darkness of the night the dispersal began. The portable bridge stuck in the mire at the first moat or cut. The rearguard had to fall back and seek refuge at their old headquarters, while those who kept on advancing had to swim across the remaining moats, with the help of beams, or by passing on top of those who were not active enough.

3

Cortes noticed that many men belonging to the rearguard remained in Mexico, but he was unable to assist them, or to save them from the death that awaited them on the Sacrificial Stone. And the story goes that on arriving at Tacuba he realized the magnitude of the disaster, almost half his army wiped out, hundreds of Spaniards and thousands of Indian allies having perished; nearly all the rest wounded, even Cortes himself; the treasure that had been distributed before the flight, and also the artillery, sunk in the moats; many horses disabled, and no food nor supplies. It is then, so the legend tells us, that the tears started to his eyes. After that he sought refuge in an Indian temple, where years later a

Brigantines built by Hernan Cortes for attack on Mexico City. Sahagun Codex.

church was erected in honor of the Virgin of *los Remedios*. And as the Aztecs were unable to keep up their pursuit, Cortes succeeded in continuing his retreat in order to seek refuge among the Tlaxcaltecs.

4

In order to offset his defeat, he managed to turn the tables and retrieve his lost fortunes in a battle near Otumba. In an open field, and

surrounded by thousands of enemies, the group of Castilians demons-
trated once more the strength of their organization and the force of
their arms. The soldiers, though wounded and tired out, desperately
kept on fighting. And their Captain, like the hero of some book of
adventure, threw himself on the leader of the enemy, cut him down
in a hand to hand fight, took from him the standard that served as
a guidon for the Indians, and by his bold stroke demoralized his adversaries and once more inclined victory to his own side.

THE FALL OF MEXICO-TENOCHTITLAN

1

Almost a whole year elapsed before Cortes again appeared to attack
the Aztecs. Just after his disastrous defeat, a number of his men openly
avowed their desire to return to Cuba, and the attitude of his Indian
allies seemed doubtful.

But little by little the fortunes of the Conquistador were retrieved.
Reinforcements of men, arms, horses, and supplies arrived at Vera Cruz,
in the form of sundry small expeditions that came in search of trade
and adventure, only to swell the ranks of Cortes' men.

The Tlaxcaltec allies, and also the Cempoaltecs and many others
nearer Mexico, remained faithful and continued to render efficient
assistance.

At Tlaxcala, in spite of the stand taken by Xicotencatl the younger,
who advocated fighting the Spaniards and joining Cuitlahuac or Cuauhtemoc, the counsels of the friends of Cortes and enemies of Mexico,
prevailed. Gainsaying the opinion of his own father, Xicotencatl openly undertook to oppose Cortes, and lost his life in the attempt.

2

Partly by main force, and partly by clever political combinations,
Cortes prepared a decisive campaign all round Mexico, having gradually surrounded the city, shut off supplies and assistance, and availing
himself of all possible resources to isolate the Aztecs. He had small
ships built that could sail on Lake Texcoco, to interfere with canoe
traffic.

3

From May 26 to 30, 1521, the siege of Mexico began. The Indian
allies, almost one hundred thousand in number, crowded round the
ancient capital of Anahuac.

Glory and credit for the defense fall to both Cuitlahuac and Cuauhtemoc. Cuitlahuac did much as chief leader of Aztec resistance. He was in command on the "Sad Night" of Cortes' defeat. But Cuitlahuac died of small pox and the "Falling Eagle" was appointed in his stead.

4

Cuauhtemoc continued to carry out all the measures adopted by his predecessor; "he won over many to his side, although some staid aloof, not so much out of fear of the Spaniards, as out of ancient enmities;" he laid in a great supply of weapons; he filled the city with warriors; he weeded out a lot of useless people whom he despatched to the nearby mountains; he exercised his men in the use of arms; he gave prizes to those who outshone the others and ever sought to know what his enemies were doing."

In a small but swift canoe, sword and buckler in hand, Cuauhtemoc flew from one place to another.

5

The Spaniards failed in their attempt to take the city by storm, and even Cortes himself but narrowly escaped death on more than one occasion.

Cuauhtemoc imprisoned and brought before Cortes.

The Aztecs once had him down on the ground and a prisoner, but as what they wished was to bear him off alive to the stone of sacrifice, to tear out his heart and offer up to their gods so notable a victim, some of his most faithful men succeeded in rescuing him.

On the other hand, the lack of food and water proved to be deadlier weapons. The besiegers advanced by tearing down house by house, palace by palace and temple by temple. Hunger and plague decimated the Aztecs.

6

An ancient writer says: "It was Garcia Holguin who took the king prisoner. Cortes said to him through an interpreter: "Ask Cuauhtemoc why he allowed his city to fall at the cost of so many lives as have been lost these days, both on his side and on ours, when overtures for peace were so often made to him.

The brave king asswered him thus:

"Tell the Captain that I did my duty in defending my city and my kingdom, just as he would have done for his, had I gone to take them from him; but as I failed and am in his power, let him take his dagger and slay me."

Cortes, however, would not then kill him. The prestige of the vanquished monarch was still of use to him in the rebuilding of a new city of Mexico, so that he thus had some share in the formation of the new nationality that then arose.

This completes his personality as a hero and as the representative of his race.

PART TWO
THE COLONIAL PERIOD

FIRST STAGE OF SPANISH COLONIZATION

EXPANSION OF THE SPANISH POWER

I

A SURVEY OF ITS HISTORICAL EVOLUTION

Discovery, conquest and colonization constitute three stages or phases of one and the same movement. According to this, the period of exploration and discovery may, so far as Mexico is concerned, be taken as beginning with the first voyage of Columbus en 1492, up to Cortes' expedition in 1519. 1519 to 1521 are years of conquest, with direct consequences extending to 1535. And after that, up to 1810, comes the period of colonization.

We shall now, along the lines above laid down, attempt to present a picture of the colonial age..

The first period embraces the conquest itself and the immediate consequences of military occupation, such as the destruction of the City of Mexico, government by Cortes and his agents, up to the arrival of the Audiencias and the erection of a regular institutional system which assumed definite form when viceregal government was established: this period is that from 1521 to 1535.

The second period is marked by the expansion, consolidation, growth and height of the colonial régime, and covers the whole of the sixteenth century and a portion of the seventeenth, until the forces of discovery, conquest, settlement and missions are spent.

And the third period is that of stagnation and decline, in which forms of government and a social, economic and constructive movement exhibit the symptoms of the crisis which eventually broke out in the form of the Revolution of 1810.

II

DIRECT CONSEQUENCES OF SPANISH CONQUEST

1

Conquest is a feudal form of activity, manifested by violence and domination by force or arms.

Before our times, the means of production of wealth, that preceded the capitalist system, consisted mainly in utilization of the soil itself, directly or indirectly exploited by the nobility, under the Crown, and by the Church with the Papacy at its head, the land being tilled by great masses of peasants as serfs or workers attached to the soil.

The Conquest of Mexico wears throughout the aspect of a great impulse from feudal Spain. The winning of precious metals greatly resembles a search for treasure, because the attempt is made to gain them without organized and systematic work.

Illusions as to gold at that time proved disappointing, because neither the treasures of Moctezuma and the Indian chiefs, nor the scanty products from surface workings sufficed even to offset the expenses incurred in military expeditions. Prior to finding means for establishing mining operations on a large scale, and for this very reason, New Spain was a land meet only for conquest. There were no utilizable resources except the land itself, and the land without serfs, or the labor of the Indians, was absolutely unproductive.

2

The right of property was based solely on force, but thinly clothed with vague formulae in the shape of authority from the Crown, under cover, in turn, of authority from the Church. Out of this system arose *encomiendas* or grants of Indians, as a sort of extension of the feudal system into the Americas.

Encomiendas were a form of slavery, which appears as an advance in the way of emerging from absolute slavery and from the wild disorder and destruction, of the conquest itself. Out of feelings of humanity, and in their own interest, the conquistadors, in order to survive in a land that hardly furnished them with sustenance, became *encomenderos*, or holders of labor grants, and left to the agents of the King and to churchmen the performance of administrative and ritual functions.

Exploitation of the land by slave labor or similar systems means rudimentary forms of cultivation. Mining operations carried out by primitive methods are as harmful, due to loss of life and incomplete benefits, as plagues and epidemics caused by war.

Cities and villages are founded with military necessity mainly in view. So, after the destruction of the City of Mexico, when the advisability of rebuilding it elsewhere, to avoid the danger of inundation, was considered, it was decided to rebuild it on the same site as before, for fear that the Indians might at some time establish themselves anew at their ancient metropolis and again constitute a center of population away from the vigilance of the Spanish authorities.

Whenever a new town was founded, which was done mainly along main roads indicated by military necessity, the first thing laid out was the *plaza de armas,* or main plaza, with the pillory and the gallows, and the cross of the church or mission.

3

During the years that immediately followed the taking of the City of Mexico, the conquerors devoted all their efforts to spreading towards the west, up to the Pacific ocean, and south, to the Isthmus of Tehuantepec and Guatemala.

And just as exploration, discovery and conquest have all the characteristics of a commercial enterprise undertaken for profit, so the system of labor grants or *encomiendas* wears the aspect of an agricultural speculation. So long as there was no possibility of improving methods of production by bringing in suitable farming implements, equipment, tools and crops, and as no movement for permanent colonization was developed on a large scale, the soil could only be utilized in the most primitive manner and by following the same procedure as in conquest by force or arms. Indian porters or *tamemes* render personal service, branded like slaves, driven and guarded by foremen and savage dogs. Land and mines are distributed as rewards for services to the conquistadors, their families or close relatives, almost as though invoking the right of the first occupant. Such things as salaries and freedom of labor are ignored. Taxes are collected as spoils of war, (one fifth portion for the Crown, and a poll-tax on the great mass of the vanquished.) Trade is reduced to exchange and barter of the produce of the soil.

4

A transition period sets in, from feudalism to absolute monarchy. From anarchy the community passes to military government, arbitrary and despotic and as yet uncontrolled by civil standards. The supreme authority of the King begins to constitute the first organs of administration, by broadening the functions of the Council of the Indies and of the *Casa de Contratation* or Colonial Office at Seville; by appointing inspectors, agents, supervisors and courts of impeachment; by combating the system of *encomiendas* and limiting the power of feudal lords and endeavoring, through the Church, to lay down the fundamental principles of educational and charitable institutions, and by religious ceremonies and moral and spiritual propaganda.

Religious ideology is dogmatic, exclusive; and intolerant the winning of souls and pursuit of spiritual and temporal control.

There are no other forms to constitute a State or a Nation; hardly even the formalities of municipal organization; the only racial differences are those between Spaniards and Indians. There is no clear knowledge of the extent of the lands being explored, discovered and conquered. The appellation New Spain is applied to a vast region, in the center of which lies the City of Mexico; it extends to other centers of lesser population on the Mexican plateau and along the great mountain ranges, and it fades away in those desert and unknown regions where dwell scattered tribes of unreduced Indians.

And this period in reality extends to 1535, as the first *Audiencia*, with Nuño de Guzman at its head did not abandon primitive methods of conquest. The second *Audiencia*, under Ramirez de Fuenleal and Vasco de Quiroga, paves the way for colonization in a better organized and more progressive form.

III

CORTES AS RULER AND COLONIZER

1

When it was decided to rebuild a new Mexico City on top of the ruins of Tenochtitlan historical continuity of Mexican culture was preserved, as it continued to develop round the same center of tradition and population. On the site where the great Temple of the Aztecs had lately stood, the Spaniards began to erect a Christian church that in after years became the Cathedral, and on the *Plaza de Armas* or main square work was commenced on a palace, the Palace of Cortes, which subsequently became that of the Viceroys. The Indians of Mexico and of the whole Valley were compelled to labor on the work of reconstruction, as slaves bound by the harsh laws of war, and under such miserable conditions that according to trustworthy witnesses, as many men perished at that work as during the siege or in epidemics of small-pox or other plagues.

Although no legal authority was vested in Cortes, he exercised the functions of Captain General and military governor. At the beginning he chose Coyoacan as his place of residence, and from there directed the fitting out of new expeditions.

2

The episode of the torture of Cuauhtemoc reveals the character and state of mind of the victors, in those times.

Certain officers of Cortes thought that Cuauhtemoc had hidden the treasure of Moctezuma, or that he could say where and how it could be found. And at the same time they accused Cortes of having kept too much for himself when distributing the treasure already found.

Gomara's story is the most authoritative:

"We never found the whole of the gold that had first come to our hands, nor any trace of Moctezuma's treasure, which the Spaniards deeply regretted, inasmuch as they thought that they would, on re-taking Mexico, find everything they had been compelled to drop in their flight. The soldiers ill-treated the citizens to extort money from them. The King's officers sought to discover gold, silver, pearls, precious stones and jewels, in order to amass a substantial fifth portion; buy they never succeeded in finding any Mexican who would reveal anything, although they had all boasted how great was the treasure of their gods and of their kings; so that it was resolved to torture Cuauhtemoc and another man of high degree, and his attendant. The courtier suffered so greatly that although he died when subjected to torture by fire, he did not admit a single thing asked of him. When he was being burned he gazed intently at the King, so that the latter should, taking pity on him, permit him to say what he knew, or say it himself. Cuauhtemoc looked at him angrily and upbraided him as a weakling and of little account, and asked whether he himself were in some pleasance or bath."

3

Cortes was not very happy in his political organization of New Spain. He was in the position of a feudal lord attempting to assert his power on his own estate, and fought against the restrictive tendency of the Crown and the ambitions of his own soldiers, who in their turn wished to become great lords. On one side, monarchical absolutism, and on the other, the anarchy of the new *caciques*, or bosses. And between both groups, leaning at times in one direction, and at others to the opposite side, were the religious orders, the clergy and high ecclesiastical officials, divided by rivalries between the different orders.

But on the less showy but more effective work of actual colonization, we find the mark of Cortes' hand; such as organization of transport services, the building of roads; the importation of cattle, plants, and new crops; inducements to skilled workmen and farmers; shipbuilding on the shores of the southern seas and opening up of new sea-routes; ordinances, regulations, petitions and suggestions constantly sent to Spain. But so soon as Cortes' personal action was wanting, everything languished. His agents, his attorneys, his lieutenants all showed their absolute incapacity for command, due to their immorality, stupidity and meanness. The names of Albornoz, Chirinos, Salazar, Rodrigo de Paz, stand out only because of their immoderate appetite for gain in a confused medley, abounding in crimes and betrayals.

4

Cortes had not succeeded in gaining approval in Spain for his actions; his enemies triumphed, with the assistance of Juan Rodriguez de Fonseca, the President of the Council of the Indies who succeeded in having Cristobal de Tapia appointed as Governor of New Spain, and that an order be issued for the arrest of the Conquistador.

The Emperor Charles the Fifth, however, finally decided in favor of Cortes, on October 15, 1522, and appointed him Governor and Captain General of New Spain. Other appointments made at the same time were Rodrigo de Albornoz, accountant, Gonzalo de Salazar, factor, and Alonso de Estrada, treasurer.

The expeditions sponsored by Cortes reached Panuco on the northeast, Michoacan, Jalisco and Colima on the west, and Guatemala and Honduras to the south. Cristobal de Olid was commissioned to seek, further south, the straits that were to shorten the route to the Indies. He sailed from Vera Cruz in January, 1524, in command of a fleet of five ships and with four hundred men on board.

Olid attempted to serve Cortes as the latter had served Velazquez, and announced that he was the chief of the expedition and acknowleged no authority but that of the King of Spain. When Cortes learnt of this, he decided to punish the insubordinate underling, and after sending along Francisco de las Casas in the van, he himself left for Las Hibueras (Honduras.)

And this is where we meet Cuauhtemoc for the last time.

5

Cuauhtemoc was appointed by Cortes Governor of Mexico, but only "to honor him and perform what he had promised him," because he allowed him not to go about alone, but only in his company, so that he might not rise up against him, and to share in the homage yet paid him by his vassals, because "the Indians greatly honored him and continued to pay him the same reverence and ceremonies as to Moctezuma."

For those same reasons Cortes made Cuauhtemoc accompany him on his trip to the Hibueras.

Bernal Diaz thus relates the story of the hero's death:

"Guatemuz, great *cacique* of Mexico, and other Mexicans of high degree that came with us, were contemplating, or had ordered, that we all be killed, they to return to Mexico, and on arriving at their city, to join their great resources and make war on those of us left in Mexxico and again see their kingdom rise..." The conspiracy was discovered.

"Guatemuz admitted that what the others had said was true; but that he had not originated that plan, and that he had never had any intention of carrying it into effect, but only that they had talked it over... Cortes ordered that the rebels be hanged.

"And when they were about to hang him Guatemuz said: "Oh, Captain Malinche! Many days ago did I realize the falseness of thy words, and that thus wouldst thou put me to death, since I slew not myself when thou didst seize me in my city of Mexico; why slayest thou me unjustly? God will call thee to account." The lord of Tacuba said that death to him was welcome since he was about to die in the company of his lord Guatemuz."

"And putting them to death thus was most unjust, and was censured by all of thus who went on that journey."

6

Aside from this, the journey to the Hibueras proved to be a formidable geographical expedition that lasted one year and seven months, through unknown lands and overcoming obstacles that seemed unsurmountable. When the Conquistador reached Honduras, Francisco de las Casas had already slain Olid. But he received news that his return to Mexico was anxiously awaited because his lieutenants and substitutes had brought about a dangerous situation bordering on anarchy.

IV

ROYAL OFFICERS AND AUDIENCIAS

1

When Cortes set forth on his journey to the Hibueras, he appointed Licenciado Alonso Zuazo as mayor of the city, and as his substitute in the government, together with the treasurer, Alonso de Estrada, and the Accountant, Rodrigo de Albornoz.

It seems that Cortes wished to constitute a kind of Council of Government to represent the authority of the Crown; his own personal interests he entrusted to his steward Rodrigo de Paz, who was in reality another governor. The conduct of Estrada and Albornoz was immoral and stupid. Hardly had the Conquistador started out on his journey when he found himself compelled to send another pair of temporary Governors to restore order. But the two new ones, Salazar and Chirinos, proved to be worse than Estrada and Albornoz; they allied themselves with Cortes' steward, seized and deported Zuazo, and devoted themselves to graft and misgovernment.

Folio of *Codex Vaticanus*, depicting the hanging of Rodrigo de Paz, from a gallows, and of Cuauhtemoc and the Lord of Tacuba, from a tree. Spanish officials looking on.

2

Besides this, they sent to Spain reports against Cortes, with mingled truths, exaggerations and slanders; they accused him of immoderate ambitions, of exercising a tyrannous control which only acknowledged the royal authority as a matter of form; they added other more or less well-grounded charges, such as that he had appropriated most of the war tribute, and grants of Indians and land; they pointed to the suspicious circumstances surrounding the death of Donna Catalina Suarez, Cortes wife, and hinted at the possibility of his revolting and establishing a kingdom independent of Spain.

In vain were attempts made to remove Salazar and Chirinos, who hung the steward, Rodrigo de Paz. Estrada and Albornoz were reinstated in the government and in turn arrested Chirinos and Salazar, but order was not restored until the return of the Conquistador, in June, 1526.

3

As far back as 1525 a judge with powers to impeach had been appointed to probe the conduct of Cortes and of other royal officers; this judge was Luis Ponce de Leon, who arrived in Mexico en June, 1526, but died twenty days later. He was succeeded by Marcos de Aguilar, who also died without making much progress in the task of judging the rulers, Alonso de Estrada, a sworn enemy of Cortes, having been appointed as his successor.

As the colony increased in area and importance, the desire of the Crown to assure its own jurisdiction grew accordingly, so that an *Audiencia* was appointed and Cortes was ordered to go to Spain.

Besides, as another means of restraining the excesses of governors, *caciques* and grantees of Indian labor, the church organization was strengthened. The first Dominican friars had come with Ponce de Leon, and taken part in the work of spreading the gospel, alongside the Franciscans, whose rivals and even adversaries they became. And with the first *Audiencia* came Friar Juan de Zumarraga, with the dignity of first Bishop of Mexico and Protector of the Indians.

4

The *Oidors*, or judges of the *Audiencia*, headed by Nuño de Guzman, one of the conquerors and Governor of the Panuco region, continued the policy of hostility to Cortes; but did not establish anything like an orderly form of government. Guzman continued over Michoacan and Jalisco, as far as Sinaloa, having founded in the west the settlement known by the name of New Galicia.

But an attempt was yet made to establish a bridge between the old regime and the new, prior to creating the Viceroyalty, by conferring on Cortes the title of Marques del Valle de Oaxaca, with twenty three thousand vassals and ownership in fee of an enormous tract of land with vague and undefined boundaries, and by appointing him Captain General of New Spain and of the South Sea.

As the first *Audiencia* not only stirred up conflicts with the authority of Cortes, but what was even more serious, with the jurisdiction and power of the Church, and as it grew to be just as discredited as the governors, the decision was adopted of appointing a direct representative of the king, and Antonio de Mendoza was selected for the post. In the meantime, and until he should be able to take over the office, a second *Audiencia* was established.

Among the new *Oidors* were Ramirez de Fuenleal and Vasco de Quiroga, who by then stood for a new class of rulers, clever administrators and animated by good intentions.

V

ORGANIZATION OF NEW SPAIN

1

By the side of the conquistadors marched the missionaries, animated by spiritual and temporal motives, being as it were an arm of the military. In the early days they are clerics like Bartolome de Olmedo and Juan Diaz, or Jeronimo de Aguilar, who serve as interpreters, auxiliaries or diplomatists, and perform rudimentary civil functions in the way of justice, besides baptizing and instilling into the Indians the first notions of the Christian religion. And just after them came the Franciscans.

These are no longer those early Franciscans imbued with the pure spirit of the Saint of Assisi, but militant Franciscans organized and with their feet firmly planted on this earth. They still are poor, but have ceased to be mendicants. They no longer despise all earthly goods, whether for the purpose of tilling the soil or cultivating the intellect. On their missions they begin by teaching and learning languages; then found schools, hospitals and workshops, tend orchards and gardens, build churches and aqueducts.

2

The conquistadors, Justo Sierra tell us, by speeding up the slow pace of Indian evolution, brought about a revolution. But from this revolution arose a feudal domain, not a Colony. The conquistadors scorned to develop themselves the resources of the land they had conquered; they had not been born to do this; this was not what they had fought for; they were warriors, not farmers (that is to say, they did not want to work); development was organized by resorting to the conquered race, it was the exploitation of the vanquished, whom the peace makers and redeemers of the Indian, and the conquistadors, quarrelled over. A compromise was effected on the basis of a more or less legal servitude of the Indians, and of their submission to the guardianship of the Church, under the supervision of the civil authority.

Europeans first, and then their descendants born in the country, engaged more especially in mining, or devoted themselves to administrative functions of a political character, to trade and land monopoly; the mestizo or half-breed engaged in minor industries, petty trading and personal service, which from domestic employment ranged up to what may be called middle class occupations; the Indians, relegated to the lowest depth, were reduced to furnishing a common fund of gratuitous muscular effort for all kinds of rough work, whether farming or mining, or transport; while friars and clerics gradually built up an organization of their own within the civil power, by continued absorption of landed property, by their ever growing control over the great mass of the Indians, and their control of the consciences of the ruling classes. (Worship, education, charities.)

3

From the time that the new world was discovered, the need was realized of creating new administrative organs. The two first were the *Casa de Contratacion* or Colonial Office of Seville, and the Council of the Indies.

The *Casa de Contratación* was in general charged with colonial matters; it granted permits for voyages and explorations, saw to supplies for the fleets, furnished information to navigators and took cognizance of civil and criminal matters.

it had warehouses for the deposit of merchandise and strong boxes for keeping gold, silver and precious stones.

The Council of the Indies, the highest court in all matters having to do with government administration of Spain's colonies, was established by the Emperor in 1524. It had jurisdiction over all land and marine business of the colonies; whether political, military, civil or criminal, and had authority over Viceroys, presidents, *Audiencias,* the *Casa de Contratacion,* war and merchant marine, and military posts.

4

The *Audiencias* were courts of justice that decided civil and criminal cases on appeal, in which were vested certain legislative powers, and they could enact laws and regulations, after discussing them in the form of orders (orders made and provided.) Besides, in the absence of a Viceroy; they acted as his substitute, thus taking over the executive power; and in awkward cases the *Audiencia,* acted as counsellor to the Viceroy himself. The members of the *Audiencia* were called *Oidores,* literally hearers, because they had to hear the arguments of litigants.

Wholesale conversions by the missionaries constituted the so-called Republics of Indians. Reclamation was effected by the curates; the Indians thus reclaimed, who constituted part of the *encomendero's* or grantee's stock in trade, erected the first building, which was the church, dedicated to some saint, who bestowed his name on the village; this building was always of fortress-like proportions, and the village spread out at the foot of the church. Lands for tillage and pastures granted to each village were not the property of individuals, but common lands. Their work, in the form of produce, went to the *encomendero,* to the Crown, to which tribute was paid; to the community, to which a part of the men's work was devoted; to the tutelar saint and teacher of doctrine or curate.

5

The legislation obtaining in Spain, was the Roman law, and that law passed to New Spain, modified as regards real property, by the principle that all the land belonged to the Crown, a principle of numberless legal, economic and social consequences to the country; for in virtue of that principle landed property in Mexico was ever subject to uncertainty, both as regards the lawfulness of its origin and the area of land covered by early titles.

A military social structure, and more so if both theocratic and military in character, to which type the social and political organization of peninsular Spain belonged, and later that of her American colonies as well, carries with it a regime of compulsory cooperation, of unavoidable regulation of all acts of social existence, beginning with the production, circulation, distribution and consumption of wealth.

From conquest to colonization.

6

The system of *repartimientos* or allotments had flown out of the same principle on which the Popes had founded their action in awarding dominion over the New World to their Catholic Majesties, for just as it was deemed right and proper to oust the *caciques* from their estates and income, it was also deemed right and proper that Indians should have to work in exchange for being taught the Catholic religion.

Hence a constant source of conflicts between the conquistadors and the Crown of Spain. The king wanted the Indians treated like free men, and their conversion to christianity, without resorting to force except in special cases; and statutes providing both these things were time and time again enacted. The adventurers who had won the land at their own expense, mainly for purposes of enrichment, looked upon such laws as unjust, disobeyed them and complained because the king did what he pleased with lands whose acquisition had cost him nothing.

Repartimientos, or allotments, deposits or *encomiendas* or grants of laborers made serfs or slaves of the Indians; they paid their tribute to the *cacique* who delivered it to the grantee of the *encomienda* up to a certain amount (the maximum was two thousand pesos annually) fixed beforehand, and the rest was collected by officers of the Crown; the holder of the *encomienda* was obliged to see to conversion and religious teaching of the Indians entrusted to him.

Spain's pleas in defense are condensed in these words of Rafael Altamira:

"As Spaniards our desire is that the treatment of the Indians be held to be what it actually was; not a condition peculiar to our colonizers or special Spanish perversity, but as a common manifestation of the economic regime of the whole world as it then was.

"As men imbued with the modern spirit, and as liberals we regret the excesses of our conquistadors and colonists, and they rouse us to indignation; but we refuse, as Spaniards, to be the only ones to bear the burden of odious acts which the whole of humanity has at one time committed and still goes on committing."

Perhaps it is more accurate to say that those practices were the crimes and errors of a class of conquerors and exploiters, if not to be imputed to a whole people or race.

ART DURING THE FIRST PERIOD OF THE COLONIAL REGIME

1

The first buildings erected in New Spain were forts. Government offices, private dwellings and even churches, had to meet needed conditions for security and defense.

The palace of Cortes, later that of the Viceroys, was a kind of fortress, consisting of four great corners and another in the middle. There were no windows on the ground floor, but only loopholes, and the parapets were pierced with embrasures for cannon.

The earliest churches erected were built with very thick walls, sometimes even several yards thick, with smooth surfaces and windows placed very high; towers were broad at the base, not very lofty but heavy in appearance, while the facades were often battlemented.

Dwelling houses were of similar construction. Openings in the walls were but few, if on the ground floor they were protected by iron grilles. Doors opening on to the outside were massively built and garnished with spikes for better defense.

Decoration in that period exhibits features similar to those of architecture; plainness, austerity and strength.

The very lack of ornamentation gives to those early structures an aspect of greater austerity.

A little later on, other more elaborate designs of ornamentation make their appearance, usually geometrical with Arabic touches. (*Mudejar.*)

2

Poetry, music, the dance, the stage, are all under the shadow of the Church, in the form of liturgical chants, mysteries and allegorical plays. Painting and sculpture drew their beginnings from the need of images for the churches, and are doubly poor due to scanty resources

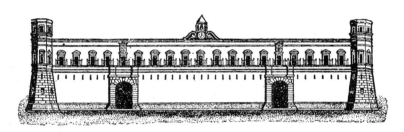

Palace of the Viceroys in the XVI and XVII centuries.

for carving and colors and the severity of religious subjects in the early stages.

The need of images for churches made it necessary to copy pictures from Europe, which began to arrive; but models for saints and mural decoration were, more than anything, taken from woodcuts in books and prints.

Pre-hispanic painting survived in part; rolls of tribute were drawn up for collection of taxes, just as paid by the Indians prior to the conquest, and geographical narrations of services rendered to the Crown and cases in courts of law, were written down in hieroglyphics of Indian type.

3

Just as the artists of this period are the painters and carvers of images, the draughtsmen of codices and the decorators of churches and articles used for worship, those who left behind them testimony for history are the conquistadors themselves, and clerics and missionaries. They hand down their own direct impressions and the narrations of very old Indians. The letters of Cortes, the histories written by Bernal Diaz del Castillo, by Francisco (Alonso) de Aguilar, by the Anonymous Conquistador, by Motolinia and Sahagun, are the most valuable sources from which we may glean a knowledge of the events, the men and the setting of the conquest. And their narratives are marked by great simplicity of style, and also by personal limitations due to political, militant or personal bias, which makes them leave out certain things and exaggerate others, out of religious zeal, interest in propaganda or overmuch ingenuity and credulity.

VI

PUBLIC EDUCATION

Bishop Ramirez de Fuenleal, the President of the second *Audiencia*, "Was the first person to introduce the practice of teaching grammar to some of the Indians, in this New Spain, to see how clever they might be." Friar Arnaldo de Basacio seems to have been the first person to teach "grammar" to the Indians, in the Monastery of San Francisco in Mexico City.

Friar Juan de Zumarraga, decided, in agreement with the Franciscans, to found a school for Indian girls and young woman. The first such school was opened at Texcoco.

As far back as 1530 "Her Majesty the Empress, at her own expense sent six respectable women to teach housewifely trades to girls" with Catalina de Bustamante at the head.

Besides Christian doctrine, they were taught to read, write and the occupations of a housewife; they were prepared to become good Christian mothers and their teachers' solicitude went so far as to find good matches for them.

2

Vasco de Quiroga in 1532 founded "a foundling hospital," to which the Indians could take their children. "Next to this hospital he built a school."

Bishop Quiroga travelled all over the province of Michoacan; he organized the villages, established hospitals and opened more schools.

He furthermore founded or planned a school of a special kind.

At the "Congregacion" mechanical trades necessary for the public good were taught. There were weavers and such like, carpenters, masons, blacksmiths etc. Each one had to learn some trade but "the common trade which all had to know and be expert in was agriculture. So that the tilling of the fields had to be common to all. The work was not too heavy nor tiring, because they were only compelled to work six hours a day on the common task and cultivation of the soil

Vasco de Quiroga.

came out at the rate of two or three days work a week for each one "according to what the fields required and the principal and Governors thought fit."

Crops were distributed among all of them and in particular to each one "in proportion to what he might require for himself and family, according to his station and needs, so that none should suffer in hospital." All were, then, entitled to what they needed, to be taken from the "common barn."

Property belonging to the "community" could neither be sold nor otherwise disposed of. The dwellers enjoyed the use of everything belonging to the hospital, which was well endowed, but could not dispose of any property; private property was not, then, admitted; all property belonged to the community.

3

All the males of each family went to the fields to work together, under the orders of the head of the family; the "grandfather" who was urged, even though he himself were exempt from actual work, to set a good example to his family, and he practically taught them how to work. Women met at certain places to spin, weave, and be trained in all occupations meet for a housewife; but always under an authority they obeyed and respected, who directed and kept the group together.

The regulations went so far as to provide that twice as much, or at least a third more, than was required for the need of the *"Congregacion"* be sown, and if a year threatened to be a poor one after giving each family sufficient for its needs for the whole year, the remainder be stored in good barns; a part of any surplus was sold and another portion distributed among the poor. The proceeds from such sales were to be kept in the "common cash." This was an attempt or plan for agrarian and patriarchal communism.

VII

TRANSITION PERIOD FROM CONQUEST TO COLONIZATION

1

That disorderly and violent exploitation that followed close upon the great drive of the Conquest, had to be checked, restrained, and transformed into a more rational regime. *Encomiendas* or grants of labor and *repartimientos* or allotments mark a comparative improvement over slavery, just as slavery was less objectionable than slaughter. Exploitation of the West Indian natives had brought about the almost total extinction of the island tribes, and had been denounced in scathing terms by noble-minded men like Friar Bartolome de las Casas.

We must now say something about the improvement in methods of conquest. The centralizing tendency of the Crown which endeavored to restrict the arbitrary authority of feudal *encomenderos*, and efforts for the diffusion of religion were joined to the highest motives that can influence humanity.

Domestic animals, for pasture and transport, were the first and humble redeemers of the Indians. Ass and cow, horse and sheep prepared the way for the reformers who were to obtain the issuance of royal decrees for protection of the down-trodden, and later the enactment of the Laws of the Indies.

In pursuit of the same end, limitations of a legal nature began to be imposed. Royal officers, became inspectors and accountants, and later judges with power to impeach and governors, and still later corporations like the *Audiencia,* in which were vested administrative functions, and lastly Viceroys who were the direct representatives of royal authority. These legal limitations, those judges and attorneys who came to New Spain bearing with them their principles of justice and legal formalities, were of course not cordially received by the conquistadors. And Cortes himself registered a protest against the "clerks and attorneys," who came to hinder or curtail his feudal powers.

2

Friar Bartolome de las Casas, moved to indignation by the *repartimientos* or allotments of Indians, decided to devote his life to their protection and defense. He raised his voice before the civil and ecclesiastical authorities of Spain, pleading the right of the natives to freedom. He instituted inquiries. He planned new systems of colonization.

It must not be thought, however, that Friar Bartolome was nothing more than an enthusiastic preacher. He also pursued aims of a strictly practical and political character, as we shall see below. A chronicle relates that Las Casas had started on a march to Gracias-a-Dios, passing through Tuzulutlan, a district belonging to the diocese of Guatemala, where he had submitted practical proof of the theory advanced in his famous treatise called *De unico vocationis modo,* that is to say, the pacification and civilization of the Indians by preaching the Gospel alone, without assistance of any kind from armed forces, rather otherwise, by dispensing with the latter altogether. The invincible faith and perseverance of Friar Bartolome had succeeded, his memory and that of his victory, having been perpetuated by the beautiful and significant name of Vera Paz, by him bestowed on that country, a name which endures to this day.

3

It is further asserted that late in 1545 several prelates met at Gracias-a-Dios. Each one presented his petitions before the *Audiencia.* That presented by Friar Bartolome, consisted of nine sections, the chief ones being: (1) That assessments of tribute from his diocese be reduced, as being exorbitant; (2) that mule trails be opened up to do away with the use of Indians as beasts of burden; (3) that Spaniards resident in Indian villages, be made to leave them with their families; (4) that compulsory personal service be abolished; (5) that Spaniards be forbidden to put land under cultivation in close proximity to Indian Villages; (6) that *calpixques* or tax collectors be forbidden to live in such villages.

Friar Bartolome de las Casas is one of the most conspicuous authors of the movement in favor of the Indians; his excessive zeal, his feverish ardor as a propagandist and fighter, led him to extremes of violence. In his defense of the Indians he even resorted to calling down curses and anathemas.

His enemies did not fail to avail themselves of his violent acts to spread the story that he clamored against Spain herself and against the King; or else that he was moved by rivalries with other orders, such as those between Dominicans and Franciscans. But in any case the foundations of his work are not impaired thereby and his personality is worthy to figure as a glory of humanity and America, rather than only of the Catholic Church or of Spain.

4

Friar Pedro de Gante succeeded in assembling in his school, a thousand Indian children. In the morning he. taught them reading, writing and singing, in the afternoon Christian doctrine and religion. He chose fifty catechizers whom he sent out to spread the Gospel and to oppose the festivals of the ancient pagan religion, and he himself would at times accompany them on their work of propaganda, founding churches and overthrowing Indian shrines.

On beginning his work Friar Pedro thought that nothing could be done with the Indians except by resorting to pressure and force, and that suavity and meekness were of no avail. His first pupils were Indian children torn almost by force from their parents, and taught with severity; they were cut off from intercourse with their families. But later on, however, the ideas of Friar Pedro with regard to the Indians must surely have undergone a change. Young people and even adults joined his school to learn manual trades, and his own victory in winning over the despised race made him become one of its warmest defenders, following almost the same lines as those marked out by Las Casas.

In his letters to Charles the Fifth he ever pleaded the cause of the Indians, and asked for leave to go to Spain to defend them personally; in a letter written in 1522, he described their miserable condition, protested against slavery disguised under the name of personal service, tribute, hiring of persons and all kinds of exploitation, including the system of *repartimientos* or allotments.

SECOND PERIOD OF THE COLONIAL REGIME

HEIGHT OF ITS SPLENDOR

I

RESUME OF HISTORICAL EVOLUTION

1

The second period of the colonial regime begins with the establishment of the Viceroyalty and the arrival in Mexico of the first Viceroy, in 1535.

From the violent impulse of the conquest itself arose the colonizing power, on its upward curve. Silver, more than anything helped to bring about this extraordinary transformation.

The enormous resources in metals of New Spain made it necessary to establish regular methods of exploration and prospecting, and at the same time furnished funds for the establishment of centers of population with stable political existence. The work of centralization and imperialism carried out in Castile under the reign of Charles V, was reproduced many thousands of miles away in New Spain and Peru, on the high plateaus with a temperate climate. From Charles V to Philip II we pass from primitive feudal conditions to a state with well-defined classes of society, the tendency to impose the supremacy of royal authority growing ever more visible, upon the power of the aristocracy and of the dignitaries of the Church, as well as on that of oligarchies of a municipal character.

This movement was not only confined to Spain, however. The transformation of the feudal world is a process that shakes the whole of European culture. The great movements for renovation, the Renaissance and the Reformation, coincided with the discovery of America, and all three reacted upon and assisted one another. The whole system of trade routes, of production of wealth, of world markets, of ideology, of thought and spirit, was in a stage of transition, building up a new world. European and Mediterranean culture, heir to Graeco-Latin and older eastern cultures, started a movement of expansion towards the lands of the Americas.

The work of colonization in New Spain is one of the most notable manifestations of that great impulse.

2

The most usual procedure in explaining that transplantation of culture may be summed up as follows; Spain transferred her institutions to America. And that same formula carries with it the explanation of the greatness and of the deficiency of her colonization.

After the stage of violence, as represented by the conquest, Spain undertook a policy of expansion, by adding to her own territory that of New Spain, almost as though the latter had been a province of her own. To this end she endeavored to introduce her own laws, customs, systems of tilling the land and of industry, her arts, science and religion.

That same attempt brought about the limitations imposed by realities. In the first place, European culture had to come to the American continent through Spain, with a pronounced Spanish tinge and features, as though directed into a channel and filtered through Spain, in the company of Spanish commerce and ideas. It could not be but feudal and monarchical: Catholic and Roman; Castilian rather than Spanish; subserving rather the interests of the reigning house than the needs of the colony or of the nation itself.

3

In the second place, such transfusion or transplanting had to be made from one world to another, by the longest route across the ocean, between two lands suffering from serious difficulties of free communication; with their centers of population on lofty inland plateaus, with but few navigable rivers, and scanty resources for sea navigation. The interchange of men, products and ideas is slow, lengthy and laborious. Spain's scanty rural population cannot easily and swiftly be directed towards the American colonies, nor can implements for cultivation and useful domestic animals be transported in sufficient quantities.

4

In the third place, the establishment of Spanish institutions in the Americas meant the transfer of the regime obtaining in the Peninsula to a continental territory. The force of the colonizing drive had to be spent over enormous areas abounding in geographical complications, and meant establishing communications between widely separated valleys and basins where Nature seemed to have delighted in piling up great wealth by the side of great obstacles.

And fourthly, Spanish institutions, more especially in Mexico, had to be superimposed or seated on an aboriginal population; a population which must be the true foundation of any organization of humanity on this particular portion of the earth. It was for a long time thought that the stronger culture would supplant and drive out the less developed. But culture is a product of land and time. Races and peoples are formed by centuries of growth and making, influenced by the fauna and flora, rainfall and temperature, the action of sun, water and food supply. It was not possible to exterminate the Indians of Mexico, on account of their number and the fact of their wide dispersion; and because the conquistadors themselves felt that it was morally ad practically necessary to avoid complete extinction. Spain's institutions had perforce to be adapted to the complications involved by all these factors.

After the conquest, which was even as a collision between two cultures, two races, two languages, two currents of vital energy, the process of amalgamation, of mingling and of multiple combinations began.

5

The area conquered, which had, in the earliest years of the struggle, been penetrated as by a violent lunge, was gradually extended by activities which continued to be a work of exploration and conquest, but which at the same time allowed of a more efficient process of colonization. New Spain, with her provincial regions of Mexico. the east coast, vaguely known as Coatzacoalcos, the southern country, known as the Mixteca, also vaguely, and the western region called Nueva Galicia or Jalisco, grew in extent until it faded away in the wild northern regions, with no frontiers other than the deserts and those marked by the hostility of savage tribes; to the south it spread down to the isthmian regions, beyond Chiapas, and the Hibueras, in a kind of zone of influence answering more or less to the Captaincy of Guatemala.

Thus to New Spain were added lands, not only temperate in climate on a lofty plateau, with their own peculiar fauna and flora, but also tropical lands along the coasts, open to the sea and sea-borne traffic and other advantages; mountain lands, great steppes and prairies, river basins and vast unexplored regions, which popular fancy placed close to the North Pole and endowed with wonderful cities and towns. But all this was disjointed, isolated by enormous distances and topographical obstacles, impossible to settle or control by a comparatively scanty stream of immigration.

6

In any event the Spanish race, when it began to mingle with the native peoples, also gave rise to racial differentiation. The first colonizers became natives of the land by the second generation. A caste of mestizoes or half-breeds, began to arise. And as each one of the races carried with it the influence of its own blood and of contacts with former races, in ever more intricate complication extending to infinity, the constitution of a new human family began. In order to ascertain wherein lay its differences and divergences one must, rather than racial features take into account the functional conditions of its economic and social position.

Antonio de Mendoza.

A Mexican is not only a blend of Spaniard and Indian, or of Castilian and Mexican. A Spaniard is also Andalusian, Catalan and Basque; he has undergone Arab and Germanic influences, through the Moors and Goths. His ancestry is traced back to Celts and Iberians, until it reaches to the borders of the Graeco-Latin world, in turn related to the Persian, Caucasian and Hindostanic Orient. The American Indian traces back his ancestry to remote but genuine Mongoloid and Polynesian affinities. But overriding all these factors of race it is the land and the time that exercise a dominant influence and imprint a final stamp of nationality.

Escudo del
Marques del
Valle de
Oaxaca

Last years of Cortes.—Arms of Marques de Oaxaca.

II

A GENERAL CHRONICLE OF THE VICEREGAL PERIOD

1

As soon as the first Viceroy arrived, the name and personality of Cortes were relegated to a less conspicuous position.

Cortes continued to send out expeditions to explore the south seas, and himself boarded a ship, and went as far as California. But those journeys did not, at that time, reveal anything but vast deserts and scattered tribes of Indians.

It was no longer a case of winning battles and carrying out undertakings of a political character with Indian chiefs and villages, but of opening up roads and settling desert tracts.

The Conquistador, with all the wealth he had acquired and all the honors heaped upon him, was not content to play a minor part. His authority was from time to time restricted and he had to struggle to have his rights as a great feudal lord, and his prerogatives and lordship over vast lands and great numbers of vassels, recognized. Until at last the Conquistador returned to Spain, only there to meet, as Columbus had done before him, with the icy reserve of the Court and the jealous authority of the Council of the Indies.

Cortes spent the last seven years of his life claiming and praying for the continuance of his privileges, and died at Castilleja de la Cuesta, near Seville, on December 2, 1547.

2

The long list of Viceroys does not amount to much more than a collection of names, with the exception of some few who deserve special praise or rigorous censure. Ignacio Ramirez rated them, as a whole, and at best. as but fair municipal officers, stewards, or university professors. He says: "The lists of Viceroys and Archbishops should only be read posted up on the pillory of history; the very best of them reached the rank of the dean of a college or of a chief of police."

This is an exaggeration, but only as regards such men as Antonio de Mendoza and Luis de Velasco, who were famous for their administrative capabilities, their lofty regard for humanity and their gifts of honesty and dignity. They stood for the tendency of the Spanish Crown to save Indian races from absolute extinction or unmitigated slavery, and the formation of a state for establishing a balance between the privileged classes and the impoverished masses.

3

If most of the Viceroys are lacking in marked personality, and even if the most distinguished among them do not attain to the rank of great statesmen with wide vision, this is also due to the fact that they could not develop any program for important work. Although they were the King's representatives, their authority was curtailed by the very fact of not possessing ample initiative of their own; by the many bounds placed on their jurisdiction, abridged by the will of the monarch, at times subject to whims or unforeseen influences; the Council of the Indies, the *Casa de Contratacion,* the *Audiencias,* inspectors or auditing judges, the Church authorities, the privileges of the nobility, and the genuine power of the great landowners. Besides all this, their term of office was short and the available resources of their power were lessened by remittances of money to Spain, by a fiscal system based on monopolies, state or farmed out, complicated by smuggling and piracy, to say nothing of the difficulty or ruling over such vast territories and scattered centers of population.

Luis de Velasco.

This is why a chronicle of the viceregal period must, in so far as concerns its political aspects, pass rapidly down the long of the Viceroys, only some few names being singled out for special mention.

During the rule of Antonio de Mendoza, in 1544, an Inspector, Francisco Tello Sandoval, came to New Spain; he had been charged with the duty of seeing to enforcement of the so-called "New Laws" which were favorable to the Indians. But the *encomenderos* or labor grantees evinced their disagreement in such a violent fashion that the visitor was forced to go back to Spain without accomplishing his mission.

Viceroy Mendoza carried out several expeditions, no longer of discovery or conquest, but in order to consolidate dominion begun in the region of Jalisco.

4

The second Viceroy, Luis de Velasco, as soon as he entered upon his office declared the freedom of mine workers, who thus nominally emerged from that condition of absolute slavery into which they had been cast just after the Conquest.

In 1563 a new royal inspector came to the colony, an attorney named Valderrama, who also failed in his attempts to make the *encomenderos* comply with the laws, and who rather leant to the side of the rich and powerful, against the Indians, for which reason he was popularly given the title, not of Inspector, but "molester of the Indians."

On the other hand, Viceroy Velasco did deserve the honor of being called the Father of the Indians.

5

In the year 1566 the peace of the colony was disturbed by the so-called conspiracy of the Marques del Valle, Martin Cortes, the son of the Conquistador. The Audiencia was then ruling until a new Viceroy should come out, and round the Marques del Valle rallied the *encomenderos* and their sons, turbulent and predisposed against the civil authorities who, despite everything, insisted on the enforcement of the New Laws.

It is not known how far the aims of the conspirators extended, but according to the most likely version, Martin Cortes encouraged the malcontents by suggesting, although without any definite plans, a seditious movement to cut New Spain loose from the Crown of Castile.

The *Oidors* or Judges of the *Audiencia* had wind of those intentions, and thought that swift repression was called for. A number of arrests were made, Martin Cortes having also been captured, and after a summary trial the two men who seemed most dangerous, Alonso and Gil Gonzales de Avila, were sentenced to death and beheaded.

The arrival of the incoming Viceroy, Gaston de Peralta, and perhaps the thought that the punishment inflicted was sufficient or that the conspiracy had not, after all, been so very serious, served to soften the harshness of the criminal prosecutions. Still, some time after that a special court sat to continue the inquiry, Judge Alonso Muñoz having distinguished himself by his severity.

III

THE END OF THE SPANISH EMPIRE

1

The Emperor Charles V, worn out and ill, withdrew to a monastery and left the Spanish throne to his son Philip II in 1557.

Philip II knew no bounds to his will other than those imposed by his condition as a man, and the disparity between human powers and the gigantic task of ruling over lands and peoples spread over half the globe.

In spite of his enormous capacity for work and of his energy, and even with incalculable resources at his disposal, the political and administrative work carried out during the reign of Philip II coincides with the beginning of the decline of the Spanish Empire. The king might and did make and unmake viceroys and archbishops, collect and spend taxes, manage courtiers and do what he willed with the life, honor and property of his subjects. But he could not shorten distances across the seas, nor do away with deserts, nor compel orders written by him on paper to be carried out regularly. He wished strictly to preserve the integrity of his kingdom and throne, under cover of the principle of political, religious and economic unity, and by bringing to bear the forces of absolute monarchy, spiritual repression and isolation of the colonies.

2

The world's activities, however, sought new ways. Trade, ideas, industries, finance could not be held back by Philip the Second's signature or a prosecution by the Tribunal of the Inquisition. Pirates, smuggling, books, gazettes ceased not to break through barriers raised to keep out foreign trade, and heresies.

The King came very close to the truth when the English wrested from Spain the mastery of the seas and destroyed the fleet baptized with the name of the Invincible Armada. The story goes that when the King learnt of his losses of ships and men, he said: "I sent them to fight against men and not against the elements."

Philip II died in 1598, and his end seems to have marked that of the political and imperialistic greatness, and force of expansion, of the feudal régime of Spain.

3

In 1571 the Inquisition was established in Mexico. This Tribunal made itself odious due to the severity of its proceedings and the heavy penalties imposed under its judgments, which even went so far as to sentence prisoners to be burnt at the stake.

In Mexico, the earliest friars acted as inquisitors and Bishop Zumarraga ordered a grandson of Netzahualpilli to be burnt alive because he had performed a human sacrifice, after which the Indians were removed from the Inquisition's jurisdiction. In 1572 the first Jesuits arrived in Mexico.

Auto-da-fe or punishment by the Inquisition.

In 1576 the first auto-da-fe, or execution of prisoners sentenced by the Inquisition, took place.

In 1573 a frightful epidemic of fever, called by the Indians *matlazahuatl*, broke out and lasted until 1577, its peculiarity being that it only attacked Indians. Almost two millions of them perished. A scarcity of foodstuffs coincided with the plague and in 1580 the city was flooded. The Viceroy, in accord with the City Council, decided to drain the water off through Huehuetoca, but when the danger was over the work was dropped.

4

As evidence of progress achieved by the colony, we may mention the fact that Viceroy Moya y Contreras, although he only held office for one year, remitted to Spain amounts larger than those sent by his predecessors; three million three hundred thousand ducats of coined silver and over one thousand marks of gold. This won him his promotion to the Presidency of the Council of the Indies.

Gaspar de Zuñiga y Acevedo, Conde de Monterrey, who entered upon his office in the middle of November, 1595, despatched an expedition to New Mexico. Sebastian Vizcaino explored the coasts of what is now California.

This Viceroy bestowed his own name on the capital of the Kingdom of Nuevo Leon, previously known as New Extremadura.

5

In 1598 orders were issued that the Indians assemble in villages and settlements so that tribute might be collected, and also to take some of their lands away from them.

A symptom of latent unrest was an Indian insurrection at the Topia mining camp, in Durango; they were driven to revolt by the harsh treatment received in their work in the mines.

6

In March, 1611, the expedition commanded by Sebastian Vizcaino sailed from Acapulco for Japan, bearing an embassy from the Viceroy, and also for the purpose of "investigating the route to the islands rich in gold and silver." Vizcaino was very cordially received, but it was very likely discovered that his expedition contemplated exploration or paving the way for conquest. English and Dutch influences were brought to bear and Vizcaino was treated with hostility and was even in danger from persecution. And only with difficulty was he able to return to New Spain in 1614.

IV

LIMITS ATTAINED BY COLONIAL EXPANSION

1

Primitive Mexican culture, starting out from that region of lakes and valleys where the confederation headed by the Aztecs by military force, actually governed, spread to the south, as far as the Isthmus of Tehuantepec; to the north it stopped at the region of mountain ranges and deserts. Its resources for overcoming distances and reducing dispersed and aggressive tribes, did not allow it to leave the high or central plateau. When the Spaniards seized the power that had previously been vested in the privileged class of the Mexicans, means for diffusion of the new culture introduced into America increased. And this work managed to grow as far as the limitations set by nature and man permitted.

The zone of domination spread from the lake country over all the central plateau and down to the coast regions, both east and west.

Map of New Spain, before division into Intendancies.

The corn crops obtained on the plateau were sufficient for the support of denser and more numerous centers of population, and in connection with the mining industry, lines of communication were established and mining camps were founded; after that military posts, missions, and villages to facilitate transit, towns and cities also grew up. Years afterwards Humboldt called the district known as the "Bajio," the garden of Guanajuato, America's Lombardy.

2

To the south, the farthest border line was only taken as far as difficulties of distance and problems of administrative organization allowed. Unity of methods, of language, of race, and of spirit, began to arise from the very inception of the Spanish American colonies, but it was not possible to strengthen political or administrative unity, for the same reason that had divided from one another pre-hispanic American cultures; that is to say, division and subdivision into isolated valleys and basins, disjointed and cut off by impassable belts with torrid climates. So that new Spain in its growth as a political and national entity, to the south met with the Isthmian barriers and the necessity of autonomous administrations such as the Captaincy General of Guatemala and with serious obstacles in the way of integral incorporation of Yucatan.

3

Towards the west, the Spanish colonizers, beginning with Cortes himself, endeavored to find a route to the Indies, and succeeded in establishing a course by sea to California, and in extending Spanish dominions to the Philippine Islands. The penetration of Texas and New Mexico by soldiers and missionaries, and the expedition of Sebastian Vizcaino and the foundation of permanent colonies in the Malay archipelago, record the maximum effort realized by expansion of Spanish colonies.

4

To the north their problems were more serious and more complicated. Starting from the City of Mexico as a basis and then from the valleys, the Bajio and the central plateau, the colonizing movement developed thanks to two fundamental sources of wealth: mining and agriculture. But that development, in its onward march, met with the following obstacles:

Agriculture became more difficult and less profitable as they advanced towards the north. Even on the central plateau it is largely dependent on the weather and on the rainfall. The farther north one goes, the harder becomes cultivation of the soil, which proves to be still more difficult or impossible in desert or remote regions.

Centers of population grew up in accordance with the needs of mining operations, and agriculture was subject to the convenience and the hazards of mining. More towards the north, the resistance of the aborigines took the form of guerrilla warfare. In addition to the strictly mining towns, other centers of population arose in accordance with the needs of traffic and of military security, but without resources of their own for their support.

All these difficulties increased as the frontier was pushed farther north and became ever more strung out, to the detriment of security and ease of communication, and of contact with the central regions of Mexico.

And finally, to all these adverse circumstances we must add the pressure or penetration of Anglo-American colonizers, who on their side effected a movement of expansion from north to south.

5

We must now mention those groups of human beings who were left outside this work of colonization. And by way of example, we shall mention the following testimony:

Captain Alonzo de Leon stated that the Indians of Coahuila lived on the mountains and in the lowlands, that the families at times joined together, at others separated, that their huts were built of canes and grass and were bell-shaped with a fire in the middle; that they went about stark naked and only wore sandals on their feet, tied with thongs to protect them from the thorns.

According to Captain de Leon, those Indians in winter lived on mescal which they made by cutting off the leaves of small cactus plants and baking the heart and thick portions of the leaves; in summer they lived on the flower of the prickly pear and on its fruit, also baked, and when it was ripe they discarded the peel and dried it in the sun. They did the same with mesquite pods, which they ate as soon as they began to ripen and when they were dry, they pounded them up in mortars, and this food they called by the name of *mezquitamal*. They also lived on other wild fruits and roots; they slept wherever night caught them and lighted fires anywhere, "by rubbing sticks against each other, without the slightest difficulty."

Alonzo de Leon goes on to say that the northern Indians often ate human flesh, both of friends and enemies; that of their friends they consumed at feasts and dances, with the idea of becoming related to the deceased, in the form of barbecued meat with the bones ground down, mixed "with the diabolical potion of their *peyote*." And that of their enemies by way of revenge, and in this case they would at times mix their bones reduced to powder, with the *mezquitamal*.

That is to say, they had, like so many other native tribes, been left in their primitive condition of nomad peoples.

V

IMPORTANCE OF MINING

1

The outstanding historical factor of this period is the rise of a mining industry, which contributed more than anything else to further the work of colonization, because it served as a basis for institutions, furnished resources and imprinted the distinctive features of its growth and of its national personality; it laid the foundations for a new nation that was to become independent, and its influence even stretched to the world of Europe to contribute to the great modern industrial revolution of the latter.

Hernan Cortes in New Spain began the work of colonization, by endeavoring to utilize the enormous wealth in metals and precious stones found in the lands which he had discovered, and which had so greatly astounded him; to this end he attempted to discover the mines existing in said lands, and prayed Moctezuma to show him where those mines were from which he extracted gold; Moctezuma consented to do this, and shortly afterwards the mines of Pachuca, Sultepec and Tlalpujahua were discovered.

2

Martin Verger and Cristobal Keiser, Germans residing at Seville, sent one Juan Enchel, also a German, and others, in 1536 "with equipment and implements for smelting metals from the silver mines, until then not properly understood, and they erected mills for grinding and melting down ores."

In Europe, and in the fourteenth century, no one knew, except perhaps very vaguely, what was the formation of deposits and veins of the precious metals.

In 1549 prospecting work was carried out at San Bernabe, near Guanajuato, by driving a tunnel or gallery along a vein and men thus began to know practically what is the structure of a "mother lode." And so it happened that the miners of the Spanish colony earned for themselves an almost magical reputation in the art of divining the course of veins of silver.

After that came Bartolome de Medina's invention, which was an original discovery on his part, although there are reasons for supposing that the system of mercury amalgamation was known a few years before in Italy, thanks to Biringuccio, or to some German miners.

3

About the year 1549, one of the mule trains by which merchants carried on trade between Mexico and Zacatecas, as it proceeded along the mule trail that passed through Queretaro and Lagos, halted at the top of a hill called La Luz. Certain prospectors from Zacatecas who were travelling with the train, eagerly proceeded to examine some out-crops that they saw and found very promising. On the following day they continued their task, and after ascertaining the strike of the vein, they called it San Bernabe, in memory of the mine of that mine at Zacatecas.

Main Plaza of Guanajuato in Colonial Period.

This find was soon followed by others, such as "La Luz," "Me-llado" and "Rayas," and a few years later by the biggest discovery of all, the famous "mother lode" which with the others, was to yield enormous wealth, that bestowed prosperity on the City of Guanajuato.

The growing skill which Mexican miners gradually acquired by observation of mineral deposits as they found them, rewards offered to Indian prospectors and the money prizes awarded by the Emperor every time a new deposit was discovered, must have been the main reasons for the discovery of the celebrated veins at Pachuca, in 1551.

4

As regards processes for reduction of metals, that of melting them down in small Castilian furnaces spread rapidly throughout the country, at the beginning. But this method which is suitable for operations on a small scale, was not sufficient to aid development of mining work. A process was sought to treat great masses of our characteristic silver ores, that should at one and the same time be suitable, simple and economical.

To the Pachuca mining camp fell the honor to see in 1557, how the celebrated and transcendent discovery was applied for the first time at the Purisima mill.

In that year, indeed, Bartolome de Medina for the first time extracted, with the greatest ease, with little expense and in a comparatively short time, large amounts of silver from enormous masses of silver ores.

His well-known and wide-spread process of amalgamation, usually known as the "patio process" and by European scientist called "American Amalgamation" was to such extent marked by the three qualities pursued, that it amounted to the realization of an ideal. Five years later, in 1562, there were at Zacatecas thirty-five reduction works employing the patio process, and in 1571 Fernandez de Velasco took it from Mexico to Peru. And in Mexico, in Peru, and throughout Latin America, the process invented in this country showed the most brilliant results, and gave a great and mighty impulse to the industry of developing the subsoil.

5

Bartolome de Medina himself, in a document signed at Xilotepec, December 29, 1555, tells us about the work done by him. What he says is worth while repeating here, because it is not widely known and refers to an event of far-reaching importance to Mexico and to the rest of the World (Old manuscript published by M. Fernandez del Castillo.)

Petition to the Viceroy, Luis de Velasco. "I, Bartolome de Medina, do say that having learned in Spain, in conversation with a German, that silver could be extracted from the ore without smelting, nor refining and at no other great expense; with this information I decided to come to New Spain, having left in Spain my home, my wife and children, and having come to try it... and the most illustrious Don Luis de Velasco having become aware of the great service thereby rendered to his Majesty's Royal Treasury and to the whole of this land generally, he did me the favor, in the name of his Majesty, to grant that no one should have the right to make use of said process, except by paying me so much per cent, which in no case should exceed three hundred mine pesos..."

It may be asserted that Bartolome de Medina began colonization of the lands of the Chichimecs, and that to his genius is largely due the effort for occupation of new lands begun in the third zone of conquest, which included northern Nuevo Leon, Chihuahua and New Mexico, no less so than in the case of the fourth and last, which includes Tamaulipas, Texas, and the two Californias.

6

Andres Molina Enriquez says:

"The Spaniards, who had come from a European nation, found in Mexico rich mines, and undertook the work of developing them, having succeeded in converting the precious metals won from those mines, into coins which they put into circulation, and remitted to Spain in great quantities. Those coins which were so swiftly converted into means of exchange, the metals torn from the bowels of the earth, as coins were struck almost at the mouth of mine shafts, at home, by means of the active circulation thus induced, worked the miracle of sustaining a really organic existence, under the management of a small number of Spaniards and their native-born descendants; and abroad, the benefit of launching to the east through Spain, into Europe, and towards the west, to the Philippine Islands, to India, China, and Japan, enormous amounts of currency of real value. The Mexican peso, brought about in the world, due to the fortunate combination of circumstances of its relative value as merchandise, of its abundance and uniformity, and of its widespread distribution, a transcendent revolution."

VI

INDUSTRIAL EXPANSION

1

The Spaniards introduced and spread the cultivation of European crops.

Sugar cane growing was pursued very successfully at Cuautla, Cuernavaca, Vera Cruz and other places in the hot lands. Exportation of sugar began in 1553, to Europe and Peru.

Some stock-raisers owned from thirty to forty thousand head of cattle and horses; the City of Puebla tanned every year eighty two thousand cowhides. And Father Acosta tells us that the fleet that entered Seville in 1587 brought with it 64,340 hides from Mexico.

The enormous production of silver gave rise to exquisite forms of the silversmith's and jeweler's art. Among the early examples wrought, was a celebrated silver cannon sent by Cortes to the Emperor. The cypress of the Cathedral, of solid silver, is also worthy of mention.

In the monastery of Santo Domingo a silver lamp with three hundred branches burnt constantly, besides another hundred lamps of the same metal. The Sanctuary of our Lady of *Los Remedios* was lighted by thirty great silver camps. The Collegiate Church of Our Lady of Guadalupe also owned very notable pieces of silverwork.

Gold ornaments and precious stones devoted to the uses of workship were astounding. The great monstrance of the Cathedral of Mexico was wrought of solid gold, it was almost a yard and a half high, and studded with four thousand six hundred and eighty seven diamonds; two thousand seven hundred and ninety four emeralds; five hundred and twenty three rubies, besides other precious stones.

2

Iron was also very artistically wrought in the form of grilles and railings for churches, monasteries and palaces. The balconies of great Mexican mansions, and even the nails that studded the doors prove the skill of the blacksmiths of those times, who were the pupils of those highly skilled master workmen who came out from Spain to the Americas, late in the sixteenth century.

Wood carving was another branch in which our workmen excelled, and in spite of so much loss and destruction, we may still gaze at notable examples in the shape of altars and altarpieces of plateresque and *churrigueresque* styles.

Manuel Gamio, referring to typical national industries, tells us that during colonial times European industries were introduced but gradually merged and combined with the native, so that by the end of the eighteenth century and beginning of the nineteenth national arts and crafts flourished, highly original in character and mostly drawn from Spanish and Chinese designs, cleverly interpreted and influenced by the ability and experience traditional in Indian ceramists. In the preparation, embossing and decoration of leather for saddles, furniture and hangings, Moorish tradition brought over by the conquistadors and genuine Mexican art, contended in friendly rivalry until merged into one. Lacquer work competed advantageously with the finest pieces from China and Japan. Gold and silver filigree work was as beautifully and strongly wrought as the Italian. Inlaid metal work made of the town of Amozoc a Mexican Eibar. The woven fabrics of Saltillo were noted for beauty and durability: cloth, drawnwork, and woollen; cotton and silk fabrics; and even for fibers of various kinds woven and braided. These and many other industries made of New Spain the chief industrial center of the Americas.

VII

ORGANIZATION OF LABOR.——GUILDS

1

On March 7, 1524, the first meeting of the Metropolitan City Council took place at the house of Hernan Cortes, at Coyoacan. On the 15th of the same month the first ordinance was enacted, the one relating to blacksmiths. From that time on began the issuance of abundant and precise regulations set down in the minute books of the Mexico City municipal council.

The authority whence these ordinances emanated was the Municipal Council of the capital of New Spain. This was the body that enacted them.

We shall, from a review of these ordinances, attempt to infer certain fundamental principles.

The ordinances legislate for each trade individually.

Rank in trades is only recognized in the case of Spanish artisans.

We shall, however, find some Ordinances that do recognize the right of Indians to carry on trades. "The "Ordinances for Ropemakers and Halter Makers" (1550) for example, do not bar Indians from practising these trades, and refer to the latter by granting them certain privileges: "that any coming up for examination pay each examiner two pesos for the examination... and Indians only half."

2

Artisans—workmen—were grouped in brotherhoods so far as the Church was concerned, in Guilds with respect to the law. Each Guild had its own brotherhood with its Patron Saint, and the law organized it pursuant to its classification of trades, by recognizing the differences between Masters, artisans, workmen, and *mayorales* 'or masters' sons. The Ordinances mention examiners, apprentices, workers and masters.

The Ordinances had many provisions relating to work in its various aspects. As regards the day's work we read in that "for hat-makers" (1571.) "that skilled artisans shall treat laborers well and not make them work on feast days nor on the eve thereof except until sundown, and on other days until seven o'clock at night, and shall rise early." And as regards wages, payable in money and not in kind, the Ordinance for the "Shearing Industry" (1574) provides that "Indian shearers shall be paid their wages in money and not in wool." The "Ordinances for hat makers" quoted above, provide, as regards the termination of the labor contract, "that youths and workmen earning salaries in a shop shall not be discharged without fifteen days notice in advance nor may they leave their work without giving fifteen days' notice in advance, so that the former may seek some one to work for him and the latter look for a position."

3

The Ordinances provide penalties for infringement, consisting in fines, whipping, disabilities for working at a given trade, and so on. In fact, each party is, by prohibitions, made accountable for the respective penalty. Penalties payable in cash are established in "pesos" or "mine gold." We may as well here appropriately point out that as a general rule, infringements, if by Spaniards, were generally punishable by fines, and if by Indians, by whipping, as was the case with the other races or "castes."

These ordinances must be considered as enactments that would nowadays be called special legislation, as there was also, even then, in force labor legislation of a general character; the laws of the Indies which may, to a certain extent, likewise be looked upon as a Labor Law, as they regulated personal service and labor bargaining, the day's work and legal days of rest, freedom of the Indian laborer, mode of payment of wages, special prices for food-stuffs for workmen, sanitary conditions for workshops, a system of safeguards for compliance with the laws, in which the workers themselves had a say; measures against drunkenness and vagrancy, and others for social welfare and charity, Saturday afternoons off, what we now call the "English week," in addition to rest on Sunday, and even an eight hours working day.

4

And in regard to the Ordinances for the Guilds, we may say that they were organized in a manner and for purposes in every way similar to those for European Guilds in those days, and as institutions controlling and monopolizing production; that they guided the worker's conscience in a particular religious direction (In the "Ordinances for Schoolteachers" (1700); one may read: "That to be a teacher a man must not be a negro, nor a mulatto, nor an Indian, but a Spaniard and a Christian by descent, life and habits, whereof testimony must be given before the Alderman appointed by the City Council.") This legislation made it easy for the State ti impose and collect taxes, and further that they fulfilled purposes of charity, mutual aid and assistance between the members of such guilds, which acquired property for that purpose, and also disciplined the worker and imposed on production standards of selection and administrative morality.

5

Through the guilds manual workers acquired or improved their knowledge of arts and crafts, such as wrought iron work, jewelry, goldsmith's work, ceramics, furniture making, weaving and embroidery, and others. Under the shade of feudalism there grew up among us, in our Middle Ages, that is, the colonial period, a new class destined to develop sturdily and to undermine the feudal régime itself; a class to which belonged decorators of cathedrals and palaces, who embellished our cities; goldsmiths, who wrought gold and silver; enamellers, makers of admirably carved furniture, workers in metal and smiths, who made weapons of various kinds; embroiderers and tapestry makers, wigmakers, silk weavers, copyists, etc.; and although the tools they worked with were certainly primitive, yet their work was fine and thorough. Division of labor began to make its appearance.

In the latter years of the colonial period, the guilds declined. At the end of the eighteenth century there were only fifty guilds left in Mexico, which constituted a burden on artisans and obstacles to industry.

VIII

COMMERCIAL EXPANSION

1

America had hardly been discovered, when Spain awoke to a comprehension of the importance to her of the trade with her colonies, and endeavored to establish regulations for such commerce, with two main ends in view; to preserve it for Spaniards exclusively, and to prevent attacks by pirates and corsairs. The ports of Seville and Cadiz were the only ones authorized for trade with the colonies, and the law provided that the vesels engaged in such traffic should be Spanish built and manned.

Mexico imported from Spain such commodities as wine, oil, linen, chinaware, cordage, paper, ironwork, vinegar, brandy, soap, etc.

Exports to Spain consisted of gold, silver, sugar, hides, etc.

From the Philippines came; raw, floss and twisted silk, and all kinds of silk cloths, cotton cloth, civet, musk, storax, amber, gold, pearls, porcelain, hardwood and bronze furniture, bone and ivory articles, diamonds, rubies and other precious stones, spices, such as cloves, cinnamon and nutmegs.

2

Trade with China and the East Indies was carried on exclusively, from the Philippines to New Spain, by the Manila Galleon, wrongly called the *Nao de China* (China Ship.) The voyage of the galleon, which was only allowed to anchor at Acapulco, in the early days took five or six months, but due to advances in the art of navigation the time was eventually cut down to three or four. Although the cargo of the galleon was not supposed to exceed five hundred thousand pesos in value it usually brought a million pesos' worth and sailed back to the Philippines with a million and a half or two million pesos in silver, and a small cargo of cochineal, cocoa beans from Guayaquil and Caracas, and Spanish oil and woollen goods.

3

This state of things, so Lucas Alaman tells us, on the subject of fleets and fairs, gave rise to a double monopoly; that exercised by the firms at Cadiz and Seville that shipped the cargoes and after that the one assured by merchants in the Americas, who combined to corner certain commodities the price of which they could fix, as new cargoes of such goods were not due for a long time; hence the high prices they fetched, especially when war at sea interfered with the arrival of the fleets for several years. This gave rise to the arbitrary measures sometimes taken by the Viceroys, fixing sale prices for the benefit of the consumer, as did the Second Duke of Alburquerque in Mexico, in 1705.

4

Prohibitions and restrictions multiplied galore, as one may see from
the Laws of the Indies, which prohibited direct trade between Spain
and the Philippines and between the latter and colonies in America,
with the exception of New Spain; they restricted traffic between the
Canary Islands and the Indies; they prohibited "China clothing" from
being taken to Peru, as it could only be brought to New Spain on condition that it was disposed of there; they prevented the ships that sailed
from Callao and Guayaquil for Nicaragua and Guatemala under the
pretext of loading pitch and other things," from proceeding to Acapulco "to take on cargoes of China clothing, however much silver they
might have on board, by resorting to many schemes and frauds;" and
they suppressed traffic between New Spain and Peru."

5

During the years that immediately followed the Conquest, trade
between Spain and the Indies was wholly free from burdensome taxes;
but this state of things did not go on for very long and a number of
different and complicated taxes were soon established.

Foreign goods on arrival at Vera Cruz were already burdened with
$36\frac{1}{2}$ per cent on their value; after paying the taxes of the colony,
and when they reached the consumer's hands, their value had been
surcharged 75 per cent. The same thing happened in Europe in the
case of colonial commodities; cochineal, by the time that it had paid
the production tax in Oaxaca and Vera Cruz, and on arrival in and
leaving Spain, paid forty five pesos and thirty cents per *arroba* or
quarter.

IX

POLITICAL STRUCTURE OF NEW SPAIN

1

The Viceroy was the direct representative of the King of Spain
himself.

His chief duties were to promote the conversion of the Indians to
Catholicism, to see that they were humanely treated, to dispense justice,
to reward discoverers and conquerors of new lands; to punish crime;

to undertake new discoveries and conquests; to supervise the conduct of all kinds of civil and ecclesiastical authorities; to order the construction of public works and to make allotments of Indians.

The Viceroy was also the President of the Board of the Royal Treasury and of the *Audiencia*, and exercised royal patronage in ecclesiastical appointments. He was empowered to fill up, *pro tem,* any vacancies in the ranks of magistrates, mayors and other authorities.

2

As time passed the power of the Viceroys was gradually reduced and limited.

One of the principal legal limitations on viceregal authority consisted in an inquiry which they had to undergo when their term of office was over, and in which their conduct of affairs was inquired into, and liability exacted for their acts.

The post of Viceroy, according to the law, was to last for three years, but as a matter of fact this was subject to the will of the king.

The lower authorities were: mayors, magistrates, deputy mayors and sub-delegates.

Executive powers were vested in all of them, in addition to certain judicial functions.

There were also Indian authorities, mainly for collection of tribute.

In the City of Mexico the Indians had a court of their own, the Indians' Court the counsellor of which was an *Oidor,* or a criminal judge, selected by the Viceroy.

3

The King of Spain succeeded in establishing the supremacy of the royal power over the clergy, through Patronage in all the Churches of the New World, which included the right to appoint clerics and to limit the authority of ecclesiastical courts.

In 1571, Pedro Moya de Contreras established the Tribunal of the Inquisition in Mexico City, and compelled the Viceroy, the members of the *Audiencia*, the University, the nobility, the religious orders and all residents of the City of Mexico to take the oath to defend the Catholic faith and to persecute heretics.

The main purpose of the Inquisition was to prosecute heretics, mainly Jews, Moriscoes and protestants, and persons of evil life, but at bottom and as a matter of fact, this tribunal became a political instrument, which in turn cloaked an economic tendency.

X

GOLDEN ERA OF COLONIAL ARCHITECTURE

1

During this period of expansion, Spanish art spread through Mexico in a fashion similar to that which we have noted as regards other cultural manifestations.

The conquest suddenly swamped early Aztec culture and with all the more reason did it prevail in the higher functions of art. In New Spain the forms, styles and fashions of European Spanish art were followed, but native influence is noticeable in the use of materials furnished by the land itself and in the contributions made by the hand of native Indian workers and artisans.

San Jeronimo Atotonilco, Hidalgo. XVI century.

In this latter sense the survival or revival of early Mexican culture becomes daily more noticeable, as may be seen from the following observations, which we quote from Molina Enriquez, (Mexico's Agrarian Revolution. Indian Aspects.)

2

Hardly had contact between the two cultures been established, when each one of them began to influence the other; perhaps the

Spanish, as being farther advanced, might have driven out the Indian altogether, if there had been more Spaniards; but there were so few of them that they had in everything to avail themselves of Indian crafts-men, and the latter, in every stroke of the chisel, in every touch of the brush, or every time their fingers modelled the clay, left unmis-takeable evidences of their own culture.

Professor Antonio Cortes, of the National Museum of Archaelogy, History and Ethnography, has searched diligently for traces of the meeting of the two cultures. Churches and cloisters, with their facades, belfries, columns, pulpits, baptismal fonts, doorways and staircases; crosses with carvings or inscriptions, mural paintings, everything built from the earliest days of the Conquest, shows traces of the hand of Indian artists, who modified the original design and the execution of the works ordered and directed by Spaniards, to such an extent as to guide the works in a new direction, very much as though intimate union of souls had taken place, similar to those corporeal unions that resulted in blending the blood of the races. From this orientation flows colonial art, revealing a positive originality which has ceased to be Spanish, or at least no longer purely Spanish.

3

At the height of colonial splendor, the higher forms of artistic activity take the form of architecture. Mining wealth left as traces of its passage through the colony, churches, monasteries and convents, official and private mansions, in numbers which nowadays seem to us excessive. We find ourselves compelled to assume that this overflow of construction work must have been achieved by the almost gratuitous labor and the lives themselves of the Indian, first in the mines, and then on the buildings themselves. And we find that this is only partially offset by the fact that that waste of human energy served to create an architecture possessing a superior and highly characteristic style, which is one of the most notable aspects of Mexico's spiritual individuality; an architecture which moved parallel to the current of social activities in historical renovation, without losing its Spanish features, but with modifications that testify to the influence of race and environment in America.

4

Just as the buildings erected during the period that immediately followed the conquest bear traces of Franciscan influence, so those of the next period seem to evoke the presence of Dominican and

Augustinian friars, who continued to carry out in New Spain the work of cultural diffusion. Stone walls, whitewashed at best, are part of even the most elaborate structures, and ancient romanesque and Gothic show new decorations with a suggestion of the Renaissance. This is the "Spanish baroque" style in its initial form of comparative simplicity. Those classical forms in Spanish art known as "Herreran" (from Herrera, a great Spanish architect) make their appearance. And as the new style is evolved, ornamentation in the plateresque style appears, the very name of which suggest silversmith's work, and consequently an abundance of the white metal. Not in vain have the arts of the silversmith and filigree work been a speciality of Mexico. This plateresque tendency, with certain features of Moorish origin (showing Arab, Asiatic and Oriental influences) in part came from Spain, and in part was a direct result of Mexican influence, added to the materials used, stone and volcanic rock, and to the imprint of Mexican artificers and workers, stone cutters and decorators. Thus did Spanish baroque evolve so as to produce native Mexican baroque, or ultra-baroque.

5

The most notable examples of the "Herreran" style in New Spain are the great Cathedrals at Mexico City and Puebla, especially the latter. The former, during the lengthy period of its construction, which lasted for two and a half centuries, underwent the influence of many and very different schools and tendencies, and is therefore lacking in unity. As regards the Cathedral at Puebla, taken as a whole, we may say that it is the most remarkable example of the Herreran style.

Designs in the Herreran style usually underwent modifications in order to make them less plain and more expressive. Moorish tendencies appear in the ornamentation.

The style that followed the Herreran was the plateresque, which greatly lent itself to the demands of the rising colonial spirit. Its traces of Gothic, its exuberant and delicate decorative work, and even its hybrid nature, easily modified and mingled with other styles, made it exceedingly appropriate for meeting the demands of those times.

6

The ruins of the church attached to the Franciscan monastery at Tlalmanalco, begun in the sixteenth century, show pillars supporting arches, composed of facings and columns markedly Gothic in style, as well as rich plateresque decorations, both on pilasters and capitals, which are also Gothic, and on the heads of the voussoirs of the arches, which are semi-circular. This group of buildings may be cited as an example in New Spain of plateresque design.

The doorway of the church of San Agustin Acolman, the two doorways of the church of San Bernardo in Mexico City are also in this style. But the outstanding example of the plateresque style, among buildings erected for religious purposes, is the Church of San Agustin in Mexico City, now the National Library.

As an architectural style for secular buildings, the plateresque produced, above all, mansions like that of the Marques de Moncada, now the Hotel Iturbide. We should also mention as belonging to this order, although of an aspect somewhat mixed, the House of the Conde del Valle de Orizaba, now known as the "House of the Tiles," and used as a cafe (Sanborn's.)

XI

THE EFFORT FOR EDUCATION

1

Friar Juan de Zumarraga was the first to guide education into a scientific and literary path. In a letter to the Emperor Charles the Fifth, he said: "What my thoughts mostly dwell on, and my will above all inclines to, is that there should in this City and in each diocese be a school for Indian boys who shall at least learn grammar, and a large convent to accommodate a great number of Indian's daughters." He lived to see the beginning of this plan, by the erection of the College of Santa Cruz de Tlaltelolco.

Antonio de Mendoza "built the college at his own expense, and endowed it with certain haciendas and farms that belonged to him, so that the income therefrom might support the Indian pupils to be taught."

On January 6, 1536, the solemn opening of this school took place.

Courses in the Aztec and other native languages were founded for theological students.

In 1539 the case of the heretic Don Carlos, *cacique* of Texcoco, a former pupil of the College of Santa Cruz de Tlaltelolco, took place, and this made a number of people think that it was a dangerous thing to impart higher education to the Indians.

From that time on, the Franciscans were left in sole charge of the school and its early magnificence declined.

By the end of the sixteenth century that great college had become a primary school for the children of the Tlaltelolco quarter of the city.

Fray Alonso de la Vera Cruz.

2

"About the year 1547 Viceroy Antonio de Mendoza and Friar Juan de Zumarraga, being aware of the fact that among the Indians of the city and near-by villages, were many children born of Spanish fathers and Indian mothers wandering about lost, without parents, ordered that this college be built and that all such children be brought thereto to be taught Christian doctrine and the Spanish language, reading and writing, and that those old enough to study be taught whatever else they might wish, and for that purpose a preceptor was appointed. Bishop Zumarraga gave them premises situated at the back of the monastery of San Francisco in this City."

At the college of San Juan de Letran boys were received and taught, while the College of Our Lady of Charity was for girls.

The Franciscans maintained a house of study at Xochimilco, of considerable importance.

The Augustinians had their great intellectual center at Tiripitio. Later, the College of St. Paul in Mexico City rose to pre-eminent rank. Houses of study at Tacambaro, Acolman, Puebla, Actopan, Ixmiquilpan, etc., were likewise of importance.

The Augustinians were the first to think of providing higher studies for their young theological students.

Fray Alonso de la Vera Cruz was the person charged with organizing studies. The course began with the religious who had just finished their novitiate under his tuition, to whom were added a few others sent from Mexico City. At the beginning Friar Alonso took the chair of Arts and Theology. He had before then, at the University of Salamanca, shown proof of his capacity.

At this college the son of the great *Cacique* Caltzontzin, Antonio Huitzimengari Mendoza Caltzontzin, was educated. He showed great talent for the arts and sciences and taught Friar Alonso de la Vera Cruz the Tarascan language.

3

The foundation of the College of St. Paul in Mexico was likewise due to Friar Alonso de la Vera Cruz, about the year 1575.

He himself taught the Theology class with enthusiasm and this school, though without a patron and lacking an income, was erected by means of the donations he himself solicited, and rose majestically by the side of the Old College.

To that illustrious Augustinian fell the glory of founding the first library with books he had "brought in the year before." There were books on all know Faculties, arts and tongues, brought from Spain, and gathered from a number of places and Universities. The first stock

consisted of sixty cases of books, to which he added all those that came
to his knowledge and not yet in his "library."

"He adorned it with maps, celestial and terrestrial globes, astrolabes,
clocks, planispheres and in fine, all instruments serving the liberal arts."

4

The University of Mexico was the first great educational establishment in New Spain. Its foundation was authorized by the Emperor
Charles the Fifth in his decree of September 21, 1551, an income of one
thousand gold "mine pesos" having been allotted to it, and the charters,
privileges and prerogatives of the University of Salamanca, which was
highly celebrated in those days, having been bestowed on it.

Colonial types.—Friars.

In the University curriculum, we are told, Latin took the first place
and was studied under the name of the grammar course. Then came
rhetoric; after the arts, by which name was known what in our day
we call philosophy; this included what man might comprehend by
means of natural knowledge, that is, without the assistance of revela-
tion; this course embraced all the positive learning of that time, and was
divided into natural philosophy and moral philosophy. In the former
was taught knowledge of external nature, not according to observation
and experience but according to the classic doctrines of Aristotle
as regards physics and Pliny as regards natural history; mathematics
were included in this section of the arts, and were confined to Euclid's
geometry.

5

Moral philosophy, which embraced the spirit of man, was divided into logic and dialectics; into metaphysics or knowledge of substance, the main section of which was pneumatology, or the science of spiritual substance, subdivided into the science of the human soul, of the soul of the Angels and of the divine spirit, or into ethics or morality.

A student who finished the arts course was graduated as a bachelor of arts, and if he continued to study, he could graduate as a Master of Arts or Doctor in any of the following faculties: the Humanities, or knowledge of the classics, especially the Latin; the faculty of Theology or knowledge of Divinity, which was in those times reputed the main or principal branch.

Neither the University of Mexico, nor the University of Guadalajara, which was also soon founded, nor a minor university founded a little later in Chiapas, were what they should have been; they confined themselves to teaching one or two native tongues and scanty technical knowledge for the Priesthood, Medicine and Law.

"The universities of New Spain were never true universities, nor were there either any centers of learning to crown the edifice of knowledge, as although the Colegio Mayor de Todos Santos made efforts to become a finishing center for turning out professors, this was never anything more than an attempt.

Theology, philosophy and even law were taught in a mediaeval spirit; they were eminently scholastic, and the triumph of the purely deductive method; and the starting-point of the first two was religious dogmas and the axioms of Roman canon and Spanish Law, and that of the Indies, without permitting the slightest analysis or observation."

6

Modern criticism penetrates deeper still:

The Royal and Pontifical University of Mexico, the science and art schools of religious orders and the institutes of divers origins and tendencies to which was entrusted higher education, were not open, except very exceptionally, to the Indians nor to the eighteen races into which the results of the blending of the three fundamental elements —white, Indian and negro—of the colonial caste system were divided; as in addition to the fact that very strict regulations exacted as a qualification for admission, proof of "purity of blood" or of "Christian ancestry, without trace of judaism, or heresy," and that futile pretexts, in practice unsurmountable, hindered their obtaining degrees, an economic situation of progressive inferiority in practice barred them out.

If we include those institutions expressly founded for the protection and education of mestizoes bereft of their parents, who constituted an immense majority, the College of San Juan de Letran for boys, and the College for Girls, in spite of their limited capacity which made them useless for the performance of their functions, were very soon invaded by creoles belonging to needy families. Furthermore, in the college of San Juan de Letran only six students could every year aspire to higher education, and they theoretically had to be selected in view of their capacity and application, but were in point of fact chosen by influence.

7

A review of public education in the colonial period, after the heroic efforts of the missionaries, does in reality show some brilliant aspects. But its fundamental deficiencies must not be overlooked. In the first place, the impulse given to education was scanty in proportion to the needs of the country. Higher culture penetrated the country to a limited extent only and was never wide spread nor profound. Besides this, any scientific knowledge diffused was hampered by ecclesiastical restrictions and by the scantiness of the financial resources allotted to education. However, the fetters placed by monarchical and religious intolerance, and the poverty of school life, are at least explicable, because they answered to similar cultural deficiencies in Spain, and almost over the whole world at that time. The most serious shortcoming of teaching and education, especially higher and university education in New Spain, consisted in the fact that is was a service exclusively reserved for the privileged classes.

It is true that the colonizing impulse did what it could, but not as much as it should have done. And this reproach will continue to stand, as regards all those in any way responsible for the education of the Mexican people, so long as a majority of the population of school age shall lack teaching on account of its poverty.

XII

COLONIAL LITERATURE

1

Carlos Gonzalez Peña asserts that the sixteenth century was the heroic age of Mexican letters. Though an attempt of transplantation of another culture, at the same time it displayed an eagerness for original creation not only not lacking in originality, but on the contrary, abounding in this quality.

To the material effort of the conquest to acquire new dominions, answered a spiritual effort designed to establish in the New World, by a mighty leap, the advanced civilization of Europe.

Study of the past and of Indian languages had added new branches to history and philosophy. Studies in the halls of learning, and perhaps also, though to a lesser degree, the influence of writers who had come from the Peninsula, promoted the cultivation of literature; a development which, though it did not in the case of poetry go beyond inarticulate and imitative stammerings by numberless amateur versifiers, was yet destined to produce, by the side of personalities of real worth who were swamped by their environment, like Terrazas, magnificent minds like Ruiz de Alarcon and Balbuena, who bestowed luster on Spanish letters. The printing press had spread books so profusely, that those worthies suceeded in forming a plentiful bibliography. To sum up, the capital of New Spain, which had proudly risen on top of the ruins of Tenochtitlan, had become the chief center of civilization in America.

Among the elements of culture received by the colony, we must in the first place mention the printing press. Rather than the authority of the Viceroy who authorized its importation, and rather than the owner of the presses first brought by Spain from Germany and then sent to Mexico, we shall set down the name of the first printer who actually tranferred the printed word to paper in Mexico: Giovanni Paoli or Juan Pablos, an Italian.

A majority of the works published were tracts, catechisms, vocabularies and grammars for the use of the friars; prayer or liturgical books; missals, psalters and such like. There were also, however, —though not very many,—books on law, natural science, medicine, the art of war, navigation and history.

3

From its very beginnings, Mexican literature was a branch of Spanish letters. And in the colonial period this subordination is closer. The art of literature was the last to show positive traces of native or Mexican influence. Colonial literature in Mexico, being a manifestation of the higher culture practiced only by select minorities, and in a country which was a colony with races strictly separated, and proletarian masses cut off from scientific education, could not but remain aloof from popular existence, without interpreting it or deeply influencing the ideas and feelings of the community.

The two most famous names that reflect the golden century of Castilian literature in Mexico, are those of Bernardo de Balbuena and Juan Ruiz de Alarcon.

In reality, Balbuena is not a great enough poet to warrant our comparing him with Alarcon. But he stands out because his work, purely Castilian and classical as to language and technique, is inspired by Mexican subjects, in his descriptions and geographical setting. His poem, called "The Greatness of Mexico" has been described as practical topography, which is poor praise for the heroic sentiments and beauty of his imagery.

4

But as regards Juan Ruiz de Alarcon, he and his works are of much greater interest, because here we have a real genius, a poet of the first

The first printing press in the Americas.

1. Before the conquest the Aztecs recorded important events by hieroglyphics in a kind of vegetable paper called *Amatl.*—2. The crude press invented by Gutemberg in the XV century was only beginning to spread through Europe.—3. Antonio de Mendoza, the first Viceroy of Mexico, imported a printing press, the first in the Americas.

class, a creator of moral and society comedy, who in his time vied with Lope de Vega and Calderon.

Mexico is anxious to present Ruiz de Alarcon as a Mexican, but we must not be blinded by this natural desire, and must ascertain just how far his quality is Mexican.

In the History of Spanish literature, Juan Ruiz de Alarcon is set down as a "Mexican" just as he might have been described as Andalusian, merely by a sort of provincial, geographical and accidental differentiation. The fact that he was born at Tasco of Spanish parents, that he studied at the University of Mexico and lived in New Spain for a part of his life, does not very greatly detract from the Spanish spiritual character of that great poet, nor did those circumstances leave any clear traces on his work. His famous comedies were written for a Spanish public, and in his poetry there is not a single setting, allusion, or manifest accent in any way Mexican or Creole.

A further study may possibly bring to light more concrete data. Or rather let us continue to assert and to believe that the author of "Truth Suspicious" was a Mexican, but none the less Spanish for that, because thus were the Creoles of his time. Political independence was still very far off and far more remote were economic autonomy and the creation of a spiritual individuality, especially the latter, as it needs centuries for formation and growth.

The influence of the land and of the aboriginal races on Mexican art has in the evolution of the country manifested itself the more slowly as cultural manifestations have been higher and more select.

The thought of the more cultured classes, and higher ideology or philosophy, were at that time represented by scholastic philosophy and theology. Scholasticism had by then become petrified and lifeless. And dialectics, after fulfilling their mission in the history of human knowledge, had become a medium for empty discussions.

In this connection we can only mention a single name, that of Friar Alonso de la Vera Cruz.

His books, devoted to university teaching, contain evidences of intellectual renovation, and to a slight extent break the prohibition raised against rationalist philosophy.

THIRD STAGE OF THE COLONIAL PERIOD

ITS DECLINE

I

CAUSES OF DECLINE

1

The third stage of the colonial period, which followed that of expansion and construction, is one of stagnation and decline.

In reality, New Spain was not as a dead tree. It is true that its territorial area no longer increased, nor were new cities and villages founded, but its population slowly increased and its trade and industry kept on growing. Its weakness or decline consists in the fact that the increase in population was not normal, especially if compared with that of other countries.

Nor was the growth of industry and agriculture proportionate to the country's needs. Even the progress of mining, although apparently unquestionable on account of the number of mines in operation and the value of the metals extracted, was in reality misleading. For as the number of mines and the yield increased, the actual value and purchasing power of metallic currency diminished. The figures for salaries, taxes, public revenue, export and import trade, do not show the real state of affairs; in the first place because they are only doubtfully correct, and very incomplete, and in the second place because currency is not an index to the true economic and social condition of a country, but only of one aspect of its finances and exchange. What the salary of the Indian was, may be more exactly estimated from his ration of corn.

2

The fact that the population of the country increased so slowly, and that the standards of living of the middle and the working classes continued stationary without showing any improvement, proves that the birth rate was low and the death rate high; and that the land did not produce sufficient to sustain the people under favorable conditions as regards food and development.

This period of colonization extends from the middle of the seventeenth century to the end of the eighteenth, and at the same time marks the shifting over to a new phase of universal history. Not only is it a phenomenon that marks the transformation of the Spanish Empire and its power in America, or more particularly in New Spain, but also a final tranformation of the feudal régime over all that portion of the globe where European culture was under development.

Colonization extended as far as Texas and California, but resources did not suffice to settle those regions, which absorbed military garrisons on fruitless work. The wandering Indians of the north became more redoubtable as they began to receive guns and ammunition from English colonists. So that the Apaches and Comanches were the vanguard of that Anglo-American invasion that was brewing for the following century.

The most serious symptom of the decline of Spain was the insecurity of her communications. The fleets that monopolized trade with America no longer sailed regularly and were not secure. When the regular and official piracy of war suspended the voyages of those fleets, trade was paralyzed and industry declined. Mining, which was the foundation of the economy of New Spain, was subordinated to the importation of mercury, which had to be brought from Peru.

3

And as Spain's power declined, her obligations as a state to watch over public services increased. The enormous area that had to be guarded with garrisons for vigilance and keeping order had been crossed by roads that had to be kept up and extended; cities and towns had been founded and in the cities corporations or groups of merchants and artisans, manufacturers, petty trades, urban property and a restless populace, full of urgent needs, had grown up. Crowding of the cities with people had given rise to unforeseen problems; when crops failed or speculators cornered grain, popular famine was provoked or came about. The populace had already begun riots and tumults due to lack of foodstuffs and of means to purchase them.

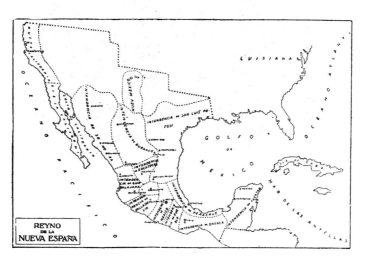

Map of Mexico in the Colonial Period; divided into Intendancies.

Artisans and merchants, public servants of the lower grades and ecclesiastics of low degree began to constitute an intermediate sub-class which awakened to a consciousness if its own existence. Mine workers, who had emerged from slavery but not altogether from servitude, constituted a discontented mass, a possible ferment of social disturbance.

4

The work of colonization developed to a possible maximum due to immigration of a new type, no longer chiefly conquerors or adventurers, but artisans, farmers, merchants and attorneys. These brought in, more than any others, means of culture, and effected the social transformation of New Spain. The Indians, on a very small scale, and the mestizoes on a larger, learned the technique of small industries. Mechanical labor, despised by the higher classes, began to develop as a means for earning their bread, among the lower classes, but in a disorganized form and by manual labor, and due to individual or family initiative.

Colonial types.—Nuns.

The mixture of races and the influence of the soil had not as yet taken from the man of Spanish race his dominant position, and although there were dissensions within his own class, they continued to stand united as superior beings, over the as yet inert mass, of the Indians and of the early generations of mestizoes who constituted the forced labor of the fields and of the mines, and the half-naked populace of the cities.

II

TRANSFORMATION OF SOCIAL CLASSES

I

The creation of viceroyalty in New Spain flowed out of the supremacy of an absolute monarch who absorbed and gathered into his own hands the power he had previously shared with the nobility and the Church.

Concentration of power in the hands of the Crown, shows itself, in the economic sphere, in the form of confiscation of the property of the most conspicuous representatives of primitive pre-capitalism; in Spain, Moors engaged in farming, and Jewish merchants and bankers.

On New Spain this struggle indirectly reacts and brings about fundamental modifications imposed by differences in economic and social structure. The Viceroy is the personal representative of the King, but his is in any case a reflected authority. The monarch also grants or delegates a portion of his authority to the *Audiencias* and religious institutions. His paramount authority is expressed by his right to appoint and remove civil officials and church dignitaries, but special prerogatives or privileges still give former feudal and religious lords power to maintain themselves, with flashes of independence, face to face with the state.

Aside from this, when the Crown concentrated in its own hands, and monopolized, military and political authority, it left to the nobility and the church the handling of public wealth and more especially of means of production, such as the land, the extractive industries, the use of credit and the utilization of revenue. The state reserves to itself the right to collect taxes, but bears all the burden of public services.

Arms of the City of Mexico. (Colonial Period.)

2

The privileged classes in the first place enjoyed freedom from taxation, or the possibility of making it fall upon artisans and proletarians. Exploitation of the land for direct utilization of its produce is modified by the appearance, in definite and systematic form, of two elements of enormous importance: rent and credit. The feudal nobility that had arisen on the strenght of military exploits, is succeeded by an aristocracy composed of great landowners and of high church dignitaries.

The church, in the form of tithes, donations, payments for civil services such as education, the administration of the sacraments, etc., had an income comparable to that collected by the treasury. But as its expenses were less, the surplus wealth thus received remained in its hands, and swollen by its own increment made the clergy the possessors of property and the depositaries of the capital thus accumulated, with the consequent benefits of active credit and handling of such resources.

3

The Crown incessantly worked to lessen the power of the nobility and of the church, but its fight had first to be directed against those who at the beginning were most powerful and most to be feared. This was why it reduced to control the *encomenderos* or grantees of labor, and the landowners. Bounds are placed upon slavery, first by abolishing it in theory and then by curtailing it gradually, by repeated orders and decrees, but slowly obeyed. Laws were passed prohibiting the abuse of Indian porters, branding them with hot irons, or disposing of them and of their families at will. The next step is servitude under the guise of fraternalism, and the laws of the Indies, to protect them, established for the laborers of New Spain, that is the vanquished Indians, a system which declared them minors, with just as much assistance as restrictions. The Indian was entitled to protection, but had no privileges. He was not subject to the inquisition, for he had no property that could be confiscated, but he did fall within the jurisdiction of the civil, ecclesiastical and military courts. He paid a poll-tax and when he did begin to receive compensation under the name of a wage, it was only just enough for a very poor living.

III

POLITICAL EVENTS

1

During this period political events seemed to be even more infrequent than during the preceding period. It is not easy to pick out from the list of the Viceroys any personality distinguished by historical importance. We should, however, mention the name of the Marques de Mancera, for he was a good ruler.

"Mancera had visited European courts as a diplomatist, and his keen desire was to show the civilized world that Spanish domination in Mexico, was not, as was generally believed, a note of infamy for Spain; that the Indian population had not diminished in the seventeenth century, that the creoles were passionately loyal to Spain, that the new element of the population, the mestizoes, was fitted to form a social group destined to grow in importance as time passed."

Friar Payo Enriquez de Rivera was both Archbishop and Viceroy. He continued and perfected the work of the Marques de Mancera. Pacification of the north became daily a harder undertaking; the unsubdued tribes of those regions attacked Spanish establishments (for example the defense of Santa Fe, in New Mexico, its desertion and the founding of Paso del Norte.) Such insurrections, and others in Chihuahua and Sonora constantly broke out. The Archbishop and Viceroy, in the midst of that enormous territory of New Spain that dwelt in peace, yet surrounded by insurrection and piracy, displayed great energy in correcting the abuses of the officers of the treasury, purified the administration of justice, watched over the interests of the Indians and spent the revenues on works of piety and charity.

We mention the names of these two Viceroys, "not because they did anything extraordinary, but because they symbolized the utmost effort possible on the part of Spain as she was then, to keep her American dominions, by defending herself against enemies, abroad and preserving order at home."

2

On September 12, 1621, Diego Carrillo de Mendoza y Pimentel, Marques de Gelves y Conde de Priego took over the reins of government.

Of him it was said that he was very energetic, and that having found the colony in great disorder, as roads were impassable because of robber bands, justice was disposed of to the influential, and society in general was displeased at the continual conflicts between the clergy and the authorities, he attempted to remedy this state of affairs.

He pursued evil-doers with such energy and severity that he succeeded in restoring public security, as in his three years of office a larger number of offenders were executed than in the whole of the period of Spanish domination that had gone before.

In 1623 corn went up in price, and as a friend of the Marques, one Pedro de Mejia, cornered this grain, the people thought that he was acting in combination with the Viceroy. Popular displeasure due to the scarcity of corn was added to the old conflicts between the Viceroy and the clergy, and gave rise to some riots.

3

In 1644 the Municipal Council prayed the King that no more monasteries and convents be founded, as there were too many of them already. And the real property owned by such religious institutions and the money lent by them on the security of real estate, amounted to one-half of the value of all the property in the country. It also prayed that no new priests be ordained, as there were more than six thousand with nothing to do, and that the number of festivities of the saints be diminished, as there was no week without one or two feast days. These petitions were not granted.

In 1647 and 1648 fresh auto-da-fes were carried out by the inquisition, an impostor who had pretended to be a priest, called Martin de Villavicencio, and nicknamed Martin Garatuza, having among others been executed.

Chronicles mention the auto-da-fe of April 11, 1649. One hundred and seven accused persons were sentenced by the inquisition, some for being Jews, others for passing themselves off as priests, a friar because he had got married and several women accused of being witches. Thomas Treviño was burned alive for heresy and blasphemy.

In November 1659 Guillen Lombardo or Lampart, a half mad adventurer, was burned alive after lying in prison for seventeen years; he purported to be the originator of a plan to make New Spain independent. He attempted to make use of counterfeit seals and signatures on royal despatches, appointing him Viceroy and captain general. His plans were to capture the *oidors* or members of the *Audiencia,* to raise troops, to apply fo the assistance of the Duke of Braganza and of the government of Holland, then enemies of Spain and to provoke a revolt of Indians, negroes and mestizoes.

In 1659 there was a scarcity of corn and wheat. On June 8, 1692, the scarcity of the former provoked a riot in the public market, in which an Indian woman was killed. Several Indians attempted to speak to the Viceroy or to the Archbishop to register a protest and submit complaints, and as their request was not granted they began to stone the Viceroy's Palace and set fire to it. The municipal archives were destroyed by fire, but Carlos de Sigüenza y Gongora managed to save the most important books. The Viceroy restored order by harsh repressive measures.

4

On the 12th June, 1702, a fleet commanded by General Manuel de Velasco sailed from Vera Cruz, carrying treasure to the value of fifty million pesos. The English and Dutch threatened to intercept it near Cadiz. It was proposed to unload the fleet at Vigo, but the merchants of Cadiz objected. The English and Dutch fleets attacked on the 22nd October. All the Spanish and French ships were lost and the whole of the treasure they carried was thrown overboard.

Juan de Acuña, Marques de Casafuerte, arrived in Mexico on October 15, 1722, and was one of the best rulers the country ever had, due to his honesty and energy.

During the rule of this Viceroy the Mint and the Santo Domingo Customs House were built, improvements were made to the Alameda or public park and other works of importance were undertaken and carried out.

IV

DECLINE OF TRADE

1

A few facts in regard to trade and finance at this particular time reveal a situation similar to that of the other activities of colonial life.

Spain attempted to establish a strict monopoly in her colonies.

A few merchants at Cadiz and Seville raised and lowered prices arbitrarily. European goods were sold at fancy prices. Some merchans made profits of 200 and even 500 per cent.

This gave rise to smuggling and clandestine commerce, from the earliest days of the colony. And moreover, the Treaty of Utrecht (1713) granted to the English the right to introduce slaves into the Spanish colonies, and also the privilege of sending each year to Portobello a 500 ton ship loaded with European goods.

By virtue of these concessions English Commissioners were stationed at Cartagena, Vera Cruz. Buenos Aires and several other ports of the Americas. These agents, who were thoroughly familiar with the internal situation of the provinces, aided that secret trade.

This was how the trade of Spanish America practically passed into alien hands, so that commerce with Spain gradually dropped from 15,000 tons down to 2,000; the fleets were almost entirely reduced to taking the Crown revenues over to Europe.

2

But the greatest danger lay in the pirates. The first of these were French, and indirectly assisted by Francis I, King of France.

The profits realized by the first expeditions attracted Englishmen, Dutchmen and adventurers from all countries.

Under the name of buccaneers, filibusters and "brothers of the coast" they succeeded in permanently occupying several of the West India Islands, such as Jamaica, the Tortugas and Santo Domingo.

A Dutch fleet under the command of one Shappenham, late in 1623 seized Acapulco, but due to sickness and want of ammunition, it had to withdraw before very long.

From 1656 on, the island of Jamaica, which had been seized by the English, became a hotbed of piracy and smuggling. The pirates, in agreement with certain merchants in the colonies, not only defrauded the treasury, but their lighter ships were bold enough to face the Spanish fleets.

The inhabitants of the seaport towns along the Gulf lived in constant fear and Belize had become the headquarters of English pirates, who had besides undertaken the cutting of hardwoods.

3

About halfway through the eighteenth century, with the ascent of the House of Bourbon to the Spanish throne, a desire was noticed of remedying so uncertain a situation. The expression of this desire is set down in the work of Bernardo Ward, Minister of the Royal Board of Trade and Currency, whose Economic Plan depicts with a master hand the situation obtaining in the Peninsula.

In his work Ward proposes to take measures to improve communications in the Peninsula, to increase the population, promote agriculture, assist industry, spread trade and generally suppress any obstacles in the way of economic recovery.

In Ward's opinion, one of the best means for attaining these objects consisted in a modification of the system of trade with the Americas. "The injury suffered by Spain"—he says of—"from the present menthod carrying on trade with the Indies, needs no more proof than to reflect on the very small profits realized from such vast possessions." And then he adds: "to burden that trade with so many duties and encumbrances that Spanish cloths reach America with a surcharge of 100 to 200 on their value, is tantamount to prohibiting nationals from trading, and to opening wide the doors to all other nations of the world, as we cannot keep them out."

By way of a finishing touch to his plan, Ward says: "in a word, so that Spain may to some extent benefit by her American dominions, it would seem necessary that one of two courses be adopted, either the one proposed, which is the better of the two, of permitting trade without restrictions, or else to allow manufactories of all kinds of cloth and goods to be established in the Americas."

A careful study of the above lines will reveal how enormously important they were. Therein is enclosed the germ of the Independence of Mexico and of all Spanish America.

V

DECLINE OF ART

1

Religious and secular architecture reached the height of its splendor in the evolution of the colonial style. This form of art grew up and developed in the manner set out above. In the period of its expansion, a style which we may call Mexican baroque made its appearance. From this it passed to what has, somewhat confusedly, been termed the *churrigueresque* or ultra-baroque style. It is, in short, Spanish baroque, strongly influenced by Mexican enviroment. It resembles the so-called Portuguese *Manueline*, but with more native and American touches.

Plateresque, with its filigree ornamentation and Moorish influences, develops, and overflows like tropical plants. Above all, what does increase is local and national influence, of native character, with oriental or Asiatic features, which are a product of the race itself, partly due to its mongoloid or Polynesian origin, and partly to the effects of trade with the Philippines. The decorative motives of Michoacan lacquer work, the ware known as *Talavera* de Puebla, tiles and feather mosaics, are in the same class as the excesses of decoration of Mexican colonial architecture.

2

The character of this riotous architecture (says M. Toussaint) partakes of wood carving, of the elaborate minuteness of Asiatic ivories, and of filigree work. In it all restraint and all rules have been thrown off and disregarded. To overcome difficulties, to pile up structural absurdities, having in view only the splendor of the work itself; this seems to have been the idea of the *churrigueresque* architects.

The great development of ceramics influences architecture, and although glazed tiles had been employed as far back as the sixteenth century, this was the time when they shed their magnificence on the churches. At Puebla, a great center of tile and pottery production, the type of the Puebla Church arises, characterized by brilliancy of coloring and the use of tiles in the domes.

The *Sagrario* and the Cathedral.

3

One of the investigators who have revealed the character of colonial architecture with most ability and penetration, was J. T. Acevedo, a true and great artist who left a number of indications of his powerful intelligence, in many plans and sketches.

We shall here set down some of his ideas in regard to the subject we are discussing.

The carved stonework of the Sagrario in Mexico City, the walls of the church of La Enseñanza, the plazas of Santo Domingo, Vizcainas and Regina, tell us more than any number of books. The Sagrario, a masterpiece of architcture, both by reason of the cleverness of its plan and the exquisite ornamentation of its façade, profoundly delights the beholder.

Churrigueresque monuments are only a minority of this noble heritage. Aside from this, what prevails is Italian baroque, not without unexpected apparitions that surprise and puzzle. These may take the form of an arcade ornamented in the style of Henry II, as in the chapel of the Salto del Agua, in Mexico City; or a reminiscence of a romantic gateway, as at Coyoacan; and so that nothing may be lacking, there is even a piece of Louis XV inlaid in one side of the Basilica at Guadalupe.

4

Late in the eighteenth century, and in the company of the worship of reason, came French styles. Tolsa, a great Spanish architect, brought them, and to tell the truth, he certainly knew them well. Due to him we have severe examples of the Louis XVI style, which must at that time have seemed too cold and plain. But one must not from this assume that specimens of an earlier date, sober in form and bare of ornament, were wanting, as the Spaniards knew how to build appropriately for the object pursued, both as regards ground plan and inside and out. And yet French architecture came to show us novel arrangements and a much purer compensation of the orders. The Cathedral towers, the School of Mines and the Citadel were finished in accordance with these principles.

Among all these works, wrote Acevedo, the Loreto Church in Mexico City and the mansion of the Condes de Rul at Guanajuato, charm us beyond measure.

5

When the colonial period come to an end, Toussaint adds, we had, as in Europe, neo-classical architecture. It was introduced by Jose Antonio Velazquez; but it reached the height of its magnificence in the hands of Manuel Tolsa, a native of Valencia, whose genius seemed to find more spontaneous expression in sculpture. He arrived in Mexico in 1791; he came while under the influence of the art favored in Europe in the the late eighteenth century, that is neo-classic architecture; as a sculptor he had also been greatly influenced by Bernini. The work of Tolsa as an architect exercised a great influence in this country. And then there arose, as always happens, a popular manifestation by the side of the truly architectural. A unique instance in this particular case was Francisco Eduardo de Tresguerras. Without artistic education, and following only examples he had seen reproduced in engravings, he succeeded in designing and building churches —like the Carmelite Church at Celaya—which follow the strictest architectural rules of his time.

6

Colonial art comes to an end when the Cathedral at Mexico City is finished. It is a summary of this art, excepting some one or two few sporadic manifestations which did not reach it, such as the plateresque, and affords examples of all its different modes of expression. Begun in the last third of the sixteenth century, at first it leant to the "Herreran" style; after that it bears the gaiety of the baroque of 1600 over its doorways and the elegant severity of the neo-classic style of the early years of the nineteenth century. If the eighteenth century left its design intact, it filled it inside with altarpieces, as though outwitting Renaissance gravity, And in regard to paintings, sculpture, furniture, jewelry, embroidery, and ivory work, it seems to be a synopsis of the art of the colonial period.

VI

DECLINE OF LITERATURE

1

Carlos Gonzalez Peña will be our guide through this period of Mexican letters:

The Golden Century in Spain was drawing to a close. After reaching the pinnacle of perfection, its decline had necessarily to ensue. The germ of this decline lay in *"Gongorism"* or *"culteranism,"* both these names being applied to this school, which is something like euphuism in English; the former appellation came from the name of its chief exponent, Luis de Gongora; the latter, because it attempted to represent what was refined and cultured, in opposition to what was vulgar and everyday, and sought to draw its inspiration more than from anything, from the discipline that constituted literary culture in those days, that is, from the study of the classics.

Painting by Roberto Montenegro. In foreground, Sor Juana Ines
de la Cruz, Carlos de Sigüenza y Gongora and
Juan Ruiz de Alarcon.

The Jesuits brought to Mexico the study of the humanities; classical studies, Greek and Latin authors. The Congregation of La Anunciata, established at the great college of St. Peter and St. Paul, publisher a number of text books; they are select compilations of Greek and Latin classical authors.

2

There is something very remarkable, so observes Menendez y Pelayo, about the appearance of Sor (sister) Juana Ines de la Cruz in the literary period which it fell to her share to live in.

"Sor Juana seems to sing with a voice like an angel" and above all, and very especially, in her profane love poems and in her religious poetry.

The love poems of Sor Juana are the softest and most delicate that ever came from a woman's pen.

Of these profane verses of hers the most remarkable are the *Romance de la Ausencia* (Ballad of Absence), the Lyres, the sonnets to a Rose, *Detente*, (Pause) *Sombra* (Shadow) and her ode on the occasion of the death of the Duke of Veragua; lastly, her celebrated quatrains entitled "O foolish men..." still popular at this day.

Sor Juana wrote but little prose, although when she did, with perfect mastery, as shown by her letters.

Sor Juana Ines de la Cruz was born in the little farm house of San Miguel de Nepantla, at the foot of the twin volcanoes, on November 2, 1651. At the age of three she began to read, at five she knew how to write and do sums; she later wished to attend the University in boy's costume to learn all that was there taught, but as her parents did not consent, she devoted her time to reading all the books in her grandfather's library; in twenty lessons she learned the Latin tongue; the fame of the poetess reached the Viceroy's ears and he welcomed her to his palace as a maid of honor and there she faced, to the great admiration of the Court, an examination by all the men of letters and savants living in the Viceroy's dominions.

3

There is scarcely a branch of the Mexican culture of his time, which does not require taking Carlos de Sigüenza y Gongora into account.

Gongora was, in fact, a loyal servant of literature. He was specially learned in physics, astronomy and mathematics; in languages, history, Indian antiquities and philosophy.

Sigüenza y Gongora by rescuing documents of incalculable value to the history of Mexico, that would otherwise have been destroyed utterly, would deserve the warmest praise that can be bestowed on any man of letters, even if he had not other claims on fame, such as the establishment of a museum of Mexican Antiquities, and his special study of the Aztec calendar for the purpose of seeking a surer basis for a study of the chronology of those ancient peoples. He assailed the error, then very widespread, of the belief in evils following in the train of comets, at that time upheld by the celebrated German jesuit, Pedro Kino, who attacked him on account of the publication of his philosophical essay against comets in 1681. "Sigüenza y Gongora popularized the soundest astronomical principles, and set forth the subject of parallaxes and the theory of comets' orbits, according to the doctrine of Copernicus and the hypothesis of cartesian vortexes."

4

Father Rafael Landivar, also a jesuit and the author of *"Rusticatio Mexicana,"* an admirable poem abounding in American scenery and color, was not a Mexican but a Guatemalan, but was closely connected with Mexico by both education and work.

Rusticatio Mexicana consists of several books, mostly devoted to Mexico, to its lakes, to its habits and customs, to its inhabitants, to the industries peculiar to the country, to the sudden upheaval of the Jorullo volcano, all described with truth, vigor and accuracy. He is a true poet. A great poet "who had he written in the vulgar tongue would have achieved something as great as Bello's Agriculture in the Torrid Zone..., and though he wrote in a tongue for the learned only, he was most happy in his touches of American local color, something that so many others have sought without success."

We should also mention the renowned historian, Father Francisco Javier Clavijero, a learned, intelligent and wise man, who, like Father Alegre, another historian, was born at Vera Cruz.

His most important work is the Ancient History of Mexico, in which he utilized all the notes and data collected during his life as a savant and investigator, besides a number of documents unearthed by him in Italy.

5

But in this sphere of action and at this time, offensive race and class inequalities were unfortunately also present; the Indians, who had in the early days of the conquest and thanks to the effort of the missionaries, received the benefits of culture, finally remained outside its current. Foreign to it were also a majority of the Spaniards who came to the country; they were either officials or rough men who thought only of work, whose mission in America confined itself to holding office or accumulating a fortune.

So that undoubtedly, of the other classes of society, it was the creoles and the mestizoes—mainly the former—who built up literary culture.

VII

TRANSITION FROM COLONIAL PERIOD TO PERIOD OF INDEPENDENCE

1

The end of Spain's colonial regime in Mexico and in the Americas, before the military and political tearing apart incident to independence, and after a prolonged period of anaemia and prostration, was marked by an impulse for recovery, restoration or regeneration.

The pressure and influence of Anglo-Saxon culture was felt in France and in Spain, as it was later to be felt in America and New Spain. The Reformation, both religious and scientific, the industrial regime of production, the appearance of the steam engine, the increase in the number of towns and in their population, the new components of society, belonging to the middle class, such as merchants, investors, property owners and professional men, leading the great proletarian mass, the swift growth of the United States, all this simultaneously brought about a spiritual reformation and the crystallization of popular instincts and aspirations, in new forms of democracy under the sovereignty of the people, popular representation by means of assemblies, votes, the division of power, resistance to oppression, private property, freedom of labor, free competition in trade, and individualistic forms of production, Masonic lodges, political clubs and parties, trial by jury, etc.

2

In the political sphere of action, this profound ideological change meant in the first place restraints upon the arbitrary power of the Crown, especially as regards the levying of taxes, and also the suppression of the privileges of the ruling classes, that is to say, the nobility and the church, that monopolized great estates and kept them out of circulation. And as a consequence of the principle of popular sovereignty, the right of protest, of rebellion and of insurrection arose.

As a defensive attempt to adapt itself to these new currents of ideas, absolute monarchy decided to sacrifice, in the first place, the nobility and the clergy, and began the suppression of privileges by working from below upwards. On its side, it admitted assertion of social rights, passing from absolute and personal monarchy to government by delegation, and to a centralized system of bureaucracy, later accepting the moral responsibility of the King himself, as though he likewise were a public servant. This is what is known as enlightened monarchy and is the first step towards constitutional monarchy. The constitution is the statute or charter of social reform, the covenant between the crown and the people to legitimize the power of the former and to admit among the upper classes, the insurgents, commoners, and the bourgeoisie or middle class backed by the proletarian masses.

The above is what in Spain and in the Americas takes the form of movement for political, administrative and economic revision, which makes its appearance wearing a brilliant aspect of regeneration and renovation, but which does no more than gild the surface and provoke, rather than check, the deep-seated work of transformation.

Mexican types, first half of nineteenth century.

3

As the attempt for political and social regeneration was in New Spain the reflection of a similar tendency taking place in the mother country, we must, to understand it better, reproduce under this head certain episodes taken from the history of Spain, as recounted by Rafael Altamira.

The ascent to the Spanish throne of the Duke of Anjou, Philip the V, involved a change of dynasty, to a French family in great part representing new ideas and influences opposed to those of the house of Austria.

Recovery is characterized by attempts to restore wealth and the public treasury, by promotion of the cultivation of the land, by a revival of traditional industries and commercial relations, and the diffusion of culture.

In this connection the struggle assumed gigantic proportions, fostered by the anti-clerical spirit of the times.

Important factors in this work were the ministers, such as Macanaz, Patiño, Ensenada, Wall, Aranda, Floridablanca, Campomanes, Jovellanos, Roda and Azara, most of whom had risen from the middle class and represented its maximum power, and the class of the lawyers or attorneys, strongly influenced by liberal currents of thought, by then very marked in French and English literature, and widely read in Spain.

4

At that time among cultured persons there was a very general but vague feeling of humanity, of love for the poor, for those oppressed by fortune and for their fellow-men in general; this feeling was called philanthropy, and induced an interest in social work and attempts to improve the fate of the less fortunate, by educating them, etc. The application of this feeling to government activities was known as enlightened despotism, the slogan of which was "everything for the people without the people" and eventually took the form of social economy, and cultural reform.

This current of thought came from certain English and French philosophers (Locke, Montesquieu, Voltaire, Rousseau, etc.), whose works exercised a very positive influence.

Kings and ministers realized that it was necessary to restore the economic life of the country. They began by the Treasury, put taxes on a regular footing, and also administration and expenses, so as to avoid extravagance, waste or graft in the handling of public revenues.

But the prosperity of the Treasury had to be based on that of the country, and they attempted to foster this by promoting industry, trade, agriculture and the increase of population, seriously diminished by war and misery.

Privileges were g·anted to manufacturers and merchants; commercial relations with th·: Americas were made easier, by removing restrictions on commerce; commercial development of several colonies was promoted by the organization of companies like the Philippine companies.

But what was chiefly insisted on was the improvement of agriculture and the reclamation, for cultivation, of that great portion of the land that was undeveloped. For this end it was necessary to assist the peasant class, sunk in ignorance and misery, subject to great landowners and holders of property in mortmain, or who lived with difficulty on small holdings of their own.

A number of laws designed to distribute farming lands belonging to municipalities among poor farmers and laborers were enacted. The most illustrious representative of all of these ideas for reform was the king's minister, Jovellanos, who condensed them in his celebrated Report on the Agrarian Law.

And in Mexico, his counterpart was the *Visitador*, or royal visitor, Jose de Galvez.

5

The inspection or visit of Jose de Galvez lasted from 1765 to 1771; he established the royal tobacco monopoly, executed the royal decree againts the Jesuits, enacted provisions for cleaning up administration of the treasury, and was commissioned to establish the system of Intendancies.

This impulse for order and reorganization increased the revenue three fold, was augmented by free trade, and climbed to the peak under the rule of the second Conde de Revillagigedo.

But Galvez, in spite of his new ideas and energies, did not succeed in penetrating to the bottom of Mexico's social problem. His best biographer, Herbert Ingram Priestley, who wrote a book entitled "Jose de Galvez, Visitor General of New Spain 1765-1771," estimates as follows the results obtained from his visit of inspection:

"It should be noted that such reforms touched very lightly or else vey late, New Spain's true misfortunes, which being of a social and economic nature required remedies more fundamental than mere changes in the form of government or in the fiscal management."

6

During the period under review some of the Viceroys erected great buildings and constructed highways; in times of plague and famine they played the paternal rôle of patrons and leaders of public charities; they pacified certain regions that were thus finally subdued, such as Nayarit, in the jurisdiction of the *Audiencia* of Guadalajara, and on the eastern side, the coast and river country that received the name of New Santander, on the Gulf shores (Tamaulipas); new towns like Linares, Nuevo Leon, were founded, expeditions were sent to Texas, the defense of the coastline was undertaken, on which considerable sums were expended, and efforts were made to remit as much money as possible to Spain.

7

On these matters Justo Sierra opines as follows:
The spirit of renovation not only stirred, to sweep away obstacles, but endeavored to constitute and carry out a new political and economic program, in which, to be sure, there was not one atom of liberty. As the requirements of the almost constant state of warfare in which the Spanish Empire continued during the reign of Charles III grew daily more urgent, the Court decided on a step whose consequences were from that moment foreboded, if not actually foreseen; the organization of a standing colonial army to replace volunteer militiamen, raised wherever needed, when danger threatened, and dissolved as soon as the occasion passed. From Spain came officers, an adjutant general, who forthwith got into a conflict with the Viceroy, Cruillas, (Joaquin de Monserrat) and instructors, who soon produced the desired results; the army recruited by enlistment, or by that kind of criminal sequestration or kidnpping known as impressment, at the beginning composed of two or three cavalry and infantry regiments, and of several minor corps, among them one of engineers (the artillery only came afterwards) in 1765 cost over seven hundred thousand pesos; the Mexicans thus took up arms and never after threw them down.

VIII

THE LAST POLITICAL EVENTS

1

Charles III, in the language of that period, desired the "reign of light" but at the same time he said, in article XVIII of his decree dated

March 27, 1767, "Individuals are not entitled to judge or interpret the orders of their sovereign," and the Viceroy added, in the decree providing for expulsion of the Jesuits "once for all, and for the future, the vassals of the Great Monarch who occupies the throne of Spain must know that they were born to hold their tongues and to obey, and not to discuss, nor express opinions on high matters of state."

2

Due to the expulsion of the Jesuits, twenty five secondary schools had to be closed. On the other hand, new centers of learning were created, like the Academy of Fine Arts, the School of Mines and the Botanic Garden; while the California Missions were entrusted to Franciscan friars, who, led by Friars Junipero Serra and Francisco Palau, founded those missions in Upper California that were the forerunners of a wonderful civilizing impulse in those regions.

The expulsion of the Jesuits gave rise to riots at Apatzingan, Uruapan, Valladolid and San Luis, and at Guanajuato, where they assumed serious proportions; but the Government soon suppressed those movements with great harshness, having sentenced more than ninety persons to death.

3

Charles III died at Madrid on December 14, 1788, after a reign which had lasted for twenty nine years and a half.

Juan Vicente de Güemes Pacheco de Padilla, second Conde de Revillagigedo, took office as Viceroy at Guadalupe, on October 17, 1789.

Aztecs used pine torches for lighting purposes.—2. In 1762, the City Council ordered that lamps be placed on front of houses.—3. Viceroy Revillagigedo in 1790 enacted ordinances for improvement of street lighting.

Revillagigedo established a police force, pursued evildoers, paved the streets, cleaned out sewers and ditches, levelled the main plaza, introduced street lighting and many other material improvements.

He established free secondary schools, improved the higher schools, founded the General Archives, promoted the arts and sciences, opened the School of Mines and the Botanic Garden, and despatched two sloops of war to the coasts of California and the Straits of San Juan de Fuca. He further had the most thorough and authentic census of the country made, ordered a monumental History of the Royal Treasury to be written, in thirty volumes, and left the fullest and most detailed secret instructions for his successor.

He ruled until the July 12, 1794, when he turned over the reins of government to the incoming Viceroy, Miguel de la Grua Talamanca y Branciforte, Marques de Branciforte.

4

Just as Revillagigedo was one of the best Viceroys, so his successor, Branciforte, was one of the worst.

War having again broken out between France and Spain, provincial regiments were raised in New Spain, which afforded the Viceroy splendid profits, through sales of commissions in said army.

With the fulsome adulation of a courtier, he asked for permission to erect a statue in honor of Charles IV and having received such permission, the laying of the corner-stone of the pedestal took place on July 8, 1796.

Finally, he was removed from office and succeeded by Miguel Jose de Azanza, who entered upon his duties March 31, 1798.

IX

THE URGE FOR INTELLECTUAL REGENERATION

1

If French influence, on science and general orientation, so critics say, was beneficial, this was not the case with art and literature. The taste of French writers and critics, very academical, cold and regulated, not only cut short the flights of inspiration, but produced among cultured people a feeling of repulsion, that sent them back to the great writers of the sixteenth and seventeenth centuries.

The advent of the Bourbon dynasty made a spirit of renovation stir through Spain. Something of this was reflected in the Americas.

The disturbance was, however, slow, and did not, in the intellectual field, begin to appear until half way through the XVIII century. Censorship having by then become less strict, or perhaps in spite of such censorhip, new ideas made their way into the quiet, and stagnant atmosphere of the Colony.

In literature a classical revival took place; this movement was mainly carried out by the Jesuits in their schools, as among them, at that time, flourished the best cultivators of Latin poetry we have ever had, as also our first great historian.

The expulsion of the members of the Society, weakened, but did not check, the cultural movement in Mexico.

2

In the philosophical field Father Benito Diaz de Gamarra distinguished himself.

Doctor Emeterio Valverde Tellez says: "It would not be fair to deny that we in Mexico owe to Gamarra, the frankest, strongest, most aggressive and efficient reaction against antiquated methods, in favor of a beneficial reform of scientific study."

3

Jose de Jesus Nuñez y Dominguez, states that the Jesuits must surely have changed their mode of action and activities, compelled thereto by the force of circumstances, and by the social phenomena that took place in their time.

"In the presence of the events that were deeply transforming society, of the force of circumstances, and of "a perfectly explicable irritation," the exiled priests brought into play all their intellectual power and became propagandists of the ideals of American freedom."

"Under the exquisite form of their historical, scientific and literary works, there'throbs unseen a tendency towards liberty, partly due to resentment because they had been expelled from their respective coun- by an alien monarch, 'or because the evolution of ideas itself impelled them thereto, imperious and overwhelming."

4

The following distinguished themselves during the period under review: Antonio Leon y Gama, an astronomer, mathematician and antiquary, who wrote essays on the satellites of Jupiter, on the climate of Mexico, and on the so-called Aztec Calendar and the Stone of Tizoc;

Joaquin Velazquez Cardenas y Leon, also an astronomer and mathematician, who made notable observations, with instruments made by himself, of the transit of Venus across the face of the sun and made a good map of New Spain, which is all the more remarkable in that even in the metropolis there were then, according to the Marques de la Ensenada, no good maps or persons able to engrave them; and lastly Father Alzate, of encyclopaedic attainments, who was, in company with Bartolache, one of the advocates of the experimental method, and who carried out valuable studies on plants and animals, which earned for him the distinction of being appointed a correspondent of the Paris Academy.

Baron von Humboldt points out that the study of chemistry was farther advanced in Mexico than in Spain; that the School of Mines boasted a good chemical laboratory, a physical laboratory equipped with instruments made in the country, and a well classified geological collection; that the best work in Spanish on mineralogy, the *"Manual de Orictognosia"* of Andres del Rio, a professor at that same school, had been printed in Mexico and that in Mexico likewise had been printed the first translation of Lavoisier's chemistry; and the Baron goes on to say: "No city of the New World, without excepting any in the United States, boasts scientific establishments as vast and as sound as those of the Capital of Mexico, I shall be satisfied with mentioning the School of Mines, with the learned Elhuyar at its head, the Botanic Garden and the Academy of Painting and Sculpture.

X

COLONIAL IDEOLOGY

1

During the colonial regime the power of the Crown was absolute and all institutions functioned by delegation from royal authority. Regalist property was introduced by laying down as a fundamental principle ownership by the Crown of all wealth. The King granted the use of property to the owners as a grant or by composition or confirmation of their ancient titles, and would just the same grant a concession covering the surface of the ground, as another for development of the subsoil, or yet another for water rights or the establishment of any kind of industry.

At that period of our history, though the religious power was still very important throughout the Hispanic world, it not only saw its temporal power lessened, but through the exercise of the royal right of patronage, appointments of ecclesiastical officers were made just as though they were members of the civil power. Popular religious feeling, the State religion, knightly ideals confused with religious ideals, the Church as a militant body, all had to fight against the tendencies of the Reformation and of the Renaissance.

The Reformation meant non-conformity and free examination of religious dogmas, and the Renaissance the restoration of dialectics, or of rationalism and of philosophy, in the problems of human knowledge. Religion ceased to be something no one could touch and endeavored to explain itself by means of scholastic philosophy.

2

Furthermore, the Reformation not only meant freedom of examination for discussion of theological matters, but also coincided with a great industrial and commercial transformation. Spain's enemies were heretics, not only to evade the authority of the Pope, but because they formed part of an economic movement that had spread after the discovery of America, and shifted commercial activity into fresh routes. The system of production and interchange of wealth which permitted the progress of Spain and Portugal, seemed to press north, through France and Holland and later chiefly to England. Geographical position, as the axis and cross-roads of the greater part of human activities, moved across the Atlantic Ocean to America, by the shortest way. The resources America furnished to Europe promoted an industrial and commercial revolution of a new type, and the drive of Anglo-Saxon colonization began by pressing against the vast body of the Spanish Empire.

In her efforts to expand, Spain increased the vigor of her forces of repression and persecution, now not only against Moriscoes and Jews, but also against Lutherans. And as symptom of weakness, she established her policy of isolation, of closed doors, which was tightened as far as the colonies were concerned. Attempts were made to avoid the contagion of heresies, which at the same time meant commercial and political competition. But as it was impossible to check the forces of the new currents of thought, breaches were opened in the walls of prohibitions, by means of smuggling, of open war which compelled the conclusion of treaties, or of irregular warfare which took the form of piratical outrages. The French pirates, after them the Dutch, and lastly the English, incessantly undermined the power of Spain, by challenging her mastery of the seas.

3

The ruling class had kept on its course in the concentration of wealth. The Crown was represented by the authority of the Viceroys, who collected taxes to be remitted to Spain; the King was likewise represented by the members of the *Audiencia,* magistrates, mayors and *caciques,* by the whole higher staff of the civil and military machinery of the State.

The Church, ever more subservient, in the civil sphere, to the authority of the State, was yet, however, an arm of the civil function, and augmented her economic power. Missions became great estates, chaplaincy funds became mortgage banks, monasteries became institutions monopolizing property held in mortmain, and the lower clergy, who did not attain to rich benefices, became spiritual allies of a middle class in process of formation.

4

The old nobility, which had fallen heir to the privileges of the *encomenderos,* strengthened its position by means of profits from

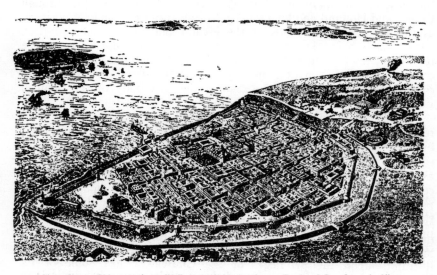

Vera Cruz.—Old engraving.—Walled city with bastions.—Castle of San Juan de Ulua (26), Verde Island (25), Sacrificios Island (24), Los Hornos (22), Concepcion Bastion (15), and Santiago Bastion (1.)

ownership of *haciendas* which grew into great estates and rents from
city realty, investments in house property being one systematic form of
exploiting centers of population. The incomplete property rights granted
to the Indians by the laws enacted for their protection were in the aggregate nullified for a number of reasons. In the first place, communal
lands were generally in the form of village common lands, close to or on
the edge of centers of population, without taking into account the
suitability of such land for cultivation, nor the water available, nor the
possibility of irrigation. In the second place, due to prohibitions dating
back to the days of the conquest and kept up for reasons of public order
and fear of revolt, the Indians had not been able to improve their
farming equipment nor freely utilize horses and live stock in general.
Introduction of improved methods of farming had been incomplete
and restricted. Tribute, which like taxes generally, is an indirect form of
expropriation, and was aggravated by restraints on trade and lack of
capital, made such lands or individual lots leave the hands of the
Indians to swell the lands of the *haciendas*. And lastly, defects in early
titles, and deeds of transfer and succession by inheritance, had reduced
the property of Indian "republics" or communities, to a minimum,
and at the same time the lack of individual property had not allowed
the rise of a true peasant class. Only scanty groups of comparatively
independent ranchers had grown up, who likewise constituted an addition to the middle classes of the cities, and were a dynamic element
on account of their dissatisfaction and ambition.

5

And the populace of the towns, together with the dispossessed mass
of the peasantry and the workers in the mines, continued to constitute
an aggregation of insufficiently remunerated labor, in a state of complete disorganization.

Aside from this, those groups or sub-classes who enjoyed the privilege of owning the machinery for the production of wealth, fought
one another in their efforts to acquire it and concentrate it in their
own hands. The Crown curtailed the resources of the Church, and
great landowners resisted fiscal spoliation or the inordinate power of
religious corporations, which absorbed the public wealth. And by
these conflicts they weakened one another. Royal authority claimed
to be founded on divine right, and by expelling the jesuits or placing
restraints upon the privileges of the Church, it lost some of its
prestige and disavowed the foundations of its own authority. The
great landowners in turn, complained that they were burdened by

oppressive taxation or by ever increasing mortgages in favor of the Church, even though their properties had originated from royal grants and were only preserved by them thanks to the military and civil protection afforded by the authorities. And lastly, the Church, on being transformed and asserting her independence in the presence of the Crown, undermined the foundations of the régime and opened wide the doors to fresh currents of thought which brought with them new forms of social ideology, and the beginnings of revolution.

PART THREE
INDEPENDENT MEXICO

I

LAST DAYS OF THE VICEREGAL PERIOD

1

In the year 1803, the viceroy, Felix Berenguer de Marquina, was succeeded by Jose de Iturrigaray, whose rule lasted until September 15, 1808, he having been the 56th of the Spanish Viceroys.

When the news of the abdication of Charles IV reached the Viceregal capital, Iturrigaray pretended to be devoted to the new King. But shortly after that other news came, that told of the captivity and exile of the Bourbons, and that the people of Madrid had risen in revolt. The Viceroy convened the *audiencia* and the members of this body decided to see which party came out victorious before adhering to his cause.

There were on the City Council of Mexico City, two men, Verdad and Azcarate, one of them an alderman and the other the clerk, who interpreted with cleverness the political ambitions of the creole bourgeoisie. These two men, well versed in the science of law, turned to good account the Spanish revolt and proposed that in Mexico, and as provided by old Spanish laws, the vacancy due to absence of the King be filled up. The Cortes should be convened, to confirm the Viceroy in the office to which the Sovereign had appointed him.

2

The meeting of the Mexican Cortes meant the separation of the colony, the full assertion of its national sovereignty, as although they were to assemble, as Licenciados Primo Verdad and Azcarate pointed out, to guard an inalienable possession of the Spanish monarchy, their plan involved, if not independence, at least autonomy and with it the rise to political power of the Creole element.

The motion made by the City Council having been accepted by Iturrigaray, despite the adverse opinion of the members of the *audiencia* he summoned a meeting for discussion of the call to Cortes.

Eighty-two persons assembled in the palace of the Viceroys on the 9th of August. The Viceroy acted as chairman at a meeting composed of the Archbishop, members of the *audiencia*, prosecutors, aldermen, members of the courts of accounts and of the commercial tribunal, canons, the nobility, rich members of the bourgeoisie and deputies from the Jalapa city council. The meeting, so Licenciado Verdad asserted, had been convened for the purpose of providing for the establishment of a provisional government. One of the inquisitors objected that the principle of popular sovereignty was "heretical."

3

The Viceroy had funds on hand amounting to almost fifteen million pesos, and more than twenty thousand men under arms. There was a moment when he seemed disposed to act energetically and swiftly.

The Spaniards, being convinced of the Viceroy's stupidity, struck a blow with but little risk. The man who carried out their scheme was Gabriel J. Yermo, a big boss who owned sugar plantations. At midnight on the 15th of September three hundred clerks from business houses, with Yermo at the head, made their way into the palace and seized the Viceroy's person

On the 16th the City of Mexico learned that Iturrigaray had been ousted from his office the previous night, and that the ranking military officer, Pedro Garibay, had been appointed in his place.

After that came the fury of repressión; in it perished two men whom our country counts among its heroes; Licenciado Francisco Primo Verdad y Ramos and a South American friar, Talamantes. The former died mysteriously in his prison in the Archbishop's palace and the latter died in the Fortress of San Juan de Ulua. Licenciado Azcarate spent three years in prison and Licenciado Prisco, Major Martin Michaus and Canons Cisneros and Beristain were also imprisoned. The ex-Viceroy, who was taken back to Spain, underwent a prosecution for disloyalty.

4

The invasion of Spain by Napoleon and the absence of the King and Queen (held prisoners in France from 1808 to 1814) gave rise to a political situation abounding in transcendent consequences.

The various regions of Spain became active centers governed by Juntas and aspired to reinstate the old Cortes as a general organ to represent all of them and to resolve as to what might be expedient in view of the needs and wishes of the nation in the absence of the

King. This was done, and an assembly composed of four classes of deputies met at Cadiz (1809-1813); these four classes represented the following: cities that had had a vote at the previous Cortes; the provincial Juntas set up anew; the people, at the rate of one representative for every fifty thousand souls, but as regard the Americas, at the rate of one representative for every hundred thousand white inhabitants.

A great number of the delegates from the Juntas had ideas on the subject of political reform.

By means of successive decrees and resolutions (the greater part of which were later embodied in the so-called Constitution of 1812) they unfolded their new liberal program, the fundamental points of which were the sovereignty of the nation, constitutional monarchy, separation between the powers composing the state, equal rights for Spaniards and Americans, the abolition of rights abusive of the Indians.

Although all of the above measures were adopted by a large majority of the deputies, they represented only a portion of their opinion.

All those classes of society and organs whose ancient privileges were assailed, stirred up contrary opinion.

5

And as regards the Spanish colonies Altamira, points out that at this stage, in the Americas an anti-Spanish party had been growing up.

It was composed of the descendants of the colonizers, and more especially of mestizoes, driven thereto not only by a tendency ever latent in the spirit of mixed races, but also by the frequent blunders, abuses and absurdities of the Spanish authorities and of the clergy. This disposition had already shown itself in the eighteenth century, and had been noticed by several ministers of the Bourbon dynasty, who pointed out the danger and even went so far as to suggest a remedy, to consist of a change of methods of government for the colonies.

The example set by England's old colonies, which had at the end of that century broken loose from the metropolis, to constitute what is now the United States of America, encouraged Spanish American secessionists, swelled their ranks and made the feeling for independence stronger.

6

Notwithstanding all this, deputies from the Americas attended the Cortes at Cadiz, and perhaps separation from the mother country could have been avoided had the political doctrines of Spanish liberals been more flexible. In fact, the latter had begun by stating that Spain's dominions in the Indies should not be considered as factories or colonies, but as "an essential and integral portion of the Spanish monarchy," for which reason they should be governed in exactly the same way as the provinces of Spain herself, and given the name of Provinces beyond the seas; the legal and juridical equality of Spaniards and American-born subjects was to be proclaimed but as in the application of this doctrine all persons not free and white (of Spanish descent on both sides) were to be excluded from citizenship and the vote, the deputies from the Americas opposed this exclusive provision, and their debates on the subject with the Spaniards produced considerable friction, the deputies from the Peninsula having resented the accusation of not being liberal enough in their views, and those from the Americas taking offense at the actual slight involved.

7

We may here appropiately mention a famous document, which has been described as prophetic and clever and is known as the report of the Conde de Aranda, which was found among the papers left by that great statesman.

In reality, that report sets forth facts that were so notorious, that even in his time only fanatics and ignorant persons could refuse to acknowledge them And the remedies proposed are nothing more then political expedients, later on tried without success. Like the *Visitador* Galvez, the author of the famous report did not glimpse the problem of Spain and of her colonies except superficially and from the political angle.

Among the most important things said by him, with reference to the United States:

"Freedom of worship, facilities for settlement on enormous areas and the advantages held out by that new government, will attract farmers and artisans from all countries, because man goes wherever he thinks he can better himself, and we shall, within a very few years regretfully see how the colossus I have forecasted will arise. That Anglo-American power once converted into a great nation, we must believe that its first aim will be possession of the Floridas in their entirety, with a view to control of the Gulf of Mexico. This step once taken, it will not only interfere with our commerce with the Kingdom of Mexico whenever it shall think fit, but will further aspire to the conquest of that enormous empire, which we shall not be able to defend from Europe, against a great and formidable power established on that continent and bordering upon that country." And in order to avoid the loss of those rich colonies, he proposed that they be made independent of Spain, by constituting one kingdom in Mexico, another in Peru and an empire to include the other South American possessions, Spain to keep only Cuba, Puerto Rico and some other point on the southern continent, that tribute be required of these new nations and that princes of the Spanish royal family be seated on their thrones, with the obligation of concluding reciprocal matrimonial alliances in order to preserve peace and harmony.

But this was not really the crux of the problem.

8

It has often been said that the deficiences of the colonial regime were not those of a people, but of the times; this argument is based on a number of circumstances, which we shall proceed to summarize briefly.

Revillagigedo wrote in the instructions to his successor: "We must not overlook the fact that this is a colony which should be dependent on the mother country, Spain, and which should yield the latter some profit in exchange from the benefits received in the way of protection, so that great judgment and tact will be required to combine the fact of such dependence and to make interest mutual and reciprocal, as such interest would cease to exist as soon as European manufacturers and products were no longer needed here."

Spanish domination endeavored to subsist, by keeping the lower classes in servitude.

The task of the worker was forced upon him, not only in public services, but also in industrial occupations.

Even at the end of the viceregal period, when the system was gradually becoming less harsh, Baron Humboldt lamented the ill-treatment served out to artisans in workshops: "Free men, Indians and colored men are mixed up with galley slaves, whom the judicial authorities distribute among factories to make them work for a wage. They are all half naked, covered with rags, emaciated and disfigured. Each shop, more than anything else, resembles a gloomy prison; double doors are always closed, and workers are not allowed to leave the premises; those who are married may only see their families on Sundays. They are all punished without recourse should they commit the slightest infringement of the order established for the factory."

"Perhaps among the reasons that brought about the conspiracy against the viceregal government, was a visit which the Magistrate Dominguez, by express order of Iturrigaray, made to the cloth mills, "in which"—says a historian beyond suspicion in this case, due to his open partisanship in favor of the colonial government, Lucas Alaman—"the workers suffered cruel slavery, after selling their freedom for an advance in cash and remaining in their prison, to be treated like slaves, until they had paid off that sum."

9

Baron Humboldt states that for a description of the political situation of the Indians in New Spain, he could think of nothing better and more exact than the summary of a memorial presented to the King in 1799 by the Bishop and Cathedral Chapter of Michoacan.

As a matter of fact, this extract reveals a great many things and is full of substance; we might almost call it the statute of independence:

"The population of New Spain is composed of three classes of men: whites or Spaniards, Indians and mixed races. The Spaniards constitute a tenth of the total number of inhabitants. Almost all the property belongs to them. The Indians and other races till the soil; they serve the wealthier classes and all they have to live on is the work of their own hands. Out of this arises that conflict of interests between Indians and whites, that mutual hatred that so easily is born between "those who have everything and those who have nothing, and between owners and slaves."

"I am not ignorant of the fact that such evils may arise anywhere where great inequality of position exists, but in America they are even more tremendous, because there is no intermediate state; "one is rich or destitute, noble or infamous, in law and in fact."

"In fact, the Indians and the mixed races are in a most humiliating situation. The sufferings of the Indians, their ignorance and above all their misery, place them at an enormous distance from the whites, who occupy the first place in the population of New Spain. The privileges which the laws apparently grant to the Indians afford them but few benefits, and might almost be said to injure them."

10

"Being reduced to the narrow limits comprised within a radius of 600 varas which an old law assigns to Indian villages, it may be asserted that they possess no individual property and are compelled to cultivate common lands. This kind of cultivation becomes a burden on them, all the more unbearable as for some years back they must have lost almost all hope of gaining anything for themselves from the fruits of their work. The new regulations for Intendancies provide that Indians may not receive assistance from community funds without permission from the High Board of the Royal Treasury. (This was a kind of "Savings Bank" into which entered the proceeds from the work of the Indians, which proceeds came from the municipal property leased by the Intendants to the Indians.)

Those funds actually built up by the villages became fictititous. To speak more clearly, that money that was not available to the Indians due to the great number of formalities required, eventually found its way to the Royal Treasury. Of these funds, which appeared to belong to no one, the Intendant at Valladolid sent to Madrid in 1798 about $40,000, telling the King that it was a patriotic gift which the Indians of Michoacan made to their sovereign as a contribution towards the expenses of the war with England.

11

"As those natives could not, under the Laws of the Indies, execute public deeds for a sum exceeding five pesos, is was impossible for them to better their condition or to live more comfortably, whether as farm laborers, or as artisans."

"The law prohibited the mixing of races; it also forbade whites from settling in Indian villages and the Indians from residing among Spaniards. This distance imposed between them was a hindrance to civilization."

"The races descended from negro slaves were stigmatized as infamous by the law and subject to tribute. These colored men being endowed with an energetic and impetuous disposition, lived in a constant state of irritation against the whites; it being remarkable that their resentment did not oftener goad them to take revenge.

"This being the situation, what loyalty can the Indians, despised, degraded, almost propertyless and with no hope of bettering themselves, feel for the Government, as the bonds of social existence do not, in short, afford them the slightest benefit? If new legislation does not take into account the lot of the Indians and people of color, the ascendency of the clergy, however great it may be over the hearts of these unfortunates, will not be sufficient to keep them submissive and properly respectful of the Government."

"Let the odious tax of personal tribute be abolished; let the legal infamy by which unjust laws have branded colored men cease, and let them be declared qualified to fill all those civil posts not requiring special proof of noble or gentle birth; let municipal property, still undivided, be distributed among the Indians; let portions of vacant lands, now mostly uncultivated, be distributed among the Indians and the mixed races; let an agrarian law like those of Asturias and Galicia be enacted for Mexico; let Indians, mixed races and whites be allowed full freedom to settle in villages now exclusively allotted to any one of them; let fixed stipends be paid to judges and magistrates. On these points the happiness of the Mexican people chiefly depends."

12

In 1809 it was estimated that New Spain annually exported twenty two million pesos to pay for five or six millions' worth purchased from merchants in Spain, favored by that commercial monopoly, which they shared with other Spanish merchants at Mexico and Vera Cruz. Those enormous profits, which amounted to about sixteen million pesos per annum, were divided by equal portions among the favored few in Spain and New Spain. To this must be added that every year six or eight million pesos (the royal revenues) left the country, the greater part as direct tribute paid to the King and the remainder to help other colonies that were unable to meet their expenses.

13

We shall, after thus setting forth the economic and social causes of independence, in a general way, note certain concrete facts connected with the same problem.

It is estimated that at the end of the eighteenth century and beginning of the nineteenth, wages ranged from nine to twelve and eighteen cents except in certain mining camps where they were higher; but an average of twenty five cents is accepted.

Baron von Humboldt calculated that after deducting taxes or excise an Indian had left an actual income of $52.00 for all expenses of himself and family.

By royal order addressed to the *Consulado* (Comercial Tribunal) at Mexico it was instructed to report on the trade of New Spain.

The *Consulado's* answer is one of the most valuable documents for the economic history of Mexico at the end of the eighteenth century. Its pages give a true picture of colonial economic existence, and are the best means for learning how taxes, and the great number of obstacles in the way of development, weighed down the shoulders of the population.

Said report stated that "The funds withdrawn from the kingdom are needed for the promotion of agriculture."

Agriculture has not, as a general thing, been of any advantage beyond feeding the inhabitants, as it has never yielded enough to encourage those who engage in it. Hence farmers confine themselves to planting only what the kingdom can consume.

It is also widely known that a majority of rural properties are mortgaged or encumbered by amounts almost equal to their full value, because they do not return enough to their owners for the latter to cultivate them.

14

We must point to another symptom that reveals the lack of equilibrium and the rise of new classes of society; the discontent among mine workers, who began at Real del Monte to rise against feudal systems of exploitation, as represented by a fortunate miner who had become an opulent landowner, Pedro Romero de Terreros, Conde de Regla. A report by *Visitador* Galvez says:

"Since the riot of the year 1766 the Count had withdrawn to his hacienda at San Miguel, fleeing from the insolence of the miners on the Viscaina Vein and at Real del Monte, who attempted to make him the victim of their unwarranted pretensions to the division of the ores, which has ever been the motive for tumult and the apple of discord at Real del Monte and Pachuca."

And we further set down these last data:

Spain, in difficulties due to her chronic fiscal destitution, in 1804, with the permission of the Pope, enacted that all funds administered by the clergy be delivered to the royal treasury, which would be responsible for them and pay interest thereon at a given rate.

This provision was obeyed to an extent sufficient to remit to Spain the sum of ten million six hundred thousand pesos, and as the colonial authorities realized that the anger of the countryfolk and of all the population would increase as spoliation proceeded, the Royal Board, in agreement with the Viceroy, decided to abrogate so harmful a law for secularization of church property, which threatened to provoke a general rebellion at a early date.

II

PRECURSORS OF INDEPENDENCE

1

The idea of the Independence of Mexico arose simultaneously with the Conquest itself, because physical separation from Spain could not but, sooner or later, bring about political separation. The very success of colonization had necessarily to give rise to the development of a new nationality, and although the transformation was slow and arduous, it had to proceed to its termination, when social and economic conditions made revolution unavoidable.

Due to restlessness, to ambition or intuition, to rebellious instincts or vital impulse of oppressed classes; conspiracies, riots, revolts of negros, Indians, *encomenderos,* mestizos and creoles constantly threatened the stability of the dominion of Spain. But the idea of a revolution for independence slumbered for centuries as hardly more than the germ of an idea; the rebellious class, lacking in consciousness and strength, and attempts at emancipation, were but suppressed symptoms of latent energy.

2

Late in the eighteenth century, thanks to all the factors studied by us in this essay, the idea of independence began to take form. Indian revolts in Durango and Yucatan assumed ominous proportions. The authorities began to realize that something serious was brewing. In the city of Mexico, the so-called "conspiracy of the cutlasses" was discovered; it was known by this name because the rebels were only able to arm themselves with cold steel.

It may be asserted that the idea of independence began to come to a head when conspiracies or plans of action included proposals to assemble or call a Congress, that is to say, to appeal to the sovereignty of the people, to a democratic formula, as against the system of absolute monarchy by divine right.

3

The forerunners of this idea were Licenciados Verdad and Azcarate, aldermen of the City of Mexico; Fernandez de Lizardi, surnamed the Mexican thinker, and Carlos Maria de Bustamante, who carried out literary propaganda; Friar Servando Teresa de Mier and Father Talamantes in that section of society in closest touch with politics. After the conspiration of the cutlasses, another plan for insurrection was discovered at Valladolid, but still inchoate in form and easily repressed.

4

We can point out still other circumstances that gradually led up to the revolution for independence.

In the city of Mexico, on August 4, 1794, when morning broke the citizens found, posted on the corner of the building known as the Provincial Palace, at the Mercaderes arcades and on the corner of the principal street, the following lampoon;

> The French are the wisest.
> To follow their opinions
> Is no absurdity.
> However much laws may try,
> They will never be able
> To stifle the cries
> Nature inspires.

The new philosophical doctrines, says Nicolas Rangel, and vehement aspirations for liberty, were assimilated and spread by the younger students of the last third of the eighteenth century. For example: the Royal and Pontifical Seminary of Mexico, was a hotbed of insurrection, and a theological student, Juan Jose Pastor Morales, the warmest upholder of the maxims of the encyclopedists of that century. The prosecution instituted by the Inquisition against this ideological forerunner, shows him to have been a young man of superior talent, learned and

National Palace in eighteenth century.

eloquent. In spite of having been ordained a priest, he insisted on professing the new ideas and in spreading them.

Very much the same may be said about Juan Antonio Montenegro, prosecuted by the Inquisition pursuant to an information lodged by one Manuel Velasco.

"The other day" said Velasco, "being Saturday the twenty eighth of September (1793) last, I having gone to visit Montenegro and being seated at dinner with him, the two of us by ourselves, he told me that a conspiracy was afoot in Mexico against the Crown."

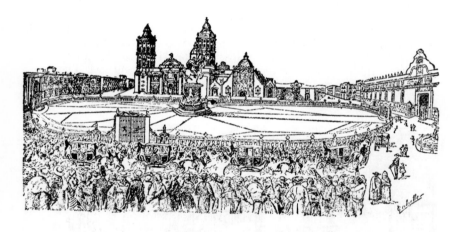

Main Plaza of Mexico City, 1808

"He said that the plan was that the kingdom should become a republic divided into provinces, with a delegate for each one; in the midst of the kingdom was to be founded a city to be the Capital of the whole, where the individuals representing the Republic and elected at certain periods, were to reside."

"The propositions I have heard Montenegro advance in regard to religion, were the following: One may find salvation in any faith. Religion is nothing more than politics of which men have availed themselves in order to reduce nations to submission."

"Such were the indications of the great storm that was ere long to break."

III

HIDALGO

1

The Valladolid conspiracy was repeated at Queretaro. One of the chief instigators was Ignacio Allende, a Captain in the Queen's Regiment.

Allende was a creole and professed liberal ideas, he had viewed the fall of Iturrigaray with disapproval and his leanings were contrary to the Spanish party.

The conspirators had on their side the local *corregidor* or magistrate, Manuel Dominguez, and his wife, Maria Josefa Ortiz de Dominguez, an enthusiastic advocate of independence.

Miguel Hidalgo, the parish priest of the village of Dolores, was invited to join the conspiracy. Hidalgo refused at the beginning, as the considered the interprise lacking in seriousness, but at last attended the meetings and consented to head the revolution.

Heroes of Independence.—Painting by Diego Rivera.

2

The Father of Mexican Independence was born in the State of Guanajuato, May 8, 1753. He pursued his studies at the College of San Nicolas at Valladolid (now Morelia) and was ordained a priest. He was a teacher and Dean of said college and afterwards occupied several curacies. In September 1810 he was parish priest at Dolores, Guanajuato.

His learning and his progressive ideas brought him under suspicion, because he used to read all kinds of books, and in his addresses his liberal ideas were always noticeable.

3

The early days of September, 1810, are extraordinarily important from an historical point of view. This is what Agustin Rivera has to say about them:

September, beginning.—It was about this stime that the following event, mentioned by Hidalgo in his statements and narrated by Alaman in the following words, took place: "Hidalgo attempted to win over to his side the provincial infantry batallion of Guanajuato. For this purpose, under the pretext of one of the feasts which he often organized, he summoned to Dolores the drum-major and music master of that regiment, Juan Garrido, and Sergeants Dominguez and Navarro: he laid his plan before them and offered to appoint them as officers of his battalion instead of the Spaniards. They all agreed."

September 13th.—*The Conspiracy at Guanajuato discovered.*—Garrido reported to the Intendant, Riaño, what Hidalgo had told him, and turned over sixty pesos that Hidalgo had given him to bribe the soldiers. The Intendant at once ordered the sub-delegate at San Miguel to arrest both Allende and Aldama, and then to proceed to Dolores and arrest Hidalgo.

Hidalgo addresses the multitude from the courtyard in front of the Church.

September 14th, early morning.—Hidalgo learned from a friend that the conspiracy had been discovered at Guanajuato.

September 14th, afternoon.—Allende was warned by Hidalgo, and forthwith left San Miguel for Dolores, where he arrived early in the evening.

September, night from the 15th to the 16th.—Allende and Aldama went straight to Hidalgo's bedroom, woke him up, and gave him a message from the *Corregidor's* wife; he then began to dress, and said to them: "Gentlemen, we are lost, there is nothing else for us to do but to go out and capture *gachupines* (term applied to Spaniards.)"

September 16th, between five and six in the afternoon.—Hidalgo, from the main doorway of the parish church, harangued the Indians inside the church and those in the courtyard, and ended his discourse by shouting: Long live America! Long live Ferdinand VII! Down with bad government! The Indians took up the cry, and joined Hidalgo, and they all went of in searth of weapons, some having taken up lances, and others cutlasses and slings.

4

The army thus improvised left for San Miguel el Grande (today San Miguel Allende) and from there they went to Celaya, the principal appointments having been made and the rank of General being bestowed on Hidalgo and that of Lieutenant General on Allende.

On September 28th they took the City of Guanajuato and the Castle of Granaditas. From Guanajuato Hidalgo left for Valladolid, and after taking the latter town he published a decree dated October 19th, abolishing slavery throughout New Spain.

The Viceregal Government had put a price on the head of Hidalgo and his principal companions; the Archbishop of Mexico and the Bishop of Valladolid had excommunicated him and a force was organized with the best troops at the Government's disposal, a Spanish Brigadier General, Torcuato Trujillo, having been placed in command. The two armies clashed at the Monte de las Cruces and the issue of the hard fought day was favorable to Hidalgo and his insurgents; and although he could have taken the Capital, he withdrew, upon which the series of his reverses began, as on being overtaken by a Spanish leader, Calleja, he was routed at Aculco. After that he proceeded to Valladolid and from thence to Guadalajara, where he arrived on November 26th. He at once tried to reorganize his forces, by establishing a government and applying for recognition of Mexico's independence by the United States of America. But Calleja was approaching and Hidalgo not wishing to engage him in the city, sallied forth to meet him, a battle having been fought at Puente de Calderon, in which the insurgent troops were completely routed. Hidalgo marched north with but few followers and deprived of military command. The road was long and arduous, and finally Hidalgo and his companions fell into an ambuscade laid for them by Elizondo, a traitor, at Acatita de Bajan, March 21, 1811.

They were taken to Monclova and then to Chihuahua, and forthwith executed.

The execution of the Father of his Country took place on July 30, 1811. His head was exposed on the Castle of Granaditas for several years, together with those of his companions Allende, Aldama and Jimenez.

5

Miguel Hidalgo, by reason of the fondness and love for him of the Mexicans, has merited from them the appellation of Father of his country. Let us endeavor to learn more about him.

Alaman says that "Don Miguel distinguished himself in the studies pursued by him at the College of San Nicolas... where he later taught with great brilliancy the philosophy and theology courses, and became the dean of that establishment;" he points that he troubled little or nothing about the spiritual administration of his parishioners, whom he had left, with half the stipend from the curacy, in the hands of a priest called Francisco Iglesias; but as he could read and understand French, something rather unusual in those days, especially among churchmen, he became very fond of reading works on art and science, and took up with eagerness the promotion of several farming and industrial activities in his parish; the growing of grapes, mulberry trees, pottery and brick making, tanning, shops for sundry trades... "All this, and the fact that he was not only liberal but extravagant in money matters, had won him the esteem of his parishioners, especially the Indians, whose language he was familiar with."

6

Miguel Hidalgo was to the Independence of Mexico what Christopher Columbus was to the Discovery of America. He undoubtedly had been preceded by forerunners who pointed out or lighted the way, beginning with Gante and Motolinia, who realized the impossibility of ruling New Spain from the far away seat of the Crown. Hernan Cortes himself must surely felt the urge to compass the independence of Mexico.

But neither in the rebellious attitute of the *encomenderos* or in the revolts of the negroes, or the isolated riots of Indians and of a starving populace, was there really a definite vision of a new nationality and of freedom.

Hidalgo was the first to envisage the full sense of independence, in the sense of emancipation and liberation, by taking up and maturing the plans of Verdad, Talamantes, and the Valladolid conspirators. The wife of the *Corregidor* of Queretaro, and Allende, Aldama, and Abasolo, are to Hidalgo as Queen Isabella and the brothers Pinzon to Columbus. To all of them fell a portion of the glory attendant upon the beginning of a transcendent enterprise.

Hidalgo is the one who started the movement for independence, in its effective and vital aspect, to be subsequently attempted in more radical form by Morelos, and consummated, though only in part, by Iturbide. Hidalgo did not have time definitely to prepare his plans, nor the good fortune and military abilities to obtain victory by the force of arms. In spite of everything, he was the real initiator, because he consciously embarked upon a mighty enterprise for the achievement of freedom, well knowing that it would cost him his life.

IV

M O R E L O S

1

Jose Maria Morelos was born at Valladolid (Morelia) on September 30, 1765.

He graduated from the Mexico City University as a Bachelor of Arts.

In order to be able to pursue his career, he was compelled to accept the offer of the parish priest at Uruapan, who took him to his parish to teach grammar and rhetoric.

Early in March, 1798, he was parish priest at Caracuaro.

In 1810 he saw the Spaniards in full flight from Valladolid and Patzcuaro, on the approach of the insurgents. He left his parish for Valladolid, and on learning that the rebellion was led by his old teacher, Miguel Hidalgo, he left in search of the insurgent troops until he met them at Indaparapeo.

Miguel Hidalgo wrote out his appointment reading as follows: "I hereby commission my lieutenant Dr. Jose Maria Morelos to raise troops on the south coast, he to act in accordance with instructions furnished him."

In the same month of October, 1810, Morelos left Caracuaro with twenty-five men from the ranks of the people, armed with a few guns and home made lances, and made his way towards Zacatula, across the Province of Michoacan in the direction of the coast.

At the town of Tecpan he received valuable reinforcements, consisting in the brothers Galeana, who not only offered their personal services, but men and arms.

The Galeanas were wealthy ranchers, and their names appear with honor by the side of that of Morelos, especially Hermenegildo, in whom kindness of heart and natural courage were joined.

2

The troops under Morelos grew in number by similar accessions, until he got together three thousand men.

By turning to account his relations with Captain Tabares, a subordinate of Paris, a royalist leader, he managed to send a part of his troops, commanded by Julian de Avila, to surprise the royalist officer in his camp, on the night of January 4, 1811, having won a complete victory.

Something similar would have happened at Acapulco, where he counted on the connivance of an artillery officer, Jose Gago, who had promised to give up the town; but Gago failed to keep his promise, and when Morelos in person attacked Acapulco, instead of meeting with facilities, he encountered unexpected resistance, and although he managed to make his way into the streets of the town, he was forced to withdraw, due to the approach of additional royalist troops.

3

On May 3rd. he began his march on Chilpancingo.

The insurgent vanguard, commanded by Galeana, turned aside to an hacienda belonging to the brothers Bravo, in search of food supplies. Leonardo, Miguel and Victor Bravo, and the latter's son, Nicolas, had had previous relations with the Galeanas, not only on account of similar social position and customs, but because they shared his sympathy for the cause of independence.

Hermenegildo Galeana, Nicolas Bravo and later, Mariano Matamoros, were each one as a host in himself to Morelos, and whenever the memory of that great general is honored, it is only right to associate with his name that of his best soldiers.

From August until November, Morelos did not rest. He directed the work of getting in supplies, mixing gunpowder and manufacture of all kinds of military equipment, having at the same time seen to the introduction of sound discipline and order.

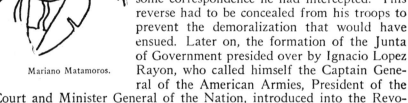

From that time large sums and great wealth began to pass through his hands, without his having ever appropriated any portion, however slight, for himself.

The imprisonment of Allende, Hidalgo and their companions came to his acknowledge from some correspondence he had intercepted. This reverse had to be concealed from his troops to prevent the demoralization that would have ensued. Later on, the formation of the Junta of Government presided over by Ignacio Lopez Rayon, who called himself the Captain General of the American Armies, President of the

Mariano Matamoros.

Court and Minister General of the Nation, introduced into the Revolution for Independence, the complications of party politics.

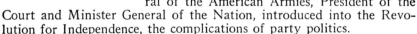

4

Due to the military successes gained by Morelos, the situation of the country was greatly altered in a little over a year, in a sense highly favorable to the cause of independence. In the secret instructions addressed to General Calleja by the Viceroy, Venegas, one may perceive the preoccupation of the Viceregal Government. In those instructions Venegas said that the City of Mexico was surrounded by insurgents, that supplies of food were running short, that communications were cut off and that the only roads comparatively open to traffic, those to Toluca and Texcoco, were in danger of obstruction. The advance guards of Morelos' army reached the city gates, and communications with Valladolid, Puebla and Tlaxcala, were only carried on under great difficulties.

Morelos had gone from victory to victory, from the southern coast into the center of the country, and had defeated all the royalist leaders who had opposed him. The Viceroy had to appeal to Felix Maria

Calleja, the destroyer of the first insurgent drive, the vanquisher of Hidalgo and the organizer of a creole army devoted to the Spanish cause, for aid.

V

THE SIEGE OF CUAUTLA

1

Morelos had fully made up his mind to offer formal resistance at Cuautla, and the insurgent garrison, under the command of Leonardo Bravo, threw out lines of trenches.

Morelos' troops, composed of the brigades under Galeana, Bravo and Matamoros, consisted of one thousand infantry and two thousand cavalry, who also fought, when necessary, on foot.

On February 18, 1812, Calleja began to surround the town with a view to taking it by storm.

At dawn the following day, Calleja decided to attack, and to that end divided his forces into four columns.

The honor of defending the position of greatest danger, was very justly granted to Hermenegildo Galeana, who defended the San Diego salient. Leonardo Bravo was in charge at the Monastery of Santo Domingo and Matamoros at the Hacienda de Buenavista. The Grenadier Corps attacked the San Diego breast-works. Galeana fought in the front rank, and slew one Captain Segarra with his own hand. The attacking force withdrew after heavy losses. The other attacking columns worked their way through the village by making holes in walls of houses until they came very close to the fortified redoubt, and for six hours, after the battle became general, both sides fought furiously. Colonels Conde de Casa Rul and Oviedo, and many officers, were mortally wounded, for which reason Calleja ordered a retreat.

2

The works for investment of the town began on March 5th.

On March 10th the bombardment of Cuautla began; it went on for four days and did not produce the effects desired on the besieged, who resisted it with great courage, constantly repairing the breaches made in their walls by the cannon.

Recourse was finally had to a blockade.

No one could believe that the siege could last for more than a month after investment began, for the climate of the region had to become daily more unhealthy for the besiegers.

The rains had to come in April, and late in March, and make the royalist position unsustainable.

Unfortunately, however, no further supplies were forthcoming, and the rainy season was that year abnormally delayed. Bravo, Tapia and Larios, insurgent leaders, did not succeed in getting a single grain of corn into Cuautla, and in spite of their pertinacity and efforts, they were repeatedly defeated.

3

On April 21st General Matamoros made a sortie from Cuautla by breaking through the enemies' lines.

Up to April 28th Morelos' men had already suffered the tortures of starvation, as provisions which had begun to fail a month before, were completely exhausted. The lack of food reached such a pitch, that vermin, the bark of trees, soap, or anything that looked as if it had any nourishment in it, was used as food.

On May 1st Calleja ordered his line commanders to transmit through the advance guards the decree of pardon issued by the Extraordinary General Cortes, in the name of the captive King, Ferdinand VII, and granted a four hours' truce for the surrender of the garrison or of an armed force belonging to it; but without admitting the surrender of any unarmed persons, nor women and children, to prevent the enemy from getting rid of useless mouths.

Morelos allowed the four hours' truce to pass without firing and even permitted certain manifestation of rejoicing, but never thought of availing himself of the pardon.

4

The sally of the besieged insurgents began on the 2nd of May at two o'clock in the morning; in the van, as always, rode Hermenegildo Galeana, with the pick of his infantry followed by many townspeople, women and children among them.

At half past four in the morning Calleja had not yet become aware of the enemy's movement, and he was, just at that time, writing to the Viceroy as follows: "It is highly desirable that the army leave this infernal country as soon as possible, and as regards my own health, it is so poor that if assistance arrive not in the short period I can hold out, it will be too late. Your Excellency will be pleased to answer telling me what to do."

And meanwhile the insurgents filed out of the town in silence, following the river bed, close to the heights of Zacatepec, on the north side of the town; on arriving at a barrier that obstructed the road, they were compelled to fire at the sixty grenadiers that defended it, forcing them to retreat and emerging into the open country, under the fire of lateral outposts. The sound of the firing roused the whole royalist army and called it to arms, and cavalry was told off to pursue the fugitives, who scattered on roads and trails, without recognizing one another and losing their bearings in the darkness, so that they were routed and dispersed. Morelos himself, closely pursued, very nearly fell into the hands of his enemies, and only managed to escape due to the devotion of his escort, which resisted until wiped out, in order to afford their leader a chance to escape.

Alaman, the historian, says: If at the siege of Cuautla victory fell to Calleja, the honor and glory fell to Morelos.

VI

THE THIRD CAMPAIGN

1

On June 4th, the defeat which Morelos' vanguard led by Galeana, inflicted on the royalist leader Cerro, at Citlala, dissipated the hopes of the Spanish party, which had relied on the annihilation of that great military leader.

Morelos swiftly made his way to Huajuapam, where Valerio Trujano was heroically defending his position, being besieged by Regules and Calderas, Royalist officers. Trujano had made up his mind to fall at his post and his only hope of salvation lay in assistance from Morelos, to whom he was able to make known his danger, by a messenger who made his may through the enemy's lines. For one hundred days Trujano's unconquerable resistance had lasted, only explicable because this brave insurgent had succeeded in infusing his own courage and resolution into all his men.

On July 13th, Morelos appeared in front of Huajuapam, without the Spanish commander noticing his proximity, so much so, that he was at loss to know to what to ascribe the manifestation of rejoicing and illuminations made by the besieged. While Trujano attacked from the front, Morelos fell upon the royalist rearguard, and obtained a victory.

2

On August 10th Morelos entered Tehuacan, and established himself in that town with three thousand six hundred men.

The first success achieved by Morelos due to this position was the defeat inflicted upon the Royalist Captain Joaquin Labaqui, who had left Vera Cruz with about four hundred men convoying a train with correspondence, and not knowing that Morelos had taken Tehuacan, he continued on his way to Mexico City. Morelos sent Nicolas Bravo to intercept him, and he took Labaqui by surprise at San Agustin del Palmar and routed him so effectually, that not one man of the royalist forces escaped death or capture, Labaqui himself having been among the slain. To the prisoners taken on that occasion were added, a few days later, others taken by Bravo at Puente del Rey.

3

The conduct observed by Nicolas Bravo in regard to these prisoners, who were almost three hundred in number, was so exceptional and remarkable, that one cannot pass it over without mention. A few days after the action at San Agustin del Palmar, the father of Nicolas Bravo who had been taken prisoner by the royalists at the Hacienda of San Gabriel, after the siege of Cuautla, was executed in the City of Mexico. The Viceregal Government delayed the excution of Leonardo Bravo, for some time, in the hope that his relatives would avail themselves of the pardon. Morelos authorized Nicolas Bravo to save his father's life by abandoning the insurrectionist party; but Nicolas Bravo refused to accept the pardon. Aside from this Morelos offered to exchange a group of Spanish prisoners in his power for Leonardo Bravo.

Nicolas Bravo.

Leonardo Bravo was executed by the garrote on September 13th, and when Morelos knew of his death, he notified is to Nicolas Bravo with the order to shoot the prisoners, by way of reprisals for the execution of his father. Bravo first thought of giving way to his natural resentment, and of obeying the orders received from his superior; but eventually decided to pardon the prisoners and set them free.

4

On the morning of October 29th Morelos with twelve hundred men appeared before Orizaba. His movements had been so swiftly and so skilfully made, that he found Orizaba defended by a scanty garrison. He at once took up a commanding position on the Borrego Hill, and ordered the attack, which only lasted two hours, because the royalist troops, who on this occasion fought bravely, retreated in disorder towards Cordoba.

Morelos managed to arrive in the vicinity of Oaxaca on November 25th.

Oaxaca was garrisoned by two thousand men. They had abundant ammunition and thirty six pieces of artillery.

By eleven o'clock in the morning of the 25th, Morelos was making ready to take the town by storm.

And at two o'clock in the afternoon, after a two hours' fight, the insurgents marched into the main plaza.

The occupation of Oaxaca and the work of organization and complete subjugation of the adjacent country, only detained Morelos until January 9, 1813. On that day he began his march on Acapulco.

5

Morelos only had three thousand men and very little artillery, without a single siege gun, while the royalists, commanded by an officer called Pedro Velez, and under cover of the fortifications and works of defense of the port and of the walls of the Castle of San Diego had ninety cannon and were assisted by several vessels that assured them supplies.

The investment of the town once completed by occupation of La Caleta, Morelos ordered the attack which took place at night with complete success.

All the fighting forces and many of the peaceful inhabitants sought refuge in the Castle of San Diego.

Finally, Commander Velez decided to surrender, and on August 20th the insurgents occupied the fort, after an honorable surrender.

On the other hand, in the territory controlled by the Viceroy, the royalists were engaged in preparations destined to change the course of events.

The time spent by Morelos on the siege of Acapulco enabled the Viceroy to reorganize his troops, to prepare a plan of campaign and to accumulate forces, which on going into action later, altered the progress of the war in a sense disadvantageous to Morelos.

6

The weakness of the Zitacuaro Junta, which did not succeed in constituting a solid center for action, compelled Morelos seriously to consider the final organization of a national government.

Ignacio Rayon had, as far back as 1812, framed the first draft of a Mexican Constitution and had sent it to Morelos so that the letter might study it and make any observations he thought appropriate.

Morelos found in Rayon's draft certain details that were not in accord with his own ideas, and although he agreed with it along general lines, he frankly rejected the proposal to keep the name of Ferdinand VII in the revolutionary program, even though only as matter of form.

And Morelos at last decided to convene a Congress.

VII

THE LAST CAMPAIGN

1

Morelos left Chilpancingo on November 7, 1813, to embark upon his fourth campaign, which turned out disastrously.

The insurgents gathered together and concentrated their forces, and made their appearance before Valladolid on December 22nd.

Calleja had ordered Brigadier General Llano to march with his troops from Toluca, with other reinforcements, to Acambaro, there to join the troops from Guanajuato commanded by Colonel Iturbide, to constitute, when all united, what was to be called the Army of the North.

The attack, begun on the 23rd by Morelos' orders and under the direct command of Matamoros, seemed likely to end in complete success.

But the sudden arrival of royalist reinforcements altered the aspect of the action.

That night took place the event that most unexpectedly cut short Morelos' military career. Iturbide having been commissioned to make a reconnoissance, he approached the enemy under cover of the darkness, with a force of less than four hundred men. Iturbide, disregarding the orders by him received, conceived a bold coup, and decided to take the insurgents by surprise at their camp on the Santa Maria heights, without being deterred either by natural obstacles, or the small number of his men, nor the twenty seven cannon that defended the enemy's camp. With lightning rapidity, each horse bearing a cavalry soldier and an infantry soldier perched up behind him, Iturbide climbed up to the fortified summit and fell upon the unsuspecting soldiers of independence.

The confusion, the surprise, the shades of night, everything combined against Morelos' troops, who even fought one another, and who, despite the efforts made by their officers to rally them, finally abandoned their positions in hopeless confusion.

2

The fourth campaign, hardly yet begun, thus practically came to an end, as the fight at Puruaran, where the insurgents offered resistance for the last time, and was really only the beginning of a battle, ended in a fresh and formidable defeat.

The rout was both complete and inglorious. The troops recruited with such great difficulty, in complete dispersion, the war material so slowly and laborious accumulated, fell into the enemy's hands; military reputation tarnished; the royalist officers and soldiers, impetuous and encouraged by the victory so swiftly won, and to crown misfortunes, Matamoros a prisoner. In vain did Morelos, to save the life of his glorious lieutenant, offer to exchange for him more than two hundred Spanish prisoners. Matamoros was executed at Valladolid.

3

In addition to the political complications to which the disaster gave rise among the partisans of independence, the military consequences alone were such that the revolution for independence seemed to have died out in abject failure, and this is what the Viceroy and partisans of Spanish domination thought.

After Puruaran, the campaign became nothing more than a pursuit on a large scale, concentrated on Morelos and the few men who yet followed him. The scouts told off by Calleja easily invaded the southern regions. Spanish militiamen from Guatemala crossed the frontier and entered the territory of New Spain through Tehuantepec. Morelos compelled to flee from every one of the towns he had but a short time before been in possession of, only had with him one hundred men composing his personal escort.

Rivalries, envy and personal hatred arose among the members of the Congress, and ill-will was directed at the Generalissimo as being the head.

His own Secretary, Rozains, was the person chosen to point out to Morelos the advisability of his resigning supreme command. At the first hint the military leader evinced his willigness to resign the rank of Generalissimo, and offered to serve as a private in the ranks.

Wihout any further military movements of interest, Morelos occupied his seat in Congress, and was later appointed a member of the Executive Power, but without command of troops. In this capacity he accompanied the errant congress on its wanderings.

After the death of Matamoros, followed that of Hermenegildo Galeana, who fell fighting in battle like a brave man, which increased the gloomy sadness of the outlook. Then Morelos said: "they have taken from me my two arms; I am worth nothing now."

On the other hand, Calleja had risen to the office of Viceroy.

4

The officials of the independent Government that had emanated from the Constitution of 1814, free of all administrative preoccupations, as they had not at their direct disposal forces of any kind, yet had more than enough reason to worry, due to the persistence displayed in capturing them by certain royalist officers, particularly Iturbide.

Aside from this, the desire to make use of the prestige and moral authority inherent in every organized body having the name and outward appearance of government, made them decide, in an endeavor to establish order and agreement between the various groups fighting for independence, to transfer the seat of power to Tehuacan.

The direction and military command of the expedition were entrusted to Morelos.

5

Morelos, at the beginning, succeeded in confusing his pursuers. He left for Uruapan with all his men on September 29th.

On the night of the 2nd November he finally crossed the Mezcala River at the Tenango ford. After allowing his worn-out men to rest for a day at Texmelucan, he proceeded to Tezmalaca, where he was overtaken and defeated by the royalists.

Morelos, without even a small and resolute group to escort him, found himself in the midst of the fleeing fugitives and had to leave his horse, which instead of being of use to him, was but a hindrance on those bush and scrub covered ridges, lacking even in passable trails.

He vainly attempted to hide in the scrub.

He stopped for a moment to take off his spurs to make his way more easily through the tangled bush, and finally found himself alone and unarmed; he was captured by a lieutenant of the royalist company at Tepecoacuilco, called Matias Carranco, who was known to Morelos, as he had formerly served under him.

6

At all the towns and villages they passed through on their way to Mexico, the multitude was moved by the same curiosity to get a good look at Morelos. Before arriving, they stopped at Tlalpan from 5 o'clock in the afternoon of the 21st November until the early hours of the following morning.

From the very moment that the first chief of the insurrection fell into the power of the Viceregal authorities, no one could doubt the fate that awaited him. Not only the laws actually in force, confirmed by decrees and special orders, but also precedents, the severe and unbending character of Calleja and the well-known personal qualities of Morelos, everything contributed to lead him to a death there was no escaping. So that the prosecution was nothing more than a series of legal, military and religious formalities.

At six o'clock in the morning on December 22nd, accompanied in a carriage by Father Salazar and an officer belonging to Concha's division, and followed by an escort of soldiers from the same regiment, Morelos left the Citadel in Mexico City for San Cristobal Ecatepec, where he was executed.

VIII

THE POLITICAL WORK OF MORELOS

1

The great significance of Morelos to Independence makes it necessary to inquire into his work and his political ideas. The fundamental acts of his action in these fields, which must be credited to him as personal achievements, in addition to his great deserts as a military leader, are the institution of the Congress at Chilpancingo and his plans for the reorganization of the country.

The results he hoped to obtain from the meeting of that Congress, were the following:

I.—The formation of a central authority that would be capable of organizing the forces of the Insurgents.

II.—To avow the program of the Revolution, by erasing from insurgent banners the name of Ferdinand VII and openly declaring for independence.

III.—To constitute an official body to represent the Nation.

IV.—To enact or legally ratify provisions in regard to distribution of property, abolition of slavery and assessment of taxes.

V.—To make through lawful channels any general declarations as to equality, liberty, good government and plans for a new regime.

2

As a result of the meeting of a legislative body, other elements arose within the Revolution that modified the course pursued by it. The deputies to the Congress at Chilpancingo had to be appointed apart from the military element. Professional and semi-professional men, who had, while the revolution had a warlike character only, played modest rôles as Secretaries, drafters of proclamations, secret agents,

Morelos and the members of the 1814 Congress. After Painting by F. de P. Mendoza.

propagandists and even members of the Junta, then rose to positions of prominence within the Revolution.

This new element, among whom were glorious representatives, like Doctor Coss and Quintana Roo, contributed the force of its ideals, informed by the scanty culture of their time and environment; it had imbibed its knowledge from forbidden French gazettes and books, as it were the bearers of the torches that had lit the French Revolution.

3

The Revolution reached its highest point in the field of ideas, when the country was enabled to hear the following words: "The Congress of Anahuac, lawfully open in the City of Chilpancingo, in North America, on behalf of the provinces thereof solemnly declares that owing to present circumstances in Europe it has recovered the exercise of its usurped sovereignty; that, this being so subordination to the Spanish throne has for ever been broken off and dissolved, and that it is free to enact the laws it shall think fit for better and easier settlement of internal matters.

"Sovereignty emanates directly from the people. Laws must extend to all alike, without exceptions or privileges. As a good law is above all men, those which our Congress shall enact must be such as to compel obedience and patriotism, moderate opulence and penury, and so augment the salary of the poor, that they may improve their habits, and do away with ignorance, rapine and theft.

"That the people shall pay no tithes other than what their devotion may prompt them to give." That is to say, that coercion be abolished for payment of Church taxes, thus beginning the separation of Church and State.

4

Aside from this, the legislative assembly framed the Constitution of 1814, which was already a liberal and democratic law.

Morelos, however, desired to go further still. He claimed to be commissioned for reconquest and new government of America, and when he spoke of new government, he not only had in mind the total destruction of the old regime, but the erection of an original system, adapted to the customs and needs of the country. This is precisely the second part of his political work. Some of it he did succeed in putting into practice, when he organized the provinces he managed to bring under control and on ordering the confiscation and distribution of property belonging to Spaniards and creoles addicted to the King, and also by modifying the system of taxation.

5

The instructions to insurgent leaders contained in the papers in the record of the case against Rayon afford an idea of his plans.

The fundamental points were as follows:

All rich men, members of the nobility and higher officials to be considered enemies, and so soon as a town was taken they were to be deprived of their property to be distributed, half among the poorer residents and half for the military treasury.

When distributing such property among the poor, to endeavor that none be enriched and that all receive assistance. From such measures furniture and jewelry were not excluded, nor Church funds.

All royal customs houses, city gates and royal buildings to be demolished, all archives and records to be burnt, except parish records, and all imported goods to be burnt likewise, not excepting luxuries and tobacco.

All *haciendas* including arable land of an area exceeding two leagues, to be broken up for small holdings and subdivision of property.

The works of rich *hacienda* owners, mines and sugar mills, likewise to be destroyed, without respecting anything except grain and staple foodstuffs.

As will be seen, the above instructions had two aims, one strictly military, and the other political and social. They are of great scope and importance, as a forecast of the radical tendencies of modern revolution.

IX

MINA

1

The movement for independence seemed to be over. The new Viceroy, Apodaca, endeavored to achieve final pacification of the country, by pardoning insurgent leaders. And with the exception of Vicente Guerrero, they almost all submitted under pressure of necessity. Then it was that Mina made his appearance.

Francisco Javier Mina was born in Spain, in 1789.

He enlisted as a volunteer in the army of his country, then invaded by the French. He was wounded and taken prisoner to France.

He returned to Spain when the King, Ferdinand the Seventh, was restored to the throne, but declared himself an enemy of absolutism and organized a revolutionary movement.

On being discovered he was driven into exile and lived first in France and then in England.

In London he became acquainted with Lord Holland, a nobleman celebrated for love of liberty, and also frequented the society of many Spanish-Americans who passionately advocated the independence of their respective countries. And above all, one who was highly eloquent and persuasive, Friar Servando de Teresa y Mier, "in whose speech reasons advanced for the emancipation of his country burnt like fire." Father Mier was a rebellious priest, who had been imprisoned and exiled for attempting to make of the legend of the Virgin of Guadalupe, a patriotic allegory.

2

His intercourse with all those enthusiasts on behalf of freedom led Mina to construe the revolutions in Mexico, Venezuela, and Buenos Ayres, and the restlessness of Spanish constitutionalists, as but different aspects of a single historical and political process. On both Continents a fight by liberty against absolutism, as personified by Ferdinad VII, was going on.

Mina decided to carry on in America that war that he had in the Peninsula sworn to wage against absolutism. Lord Holland put him in touch with an American General, Winfield Scott, who hastened to point out to him the ready assistance that an expedition designed for liberation of Mexico, could count on in the United States. Several peers belonging to the Liberal Party helped him to charter a ship, and to obtain arms, ammunition, clothing and also the first nucleus of an expeditionary force. And the result was that Mina and Mier, with a company composed of over two dozen Spanish, English and Italian soldiers, set sail for America on May 5, 1816, fully decided to second the campaign begun by Father Hidalgo in New Spain.

3

Mina published at Galveston a manifesto setting forth the reasons that induced him to fight Ferdinand VII, and in which he pointed out —by way of defense against the charge of being a traitor—that Mex-

ico's independence enjoyed the sympathy of all liberal minded and cultured Spaniards. And obvious proof that this was his true mental attitude, was by him afforded on his trip to New Orleans. Local merchants at that place offered him money, arms and ammunition for an
expedition to seize Pensacola, in Florida; but when he realized that
it was only a case of establishing a new pirate lair to attack Spanish
commerce, he refused and said "that he waged war on the Spanish
tyrant and not on Spaniards."

Mina took advantage of the fact of touching at that port, to ad-
dress a proclamation to the Mexican soldiers. It was not his intention,
he said—to conquer the country, but quite the contrary, to help it to
become independent. "I am" he added, "the same Mina who began in
Spain the method of small bands and guerrillas and organized a division that kept the enemy pretty busy. When Ferdinand, with all the
pomp and circumstance of a conqueror, invaded Madrid, imprisoned
the representatives of the Nation, and abolished the Constitution, which
had cost so much blood and so many costly sacrifices; when he banish-
ed virtue and patriotism and bound them in chains... I was the first
who dared resist him. The cry of all Spaniards with reasoning faculties, is that America must win her independence from Spain. The slavery of the latter coincided with the conquest of the former, for the King
had to pay mercenaries a wage. Let America be separated, and the
colossus of despotism will them be humbled, because through independent of it, the King would not be independent of the Nation. Mexico
is the very heart of the colossus and is the land whose independence
we must most ardently desire."

4

He reached our coasts on April 15, 1817, landed at the mouth of
the River Santander and thereupon undertook a fatiguing march, suffering hardships from lack of water and going a long way round because his guide had lost his way. He reached Soto La Marina, and de
la Garza, a royalist officer, retreated because he had not sufficient
troops to face him.

At the Hacienda del Cojo he seized seven hundred horses belonging
to Quintero, a royalist. The Government assembled troops to attack
him, but Mina won the battles of Valle del Maiz, Peotillos and Los
Arrastres, all three in June, 1817, having therein defeated Villaseñor,
Armiñan and Ordoñez, captured arms and supplies and enhanced his
own fame.

With increased forces he attacked the city of Leon, but was repulsed
and then proceeded to the Fort of "El Sombrero" where an illustrious

insurgent, Pedro Moreno, was intrenched. Marshal Liñan, just out from Spain, besieged the fort with 2,500 picked and well-armed men and 14 guns, and attempted to storm the fort, having been repulsed by the insurgents. Mina on his side made a sortie on the night of the 7th August, in order to obtain provisions and communicate with another insurgent, Torres, but was driven back. He managed to sally forth the next night, however, and to get together a convoy at the Los Remedios Fort, but Rafols cut off a part of it. And finally, on August 20th, Liñan succeeded in taking the fort.

5

Mina and Moreno continued to fight Liñan at the Los Remedios Fort, as he marched thither to attack them. Mina managed to make a sortie and after hard fighting marched on San Luis de la Paz. He was caught up almost at once by a strong royalist force commanded by Orrantia, who routed him. Mina kept going, pursued hotfoot, by Orrantia but was caught up by the latter at the Venadito ranch, where Mina, thinking that he was safe, had lain down to sleep for a few hours. He was taken prisoner October 27th.

The news of Mina's capture was celebrated with great rejoicing by the authorities of all the provinces.

Orrantia was promoted to the rank of colonel; the trooper who captured Mina was also promoted and a reward of 500 pesos was bestowed on him. The Viceroy, Apodaca, was honored with the title of Conde de Venadito.

On November 11th of the same year, Mina was executed, being shot in the back as a traitor, in front of the Fort of Los Remedios.

6

Mina's campaign on behalf of the independence of Mexico was a dramatic episode thrown into relief by the personal prestige and the reckless courage of the young and dashing guerrilla fighter from Navarre, but could not be directly connected with the social movement and the impulses of Mexican insurgents.

Mina was a champion of liberty, who first fought in defense of his country against the French invaders and after that rose against the despotism of Ferdinand VII. His attitude as a Spaniard who had revolted against the King made him sympathise with the cause of the American creoles, who were also rebels against the Crown.

He succeeded in making his way into Mexico, but his troops were largely composed of adventurers, one might almost say filibusters and soldiers of fortune. His lack of knowledge of the land was another great obstacle. He had great difficulty in getting into touch with the various groups of Mexican insurgents, who were just at that time in a very depressed and disorganized condition. Mexican insurgents received Mina coldly, on account of his troops which included many foreigners, his position as a Spaniard and as a soldier, torn by the duties of nationality on the one hand, and the imperative needs of war, on the other. On his side, Mina suffered by reason of the contrast between his aspirations and the reality. To him the political aspect of Mexico's independence, was but the action of the creoles or the liberal middle class against the tyranny of a bad king.

He was a brave and generous fighter. He embarked on an adventure bordering on sacrifice, in behalf of a dream of liberty and passionate hatred of oppression. This is why, though Spain refrains from counting Mina among her favorite sons, Mexico includes him among her liberators.

X

GUERRERO AND ITURBIDE

1

Vicente Guerrero was born in the village of Tixtla, now called Ciudad Guerrero, in August, 1782, of Indian and peasant parents.

He began his military career in 1810.

His distinguishing quality being faithfulness, Morelos trusted him and instructed him to raise troops and to diffuse the idea of revolution.

He took part in the battle of Tesmalaca and escorted the Congress to Tehuacan. When the Revolution began to decline, he sustained a defeat in the Los Naranjos Canyon; having broken his way through, he was very nearly slain, but shortly afterwards managed to turn the tables in another battle.

He was forced to fall back to the coast, after a number of raids. Proclaimed Commander in chief of the Armies of the South, he had to hide for a number of days with only a few soldiers and suffering all manner of hardships. He had cannon cast from church bells melted down, and got in touch with the Commanders of Michoacan and Guanajuato to carry on the campaign.

Deserted by fortune, betrayed, without arms or funds, he was, during the time of gloom and depression, the sole supporter of the cause of independence; and then his qualities, such as courage, wisdom, sagacity, untiring activity and heroic tenacity, stood out all the more strongly.

2

The story goes that Pedro Guerrero, Vicente's father, had from the beginning sided with the royalists and fought against the forces commanded by his son.

The Viceroy assumed that the presence of his father would have some effect on the leader and authorized Pedro to go and see him, to offer him a pardon and induce him to submit. Guerrero was deeply moved on seeing his father whom he regarded with deep affection and veneration, and heard him say how the Spanish Government would recognize his military rank and bestow on him a substantial sum of money; the sad position of his wife and daughter was pointed out to him. The father kneeling before his son and embracing his knees, prayed him to return to the bosom of his family and accept the offer of the Government. The leader heard his father out calmly, and even wept with him, and without answering his supplications called his soldiers and said to them: "Companions, this old man is my father; he comes to offer me positions and rewards, on behalf of the Spaniards. I have always respected my father; but my country comes first." He kissed his hand and besought him never to seek him out again, if the purpose of his visits were to try to convince him to accept a pardon.

3

The final events of the war of independence are a complicated series of political manoeuvers which have not yet been satisfactorily cleared up. Rather than historical facts, they seem to be the chronicle of a series of adventures, mixed with conspiracies, plots, personal intrigues and the activities of masonic lodges and political parties in process of formation.

Iturbide, as a royalist officer, always treated the insurgents with excessive harshness, and detracted from the brilliancy of his victories by acts of cruelty and greed for wealth, to enrich himself; this drew upon him an accusation by several of the principal business houses of Queretaro and Guanajuato, for which reason he was deprived of his command and summoned to answer the charges brought against him. As he was clever and astute, he became a friend of the Prepositor of the Church of La Profesa, Doctor Matias Monteagudo, and even with great devotion attended a spiritual retreat, in order to obtain recommendations for the *Oidor* or Magistrate, Bataller, who as Auditor General had to handle the case brought against him.

4

The insurrection had been brought under control and only Vicente Guerrero and Pedro Ascencio remained in the south. It is said that the Viceroy, Apodaca, received a letter from Ferdinand VII, ordering him to do everything in his power to make this kingdom independent of Spain, by proclaiming as a basis, the union of Mexicans and Spaniards and the Catholic religion, and that he, due to the pressure brought to bear on him in Spain by the Constitution, thought of coming to these dominions, where he expected to find vassals more loyal and obedient.

The Viceroy, in strict secrecy, called together a few friends to consult them in regard to the best course to follow so as to carry out the plan proposed. These worthies began to meet at the Church of La Profesa, at secret meetings presided over by Monteagudo. The meetings followed ever closer on one another; they were attended by many members of the clergy, great landowners, merchants, public servants and military officers.

As soon as these meetings began at la Profesa, Iturbide conferred with the Viceroy in his palace, and was by him appointed Commander in Chief of the South and of the Acapulco region.

5

Apodaca gave out that Iturbide was going to wipe out the only rebels left in the south; Vicente Guerrero, Pedro Ascencio and the bands led by Montes de Oca and Guzman, and placed him in command of the largest army that had until then been got together; Iturbide cleverly increased the number of his troops, ever helped by the Viceroy, who denied him nothing he asked for, whether more men, ammunition or money.

Iturbide forthwith displayed all his activity to win over Guerrero and his men, and invited them to an interview to put an end to the war; but Guerrero distrusted him, knowing as he did, what bloody outrages he had always committed on the insurgents; but Iturbide eventually, by clever go-betweens, managed to induce Vicente Guerrero to adhere to the plan he had drawn up, and so he informed the

Viceroy Apodaca, who answered him, highly pleased, among other reasons, "that he had desired nothing so much as the restoration of general peace, in accordance with the orders and pious intentions of the King."

6

Iturbide showed great cleverness in getting a printing press in Puebla to print the Plan of La Profesa, amended in the sense of independence, by Licenciado Juan Jose Espinosa de los Monteros; he obtained over twenty five thousand pesos from Bishop Cabañas and deceived and misled the Viceroy to induce him to order the departure from Mexico city of the mule train called the Manila train, which was taking to Acapulco over five hundred thousand pesos, being the proceeds from the sale of the goods brought by the Manila Galleon. He was already in agreement with Lieutenant General Vicente Guerrero to join him and proclaim Mexico's freedom; at Iguala was published a proclamation, the essential articles of which are union between Europeans and Mexicans, the preservation of the Catholic religion, no other to be tolerated, and the establishment of a constitutional monarchy under the title of Empire of Mexico, Ferdinand VII to be called to occupy the throne; but that should he not come personally to Mexico to take the oath of observance of a Constitution to be enacted by a Congress, the *Infantes*, his brothers, and failing them the Archduke Charles of Austria or any other member of a reigning family to be chosen by that future Council, would successively be called.

These principles were called the "Three Guaranties" and a white, green and red flag was adopted.

This plan was proclaimed in the midst of wild enthusiasm and rejoicing, and the whole of the large army encamped at Iguala swore to uphold it and to shed their blood if need be.

7

The Plan of Iguala was disavowed by the Viceroy Apodaca and those Spaniards who were upholders of absolutism.

The royalist officers at first signified their adherence to the viceregal government; but little by little they deserted its ranks and went over to the independent side. Among these officers, some of whom later took a prominent part in politics, we should mention Jose Joaquin de Herrera, Antonio Lopez de Santa Anna and Anastasio Bustamante.

The insurgents also hastened to rally round the tricolored flag: Nicolas Bravo, Ramon Rayon, Guadalupe Victoria and several others.

Within a few months insurrection had spread from north to south throughout the colony.

The officers of the regiments that had come from Spain ascribed the spread of the revolution to Apodaca's blundering; they revolted, broke into the palace and deposed the Viceroy and appointed Francisco Novella in his place.

Several important cities had fallen into the hands of the Independent party: Monterrey, Durango, Guadalajara, Queretaro, Valladolid and Cuernavaca.

Early in August the last Spanish Viceroy to reign in New Spain, Juan O'Donoju, landed at Vera Cruz.

Iturbide flew down to meet him and they had an interview in the city of Cordoba. The result was the treaty bearing the name of that city, confirming the Plan of Iguala, but suppressing therefrom one

Swearing of the Plan of Iguala by Iturbide and his officers, March 2, 1821.

provision, which was later to redound to the benefit of Iturbide himself; where reference was made to the person who was to be substituted for Ferdinand VII, should he or some member of the Spanish Royal Family not accept the throne of New Spain, the article "or some other person a member of a reigning house in Europe," was altered to read "him whom the Cortes for the Empire shall appoint."

Meanwhile, the independent troops began to assemble round the capital, to lay siege to it, as Novella refused to recognize O'Donoju, because the latter had signed the Treaty of Cordoba.

But in the face of the imposing aspect of the Army of the Three Guaranties, and of the Viceroy's threats, Novella was compelled to throw open the City gates.

8

On September 27, 1821, the houses of Mexico City were adorned with flowers and bunting, palm leaves and tapestries, in which shone the colors of the flag of Iguala.

At ten o'clock in the morning Iturbide rode in through the Belen Gate, on a black charger followed by the officers of his staff. At the corner of the Monastery of San Francisco, the City Council awaited him, under a triumphal arch, and the oldest alderman delivered to him a set of golden keys, emblems of the City. He reached the Palace, where he received the congratulations of the authorities and corporations, and forthwith came out on to the balcony, in the company of O'Donoju, to witness the grand parade of the troops.

Sixteen thousand men marched past.

Iturbide issued a proclamation whereof these were the most notable words:

"Now ye know how freedom is won; to you falls the task of achieving your own happiness."

The first stage of the movement for independence had been consummated.

XI

LITERATURE OF THE EPOCH OF INDEPENDENCE

1

The revolution in its early stages had to elaborate its own ideology and to spread the new doctrines.

We shall attempt to summarize the outstanding features of this intellectual movement.

The revolution of 1810 brought with it the rise of an insurgent press. Between 1810 and 1812, the Royalists who carried on their propaganda against the revolution, mainly by pamphlets, issued several periodical publications: Beristain edited *"El Verdadero Ilustrador Americano,"* by way of answer to an insurgent sheet of the same name; Fermin Reigadas, *"El Aristarco;"* Ramon Roca, *"El Amigo de la Patria,"* and a short lived-literary magazine, called the *"Museo Mexicano."*

Freedom of thought, sanctioned by the constitution of Cadiz in Mexico provoked a passing outburst of journalism in 1812. The *"Diario de México"* greeted "Freedom of the Press, the foundation of political and civil liberty."

2

Literature could not let the revolution pass by unnoticed. If letters had, during the colonial period and New Spain, been a field almost exclusively within the province of churchmen, and cultivated by them in the privacy of their studies, without close touch with the popular mind, their physiognomy and character was destined to undergo great modifications in the period under review. Political literature was born of the heat of the struggle. In Mexican letters a transcendent change took place, which coincided with the fight for independence; the awakening of national sentiment. Religious literature kept almost silent, and satire was rampant. During the course of the War of Independence poetry became epic.

In Mexico, wrote Luis G. Urbina, people lived and sang in an old-fashioned way. The education imparted by the jesuits left a deep imprint on the soul of Spanish colonists, on creoles and on those mestizos who had been through the university of Mexico, where metaphysics swamped the thought of man in misty twilight, and dialectics were as a web of reasoned out subtleties. Scholastic philosophy reigned in all its splendor. Aristotle and St. Thomas divided between them spiritual lordship. Plato was excluded from those halls of learning, and sought refuge in the minds of certain idealistic thinkers. By the time that the eighteenth century had run half its course, the jesuits, consummate Latinists and theologians, had strongly influenced the mental leanings of the inhabitants of New Spain.

3

Friar Manuel Navarrete expressed the delights of the tenderness and serenity of his mind. These are the qualities that distinguish his poetry.

In Navarrete, among the flourishes of highly conventional and artificial rhetoric, which at that time constituted the primary element of poetry, we are surprised to find vivid, vigorous, animated and sincere outbursts.

The feeling reveals itself, and breaks forced patterns and tinsel ornamentation. Under the sonorous and mellifluous fabric of conventional versification, there beats the heart of a man, tender and passionate. Rich and sincere imagination shines out amongst the glass beads of delicate and graceful erotism.

Melendez Valdes exercises an almost complete influence over Navarrete's poetic manner. "Neo-classical taste, delicate to the point of insincerity, symmetrical to the point of monotony, and cold to the point of tediousness, pervades almost all the work of that Mexican Friar."

4

The insurgents founded at Guadalajara, in 1811, a periodical called *"El Despertador Americano,"* with Dr. Francisco Severo Maldonado as editor. He was an extraordinarily eccentric individual and his arrogance and presumption were unbounded. At bottom a restless mind, a superior intelligence that embraced what was at that time undiscovered country, and who, in a province of New Spain, forestalled the doctrines of Fourier and Saint Simon.

The secret band called the *"Guadalupes,"* who advocated independence, seized a printing press in the City of Mexico in a manner that reads like a page out of a novel. It was sent to the insurgent camp, and Dr. Cos, in May 1812, founded *"El Ilustrador Americano"* to which two other famous patriots contributed: Ignacio Lopez Rayon and Andres Quintana Roo, the latter a venerable figure in the history of Mexico. When he was merely a practicing student in the law office of an eminent lawyer and enemy of the revolution, Dr. Agustin Pomposo Fernandez de San Salvador, he won over a son of the latter and together they went off to the insurgent camp. Leona Vicario, the lawyer's ward, also fled with her fiancé, young Quintana Roo. They were married and lived the most delightful romance that can be found in the annals of the revolution.

Quintana Roo while in the insurgent camp founded the *"Seminario Patriótico."* He published articles of all kinds: proclamations, manifestos in a style eloquent, warm and vigorous. He was quick to think, expressive and forceful in what he said.

Quintana Roo had already blossomed forth as a poet, in an ode published in the *"Diario de México,"* on January 14, 1810, a piece of classical verse, in the fashion of the times.

5

The constitution was sworn on September 30 1812. The decree for freedom of the press was proclaimed on the 5th of October following.

Three days after the liberal decree was published, a celebrated weekly, the most famous of the period of independence, made its appearance. Its name was *"El Pensador Mexicano"* (The Mexican Thinker.) The editor was a clever, bold and courageous man: Joaquin Fernandez de Lizardi

He wrote the following words:

"If we had always had a protecting government, ministers that were wise, politic and lovers of humanity, that had not bound the bands of the Americans, but opened wide to

Jose Joaquin Fernandez de Lizardi.

them the methods of industry and the resources of nature to enable them to make a living with less difficulty; if the Indians had been treated as what they are and not as they were desired to be, if they had been granted the privileges of manhood, by removing from them exemptions granted to neophytes, exemptions which have done them enormous harm, as I can prove if necessary; if we had, lastly, enjoyed the general benefits of that freedom which the nation has just bestowed upon us, I won't say Hidalgo, but not even Lucifer himself, could have assembled in so short a time the many bands which sprang up as insurrection broke out."

Jose Joaquin Fernandez was born in the City of Mexico in 1774.

When he finished his Latin grammar studies he entered the College of San Ildefonso.

Ignacio M. Altamirano tells us that Fernandez de Lizardi was wont to visit the house of Josefa Ortiz de Dominguez, at that time living in Mexico City with her husband, and that in conversation with that distinguished woman he often discussed the subject of Mexico's independence.

6

Prior to the proclamation of the Constitution of 1812, every piece of written matter intended for publication was subject to civil and ecclesiastical censorship; no book could be printed pertaining to matters in the Americas, without the previous consent of the Council of the Indies, and Alaman himself tells us "that Clavijero was unable to obtain permission to print in Spain, his history of Mexico, and was compelled to publish it in Italy, in the language of that country; "lastly, no books printed in the Peninsula or any other European country, dealing with happenings on the new Continent, could be sent to the Americas without the permission of the competent authorities.

Fernandez de Lizardi started publication of a highly interesting journal in which he set forth ideas very advanced for that time, and which bore a name later applied to the author: *"El Pensador Mexicano"* (The Mexican Thinker.)

In the two first numbers of that sheet he proved how necessary and advisable was freedom of the press, and enthusiastically praised that right granted by the Constitution.

From number three to number seven, under the title of "Essay Number Two, on the Exaltation of the Spanish Nation, and the Overthrow of Ancient Despotism" he published a series of articles in which he denounced the injustices of the viceregal government, the abuses, the outrages and infamous acts committed by mayors and justices, and subdelegates; the courage of his opinions reached the point of proving, in number five, that in spite of the sovereigns, there was no civilized nation that had had a worse government than ours, the worst in America, nor vassals that had suffered more severely from the chains of tyranny.

7

"His most celebrated work" says Altamirano, on the subject of the writings of the Thinker—is the novel called *"El Periquillo Sarniento."*

This novel was written in the times of the Viceroys and of the Inquisition, and yet it is a terrible satire against that backward and ignorant society, against the then prevailing fanaticism, against the vicious and unwholesome education imparted, against those vices that would have devoured the life blood of this youthful nation, had not the upheaval produced by revolution come to its salvation.

"El Periquillo Sarniento" is the "Thinker's" most popular and most important work and consequently the one worthiest of attention.

On this work, as on others written by Lizardi, critics have vented their fury, hatred has assumed every form from religious to literary, and the retrograde party was unable to repress its indignation when that book arose like a victorious banner, after their efforts to brand it as beneath contempt. *"El Periquillo Sarniento,"* in the style of Gil Blas, and with reminiscences of that genial rogue, Guzman de Alfarache, or of the Lazarillo de Tormes, is a great Mexican book. It is a bold personification of society as it was at that time.

8

We cannot omit to mention another sheet that was published almost at the same time as the preceding: *"El Juguetillo"* by Carlos Maria de Bustamante.

Bustamante's paper was received almost as enthusiastically as Fernandez de Lizardi's.

"As simple and plain in style as the "Thinker," but rather more careful and elaborate, is Bustamante; and yet his learning, his profession, what he had read, served to embellish his style and develop his ideas. But what is most attractive in the articles that appeared in *"El Juguetillo,"* is that from all of them arises like a perfume, his love of country. The mistakes, hesitancies, and contradictions into which Carlos Maria Bustamante occasionally fell, never obscured the strength and purity of his patriotism."

9

In 1817, with Mina's expedition, came an insurgent book that had already caused a sensation in Spain. The author, who had written it in London, brought it out to Mexico in his revolutionary baggage. The title of that book was "A History of the Revolution of New Spain." It purported to be by one Jose Guerra, a doctor of the University of Mexico City. Under that pseudonym was concealed a notable author, a patriot and an adventurer out of the pages of fiction; Friar Servando Teresa de Mier.

Friar Servando de Teresa y Mier.

He was a passionate student of the encyclopedists. And the spectacle of the French revolution and of the independence of the United States of America, had engendered in his heart the love of liberty.

The life and works of Father Mier placed him in the front rank as an intellectual of the revolution.

XII

IDEOLOGY OF INDEPENDENCE

1

The revolution for independence, judged by its essentially political aspects, has always been looked upon merely as a struggle to throw off foreign rule, almost as an offset to the conquest, to restore to Indians nationality its usurped sovereignty. These features did undoubtedly exist, but were not the only ones, nor were they decisive.

The political aspect has stood out more prominently, because independence began and was consummated according to the formulas of a political uprising, of an impulse of insurgency against the Spanish authorities and to obtain the independence of Mexico as a province of the Spanish Empire and to create a free organism with a new nationality.

But there are besides, at bottom, other causes and other impulses that have not been properly taken into account. The economic factor is not the only one involved, but also all those factors bound up with economy, as understood in its broad and complete aspect of human activity that sustains institutions making for permanent culture.

2

At first glance the movement for independence seems to be a rebellion by creoles with the support of the Indian masses, to free Mexico from Spanish rule.

As regards military activities the distinction would have to be drawn between insurgents and royalists. In yet another aspect, the fight would seem to be one between the partisans of moderate or constitutional monarchy and the insurgents, and after that between constitutional monarchy and the republic, of centralization against federalism and between conservatives and liberals.

If we apply the method we have essayed for the study of previous periods, we shall find the thread that is to guide us.

The movement for independence continued evolution of nationality, and at the same time reflected renovation of the cultures taking form in the territory of Mexico, and the pressure of outside factors. The ancient feudal theocratic regime, with absolute monarchy by divine right, a hereditary nobility of military origin and with religious institutions exercising civil power, had passed through its period of growth and maximum development, and was definitively declining, to give way to a new era of organization.

3

The ruling classes lose power due to their own growth and opposing tendencies of concentration and centralization. The movement for democracy, engendered by the Reformation and the Renaissance, is politically victorious in England, where the foundations of the new regime of constitutional government are laid, rooted in the industrial system of modern times (coal, iron, steam engines, cotton spinning, spread of silver currency, exchange and credits, middle class with small investors and merchants, and firearms and horses for the many.) From that same movement arose the independence of the United States, assisted by the monarchical governments of France and Spain.

4

National types.—Period, beginning of century and War of Independence.— Infantry soldier.

These same phenomena are reflected in Spain and even farther away, considerably distorted, but still with efficient vitality, in Spanish America, Colonial isolation was of no avail; systems of production, cartesian philosophy, revolutionary literature, had to come to Mexico, wrapped in the fashions of French decorations and of the styles of academicism and of so-called neo-classical art. The encyclopedias and freemasonry laughed at frontiers and evaded ecclesiastical persecution.

The strength of the Spanish monarchy waned due to the expansion of its dominions; because it threw off the prestige of its divine origin and close alliance with religion; due to the unavoidable decline of institutions which did not change in accord with the rhythm of the times; due to the supremacy of other types of culture flourishing in other countries. The monarchical State could no longer fulfill its essential functions of maintaining order, vigilance and affording protection, and when it lost its sea power it was practically cut off from its dependencies. This is why the first step of the revolution was political emancipation, the separation of Mexico from Spain; the drive of renovation had attacked the most vulnerable point of the whole system.

For that same reason the work remained unfinished. Class renovation was only carried out by eliminating the monarchy, the hereditary nobility and official bureaucracy directly bound up with the Crown.

The other two dominant elements were left intact and became even stronger than they had before been; the clergy and the great landowners, face to face with a State that was weaker and less exacting.

5

According to the opinions now held, the middle classes rose in rebellion late in the eighteenth century, as the advance guard of the masses, in the compaign against the old regime, with a new ideology, and with ideas of its own. The eighteenth century man of the middle classes proclaimed the reign of reason as against the reign of religion and superstition, and was an optimist who believed in the force of progress, in the moral virtues of man.

By natural law was understood the régime that prevailed in some age prior to feudalism when mankind knew not yet the law of the strongest. The conviction prevailed that the State, the social order, had begun as the result of an agreement between men, the result of a "social contract," and that as soon as the regime of a society failed to meet the requirements of the citizens, the oppressed were entitled to revolt against the existing order.

In its struggle to overthrow the régime of force of feudalism, the bourgeoisie of the eighteenth century sympathized with the people and waved the banner of equality, liberty and fraternity. But the man of the middle class owned property of his own, he possessed something, and his ideology was rooted in the fact of such possession. Proud of his property and of his middle class culture, he was an individualist.

6

It has been asserted that the emancipation of the Spanish-American peoples was directed by the creole landowning class, who wished to throw off the economic and political yoke of Spain. This is only partly true, in so far as concerns the consummation of independence, and only if we look upon the revolution in Mexico as terminated by the action of Iturbide. It would be more accurate to say that the Revolution in Spanish America and in Mexico, reflected a world-wide revolutionary movement, but with delays, distortions and hindrances due to the distance and lack of communications; to colonial isolation and resistance, poverty, ignorance and the ancient traditions of our geographical and social medium.

In fact, as far back as the early eighteenth century economic power in Europe was already in the hands of the bourgeois classes, who handled commercial and banking activities, while the feudal nobility preserved political power. And this want of balance between politics and economy provoked the French Revolution, the transformation in England having taken place very differently. The same movement reached Spain much more slowly and acted upon a different medium, and still more so, in the case of the colonies or sub-colonies in the Americas.

Night watchman.

7

This is how we explain the fact that the revolution for Independence was started by the creole class, not the upper classes, but the lower clergy and the countryfolk who were not among the big landowners, with the support of the proletarian masses of the fields, the mines and the cities. But as the insurgent middle class was a small group and lacking in power, and the proletarian masses were completely scattered, unarmed and weakened, the Revolution for Independence, in its initial and effective aspects, was practically crushed together with its first leaders, Hidalgo and Morelos. It was the creoles of the upper classes, great landowners and princes of the Church, who contributed to the consummation of independence, in its purely political aspect of separation from Spain. Thus the driving force of the Revolution, not in plans or Constitutions, remained buried deep down in the popular sub-conscience, repressed but ready to spring up anew in fresh movements for renovation, which were later on to assume the name of revolution for Reform.

8

The better to understand this revolution, we must repeat that Mexico not only reflected the social, ideological, political and economic movement going on in Spain, but likewise similar movements in France, England and the United States. These influences were mostly filtered through Spain, but were also introduced by means of direct contacts due to trade, interchange, smuggling and war. This is shown by the adoption of political and ideological forms that had sprung from the English Revolution and Magna Charta, from American independence and the Federal Constitution of the United States, the French Revolution and the Declaration of the Rights of Man; from the Spanish Revolution and the Constitution of 1812.

Underneath all these forms and doctrines, throbbed the vital process of production with all its complications and combinations. For Mexico, the outstanding features in this connection were the disorganization of her main sources of wealth; mining and agriculture.

9

Mining in Mexico, like any purely extractive industry, yielding only comparatively and occasionally satisfactory returns, carried on according to colonial methods and on the basis of starvation wages, without proper technical methods for development and with consequent waste of resources and human life, was only of minimum benefit to the country, due to heavy taxation and salaries kept down to the lowest point.

10

Cultivation of cotton in the south of the United States, with machinery allowing rapid development, directly promoted immigration into that country. In the American Revolution for Independence three fundamental aspects have been pointed out:

Civil war of colony against England.

International war with support lent by France and Spain to the Colonies.

Class war to give form to a new economic structure.

And it is commonly held that these features did not exist in the Mexican war of independence, judging from the way it burst all bounds, and its apparent consequences of anarchy and economic and political breakdown.

In the first place, those fundamental aspects are only condensed as above for convenience in setting them out, but in reality they represented movements, actions and reactions that were a great deal more complicated. In the United States, political emancipation, the pressure of foreign powers and economic renovation stood out more clearly, because they developed on ground open and favorable to new economic forms.

Lady of position. Her son wearing habit of St. Francis.

In Mexico the same tendencies and the same phenomena existed, but more complicated, more laboriously developed, with greater distortions and irregularities.

There was a civil war of the colony againts Spain; pressure from outside on the Spanish Empire that resisted disgregation, and a class war to introduce a new economic and social structure.

But the civil struggle was not between two well-defined and powerful groups who attempted to decide the contest by swift military action, but between confused and scattered groups and was a contest, in which the parties were both of them weak, a colony not yet fully organized and a metropolis in the midst of a crisis of prostration and decline. The civil struggle was not only colonists against Spaniards, but minorities of both groups who dragged along with them on one side and the other, portions of the proletarian mass.

The fight against outside pressure was not openly and frankly hostile, but against pressure and manoeuvers on the part of England and the United States indirectly to assist the independence of Spain's colonies, first by means of piracy, then by the sale of arms to the Indians on the northern border and to the insurgents, then by diplomatic intrigues and moral support.

And lastly the fight for the formation of a new economic structure and the integration of a new class system, was sought with less precision, but just as keenly, and took place in broken and uneven country, disconnected and in the face of obstacles of population and of a geographical nature, to make room for new industrial, commercial, political and cultural methods.

11

The above statement of the causes, antecedents and course of the war of independence, will allow us to draw a picture of the great movement along general lines, the better to study and understand it, not only in chronological order but for the clarification, explanation and proper ordering of its various stages and its relations and affinities with the previous and subsequent periods.

We must not, of course, confine ourselves to a review of military and political events, with a narrative of conspiracies, uprisings, tumults, battles and personal glorification of heroes and military leaders.

We must make a beginning at applying those modern concepts that define the doctrine, that is to say, the methods, science and technique of Revolution, considered as a transcendent and universal phenomenon.

It is obvious that the Revolution for Independence does not exhibit as well-marked and clean-cut features of social, industrial and economic renovation as are shown by contemporaneous revolutionary transformations, but the causes and essential aspects are now discernible, although still with obscurities and aberrations originated by lack of documents bearing on this particular aspect, the prejudices of antiquated methods of history writing and the rudimentary and formless character of classes of society in process of growth and organization

12

We shall thus see how the fundamental cause of the Revolution formally begun in 1810 was even then a conflict between the forces of production, and the relations of production, and the upsetting of the balance between these relations of production and the political forms expressing them. We shall also see how the Mexican Revolution was a reflection of similar movements, in England in 1688, and in France in 1789, which were not purely national, but of European scope, and consequently of far-reaching importance to Spain and her dominions. The destruction of the feudal State to put the bourgeois State in its place meant the triumph of a new social order, which structured vaster and more coherent nationality on top of a provincial, sectional and feudal organization, and which made the individual property of the bourgeoisie prevail over the feudal property of the great landowners; commercial and industrial competition over the system of guilds and corporations; subdivision of land over the privileges of primogeniture and entail; the new standards of working over mediaeval backwardness and routine, sunk in stagnation due to the decline of religious mysticism and the remains of old superstitions.

13

Cavalry soldier.

All this constituted a dyke holding back the forces of production, and brought about the overflowing of the revolution, by means of contradictions, collisions and international, national and civil conflicts; British culture versus Spanish culture; Spanish-American independence, due to decline of the metropolis, civil war between conservative elements and groups intent on liberty.

Consequently we must seek and outline the various stages of the Revolution in the four phases that modern doctrine lays down for us. First, the formation of an insurgent class, the standard bearer of new social forms, which begins to gather strength and organization, numbers and consciousness of its own existence. This is the ideological phase of the Revolution, without which the succeeding stages would not be able to develop; these later stages are the following:

Political and, military phase, attack on and destruction of old political forms and of the army that upholds them;

Economic phase for the destruction of old methods of production; and

Technical phase, accompanied by creation of stable and definite standards, social equilibrium, realization, reconstruction, organic and moral process or evolution.

14

We must say it again, these phases or stages do not develop with geometrical precision and in perfect order, but at times overlap one another and their currents cross or mingle. But in any case they must serve as a guide and prepare us for the study of the historical evolution of Mexico, until by a logical process we arrive at the modern Revolution.

Thus we find that the movement for independence was only the beginning of the ideological stage or phase, in an incomplete and embryonic form, because the insurgent class hardly yet began to acquire force, numbers, organization and consciousness of self; the military and political phase developed with all the greater vigor due to the weakness of the conservative elements, by then disintegrating, and yet it was only possible, after the first great failures and by a military combination, to achieve an apparent victory in 1821, which was nothing more than formal independence and hardly brought with it anything more than a partial political and military renovation.

And we shall see how that same revolutionary process, hindered by external factors and distorted by internal difficulties, was the one that continued to advance through stages of political and military renovation, until it compassed the destruction of the old State and of the old army, in the fight for Reform, which reached its height in the middle of the nineteenth century, and was not consummated until restoration of the Republic, thus reaching the technical phase of its consummation, realization and decline, to enter upon a fresh cycle of social Revolution that marks a new historical period for Mexico and for the world.

NATIONAL INTEGRATION

I

THE DAWN OF A NEW EPOCH

1

We must now begin by finding our bearings, so to speak, in the history of Mexico after independence.

We must not overlook the fact that stages or phases of evolution overlap and are defined by their most notable feature, but are not separated nor marked out with geometrical precision. Thus, the roots and antecedents of Independence dated back to the end of the Conquest, and even in Cortes's time and that of his immediate successors we find the first designs at separation of New Spain from the Crown of Castile.

But independence, with a specific program and on its way to actual realization, began on September 16, 1810, and the period of war and violent separation was prolonged until 1821, when emancipation was officially declared.

2

Rancher of the *Bajio*.

The Revolution having been incompletely consummated, the work of national integration began to develop in great distress and fighting with enemies at home and abroad. The revolutionary impulse, in the early days almost unconscious, formless and lacking in program, gradually condensed and crystallized into political formulae and institutions.

The industrial and commercial change took place very tardily and with incomplete adaptation. The system of democracy gave rise to new forms of political contest, waged by parties and factions; but none of the parties succeeded in building up a State powerful enough to establish permanent institutions. The victory of a party raised a personality or a group to power, who met with the opposition of enemies and hostility in his or its own midst due to divergences between radicals or moderates.

3

In reality, this period reaches to 1867, when restoration of the Republic was finally achieved in accordance with the principles of democratic revolution, set down in fundamental laws.

The period from 1821 to 1867, is so confused and agitated that it does not allow one clearly to distinguish the various phases of social and economic evolution, in the midst of the disorganization provoked by the gigantic internal crisis of production, politics, class readjustment and new currents of thought, art and customs.

After anarchy, misery, rioting and military coups, the disorganization caused by two foreign invasions, loss of territory and waste of energy, the transformation begun in 1810 by the War of Independence was fully consummated by the restoration of a Republic, federal and democratic in form, and by the predominance of a group of the middle class supported by the proletarian masses. The wars of Reform, French intervention and the Empire brought to a close the undertaking begun by Hidalgo and Morelos.

4

The ancient ruling classes of feudal origin, by the force of arms, and due to the destructive effects of time and the rise of new generations with new ideas, lost ground in the political sphere, although they preserved the remains of their economic and moral power.

On the other hand, the heirs to the ancient class of great landowners, favored by the system of private property, and by their control of money, rent and credit, succeeded in keeping their advantageous position.

5

The privileges lost by the high officials of the old order had passed into the hands of the military and official class of the Republic, and the benefits of property and capitalism to a new class of landowners and investors composed of the remains of the ancient mining and hacienda owning nobility, and of the new rich of the era of Civil War; money-lenders, landlords, army contractors, purchasers of church and national property. And also fortunate merchants, professional men and politicians, who had managed to rise from the lower and lower middle classes, to the higher strata of the bourgeoisie.

6

When independence was consummated, in the political aspect, by exclusion of the Spanish government from the administrative func-

tions of her old colony, two great portions of the dominant class succeeded in bettering their position, thanks to their participation in
coups d'etat, and in the political manoeuvers thereby produced. The
church kept all her property and privileges, but without the obligations
and functions that had theretofore kept her in subjection, and the
great landowners, merchants and the wealthy middle class, not only put
their property rights on a more stable footing, but strengthened them
as well.

7

Seminarist.

The regalist system of land
tenure that granted to the owner
the use and enjoyment of property,
but reserved to the crown paramount right to grant and revoke,
was in the democratic system replaced by provisions sanctioning individual, inviolable and absolute
property. Property thus became a
"guarantee" with respect to the
State, in the form of a natural right
or right of man.

Thus was nullified one of the
reasons for independence, that is the
intention to open markets and commercial routes to world traffic, and
more especially to trade with England.

This is why, in the early stages
of Mexico's independent existence,
although the presence of English
merchants was noted, and in less
number, of American and French,
they met with open or veiled resistance and hindrances. At the same
time the tendencies of the conservative party began to show themselves,
its design being to uphold privileges of colonial origin, by perfecting the
alliance between the heirs of the former ruling classes, to which the new
owners of wealth and privileges, such as military officers, political bosses, property owners and money lenders, gravitated by a natural law
of attraction.

8

In opposition to the above, the tendency of the liberal party, which rested on the proletarian mass, led by a minority consisting of intellectual leaders, anxious for personal and class betterment, the dissatisfied, and partisans of renovation, also began to be noted. The conservatives sought the continuance of the old regime, including solidarity with Spanish elements, not exactly with Spain as a people, but with the representatives of ancient feudal Spain.

For similar reasons, the liberal party met with the support and the somewhat interested sympathy of the English, and later on of the Americans. Freedom of worship, freedom of contract and open markets, were combined and made their influences felt by investment of capital, the so-called Monroe Doctrine, the opening of steamship lines, foreign loans and the activities of alien companies engaged in operation of Mexican mines.

The above factors, by action and reaction, gave rise to the international and national complications of the history of Mexico, during the period of its integration as an independent nation, from the year 1821 up to the restoration of the republic in 1867, which meant the final political defeat of the conservative party.

II

ITURBIDE'S EMPIRE

1

On October 27, 1821, one month after the entry of the army of the three guarantees into the City of Mexico, while popular enthusiasm yet throbbed with satisfaction of the consummation of the nation's independence, and while the illusions that held out promises of a new era of progress, peace and liberty, had not yet lost their freshness, the ceremony of taking the oath solemnly took place.

The constitutional mayor of the city, after reading the plan of Iguala, the declaration of independence and the treaties of Córdoba took the new flag with the three colors, and addressed the people as follows: "Mexico swears the independence of the Mexican Empire on the fundamental basis of the plan of Iguala and the treaty of Cordoba." And all those that were standing in front of the palace answered as one man: "We swear it."

2

This oath re-echoed more or less confusedly over the whole area of the former colony, and spread such words as Union, Independence, Liberty, Sovereign Junta, Constitutional Congress. And these fine words likewise meant public power for the creoles, free trade, reduction of taxes and tribute, open frontiers, new machinery for the mines and new roads for industry and farming.

The immense regions included in Texas and California, Jalisco, Yucatan, Guatemala, with Chiapas, Honduras and Nicaragua, decided to unite with Mexico, in spite of the enormous obstacles of distance and lack of communication, with a spiritual brotherhood and good will that never could have existed in colonial times.

But all these illusions and good intentions were very soon upset by harsh reality. The war with Spain was not yet over, because San Juan de Ulua was still in the power of the Spanish garrison; the treaties of Cordoba were not fulfilled, because the King of Spain refused to accept that agreement; constitutional monarchy was not established, and worst of all, certain political methods were resorted to, that in course of time were destined to become a chronic disease.

3

Alderman.

So long as the Spanish government refused to recognize the independence of her former colony, Mexico continued to be subject to all the privations of colonial isolation, because other countries were too distrustful to establish active trade and formal relations with a nation that had hardly yet come into being.

There was only irregular and scanty communication with Europe, and deserts cut us off from the United States.

4

The depression of culture, the neglect of public education, the decline of industry due to lack of capital and of technical management,

were notorious during the years that followed the consummation of
independence.

It must not, however, be thought that this crisis was due to independence itself, because the causes of the depression dated far back, and
had been the very ones to provoke the liberating revolution. Industrial
poverty and financial ruin had weakened Spain and her colonies, and the
whole organism of the Spanish Empire was in a debilitated condition.

5

The historians of that period concerned themselves exclusively
with narrations of rulers who rose and fell, battles and political plans.

Public administration was carried on by a disastrous system, that
was, absolute destitution, usurious loans, reckless extravagance, a discontented army, political confusion and revolutionary agitation.

As was only natural, nothing sound could be built up on such a
foundation, nor could schools be established, roads be built, statistics
be gathered, nor the public treasury be put in order.

We shall, however, endeavor to point out more clearly the two
fundamental tendencies that differentiated the groups contending for
power.

6

As we have seen above, when we dealt with the problem of the
parties, there were two main divisions; on one side those who called
themselves conservatives or reactionaries, and on the other, the liberals, radicals and reformers. The first party enjoyed power due to its
wealth, to class privilege, to strength of organization, and was anxious
to keep power and place. The latter wished to rise, and make changes,
due to a spirit of reform and to that natural instinct for betterment
that all men feel.

Iturbide at the beginning was supported by the liberals and looked upon with disfavor by the conservatives. The people were grateful to him for freedom won, the former insurgents looked upon him as
finally instrumental in achieving their victory, and reformers expected
from him a constitutional monarchy. The conservatives, on the other
hand, were only disposed to look upon him as a lesser evil, and as a
compromise.

7

When the treaties of Cordoba became null and void, Mexico was
left free to determine her own form of government.

Then the whole of the Spanish element or that with Spanish sympathies, the conservative class, the officers who had belonged to the Royalist army and a few insurgents attracted by Iturbide's prestige, constituted a kind of party that advocated the establishment of a constitutional empire.

But as a constituent congress had already been convened and although the basis of this assembly consisted in the idea of making it a moderating element within the monarchical regime, this first attempt at democratic procedure led directly to the idea of a republic.

The congress dreamt of by the forerunners of independence, incompletely assembled at the cost of great sacrifices, meant recognition of a new principle: that sovereignty was vested in the people. The plan of Iguala and the treaties of Cordoba, had been only a compromise. And inasmuch as Spain refused to accept that compromise, Mexico was left free to establish a republic, if it suited her to do so.

Public scribe, main Plaza of Mexico City

8

The fortunate part played by Iturbide in the consummation of the political triumph of independence, apparently at the beginning modified the course of the revolution, which was not only directed agains Spanish domination, but rather against the exploiting classes and the system of privileges, despotic government and colonial stagnation.

But it very soon happened that Iturbide found himself supported by his former adversaries and opposed by his former friends. The congress he had convened turned against him, and became the starting point of a republican movement.

9

Iturbide aspired to be emperor, even though his ascent to the throne were achieved by street rioting and a *coup d'etat* that assumed the proportions of military sedition.

He made yet other mistakes; instead of attempting to have himself crowned emperor by a popular vote, he preferred violence; he disappointed the people, nullified the congress by capturing its members and compelling them by force to sanction his rise to the throne, and after that dissolved it by the force of arms; he abdicated while still strong; he again assembled congress and gave it a new lease of life, but without appeasing its rancor; he left the country an exile, and later attempted to return, in the belief that a reaction had set in his favor and giving grounds for the enactment of a law declaring him an enemy of his country.

When he attempted to return in triumph, he was taken prisoner and shot near the town of Padilla, in the State of Tamaulipas.

In spite of his success in politically consummating independence, Iturbide did not achieve final glory. His name is associated with the tendencies of the conservative or reactionary party, and popular sentiment has not forgotten his antecedents as an enemy of the insurgents.

10

The formula composing the plan of Iguala consisted of the words "Union, Religion, and Independence." Union purported to be a compromise with the exactions of the insurgents, by granting the Mexican people the advantages of emancipation and political freedom as regards official domination by the Spanish government. At bottom, however, by union was meant the preservation of vested rights, a system of government still resting on religion ,and protection of the commercial and property interests of European Spaniards and of wealthy creoles; in a word, the preservation of the colonial system, modified only by a change of persons and of formulas in the high spheres of government. By religion in the plan of Iguala, was meant respect for the interests of the church and the preservation of the privileges and properties of the sacerdotal class; and respect for the Catholic church as the only religious institution authorized, meant a continuance of commercial and spiritual separation from non-Catholic countries, or more bluntly, from England and the United States, which thenceforward became for Mexico a source of danger and of attraction at the same time. Of danger, due to ambition for territorial and economic expansion, and of attraction, due to the example of democratic freedom and industrial and progressive reform.

III

FIRST STEPS OF THE REPUBLIC

1

Iturbide was overthrown by the Republicans, although a number of others lacking in firm political principles, like Antonio Lopez de Santa Anna, joined them for personal reasons.

After Iturbide's abdication, an executive power was formed composed of Negrete, Nicolas Bravo and Guadalupe Victoria.

The function of this executive power was mainly designed to be the direction and preparation of a constituent congress, but even before this assembly was formed, the new division of the parties became apparent. Bourbonism and Iturbidism had died out, and dragged

down in their fall the idea of monarchy. Republican principles had asserted themselves. But the conservative party invented centralization, and the liberals or progressives proclaimed federalism. At the beginning this was only an artificial division. For the time being the remains of the Monarchist Party joined the Federalists, not from conviction, but out of opposition to the provisional government.

2

Butcher Boy.

The division between Centralism and Federalism, was of great political significance to the life of the Republic. But we must not overlook the fact that one of the fundamental principles of modern history is to seek, beyond or beneath formulas or written programs, the true causes of political and social events. Centralists and federalists continued to form the contending parties that ruled the destiny of the country. Those opposing tendencies had made their appearance ever since New Spain had developed an individuality of its own, and well-defined social classes had begun to rise with conflicting interests.

Thus we have seen how the division began between European Spaniards and American or Creole Spaniards; and after that between

Royalists and Insurgents. The slogan adopted by Hidalgo was: Long live Ferdinand VII! Down with bad government!

Beneath these words the actual reality of the insurgent program was independence and reform, the rise or insurgency of the oppressed masses, and rebellion against the ruling classes, ensconced behind their wealth and privileges.

3

The program became clearer and more definite under Morelos, and when independence was consummated Vicente Guerrero became the representative of that popular and effective tendency, while Iturbide stood for a purely political compromise or combination.

The onward march of these tendencies became more clearly marked under Iturbide, whose reign was a continuation of Bourbonism, of dominant and oppressive hispanicism, of absolute and exclusive rule, of unpopular clerical reaction. And the difference became more clearly evident still in the breach between centralists and federalists, and later on between liberals and conservatives. Federal or central government apparently meant a problem of administrative organization, of different shading on maps, or names of officials and public servants. But round Federalism rallied many other items of a social, political and economic program. For example, the great problem of commercial systems, the struggle between free trade and protection, which at the same time was closely connected with the existence of the thinly settled northern regions. The question of importation and tariff duties, was bound up with the conflicting interests of Spanish merchants and of strictly Mexican commerce, which felt at one and the same time the dangers and attractions of throwing open communication with England and the United States.

4

On the side of federalism was the reformative tendency that endeavored gradually to deprive the Church of her civil functions and of her exemptions and privileges, of breaking up properties that constituted vast haciendas or great estates, poorly managed, and which needed new forms of cultivation, by substituting for the work of slaves, serfs or peons, the machines that industrial revolution was turning out all over the world.

These events become more complicated on the surface of politics, because in them mingled the self-seeking passions and trickery of sects and factions, and errors and occasional and momentary aberrations. Thus we see how parties suddenly divide into republicans or iturbidists, and former royalists or insurgents joining either one. This is why we had better seek the right path by going right to the bottom of events; not the outward appearance of changes of government, or plans and programs, but actual realities.

IV

FEDERALISM

1

The struggle between federalists and centralists produced immediate consequences of a serious character. The first of these was the secession of Guatemala with the whole of Central America.

The centralizing tendency also began to foster the estrangement of Texas, to produce later on mutilation in the north, just as it had already brought about the dismemberment of the south.

After that of France and Spain, Anglo-Saxon influence began to be more directly felt. The expansive force of England, the proximity of the United States, trade and the attraction of novelty for both sides, increased Anglo-Saxon interest in the Latin Republics, as fields for enterprise, exploration and exploitation, and induced among us a feeling of admiration for the constitutional forms of the British Monarchy and of the North American Republic.

Thus grew up federalism in Mexico, and precipitated the framing of a Constituent Charter in 1824. which anticipated the final Federal Constitution of that same year, in which the Executive, Legislative and Judicial Powers make their appearance, vested in the President of the Republic and the Governors of the States, in the two Chambers, of Deputies and Senators, and in the Supreme Court of Justice, respectively. But the supremacy of the Church was as yet respected, because the Catholic religion was preserved as the sole official form of worship.

2

The origin of the celebrated Monroe Doctrine was similar, it having arisen as a defense of the republican institutions of the Americas, wielded by the United States without the express consent of the Spanish-American Republics, against the intervention of the absolutist rulers of Europe, joined in the Holy Alliance. The Monroe Doctrine, at birth was an act opposing re-conquest by European imperialism. But it even then rested on a foundation of American imperialism, and of pride.

Hopes of establishing in Mexico a strong, liberal and progressive government revived with the election of Guadalupe Victoria, an old insurgent general, for President of the Republic, with Nicolas Bravo as Vice-President.

England and the United States forthwith recognized this Government.

The rise to office of Guadalupe Victoria really meant a victory for the popular party, one step further in the consummation of independence, as this was felt and understood by the insurgents. The defeated party, after having been bourbonists, iturbidists and centralists, their ranks augmented by the inevitable malcontents who had failed to get jobs and salaries, constituted an active opposition to the government.

3.

Victoria's Government, lacking in energy, yet evidenced its principles by decreeing that Independence Day should be celebrated on the 16th September; it adopted violent methods against the Spaniards, even to expulsion: it expressly declared the abolition of slavery; it admitted the formation of an American Confederation, in accordance with Bolivar's plan. Aside from this, it endeavored to obtain funds, and found no better way than to contract loans, thus creating the Foreign Public Debt.

Guadalupe Victoria.

Guadalupe Victoria would have finished his term of office without any difficulties other than reactionary attempts which took the form of the tumult of La Perpetua, headed by General Bravo himself, in spite of being the Vice-President, and by an absurd conspiracy hatched by Father Arenas.

4

But the disastrous part of his term of office was its end, not only on account of the immediate consequences, but because it marked the beginning of a lengthy period of civil war, coups d'état and pronunciamentos, the era of Santa Anna.

The popular federalist party had triumphed with Victoria, but when the presidential succession began to be discussed it divided into two groups; the extreme party, that took its enmity to the Spaniards to the maximum pitch, and which presented a hero sprung from the people, Vicente Guerrero, as its candidate; and another and moderately liberal group, with Manuel Gomez Pedraza as its candidate.

He was a former royalist officer, not only acceptable to the moderate party, but also to the conservatives, on account of his antecedents, his disciplined character, and above all because he opposed Guerrero, who was the representative of the insurgent cause, and was looked upon by the multitude as invested to a certain degree with the legendary glory of Hidalgo and Morelos.

5

Manuel Gomez Pedraza.

The masses sided with Guerrero, but the weight of the government was thrown on the side of Gomez Pedraza and he officially won the election.

The weakness of our imperfect democracy for remedying electoral frauds otherwise than by force, made the most restless partisans of Guerrero, Santa Anna, at that time a federalist, among the first, resort to revolution, aggravated by a popular riot in the heart of the City of Mexico.

Guadalupe Victoria was only able to serve out his term of office by appointing Vicente Guerrero, as his Minister of War.

The popular party seemed to have triumphed, but unfortunately the defective way in which it had risen to power was the cause of regrettable after events.

The brave and loyal military leader from the south had a remarkably intelligent assistant, Lorenzo de Zavala, Minister of Finance. But Zavala was just as cultured as he was unpopular, and his financial plans, which aimed at obtaining resources by attacking, among others, the property of the clergy, increased the dislike for him of the wealthier classes, who were already sufficiently annoyed at seeing General Vicente Guerrero, a true son of the people, installed as President in the National Palace.

6

The popularity of Guerrero and Santa Anna persisted thanks to the brilliant success obtained by the arms of the Republic over a Spanish General, Isidro Barradas, who attempted the re-conquest of Mexico, by imitating, with sad results for himself, the daring of the first conqueror, Hernan Cortes.

But the power of the Government was undermined at its base. Without funds, nor facilities for raising them, the country's credit stillborn, due to the loss of prestige caused by the ruinous loans raised in London, which were neither utilized nor could be paid, there was no way of keeping the army quiet, nor of undertaking any serious administrative reforms, by attending to education, public health or the needs of the nation.

7

Revolt once more raised its head, this time led by General Anastasio Bustamante, promoted by the conservative party and seconded by a portion of the army with old royalist connections, and by the clergy, which was not in agreement with the renovating tendencies of ultra-radical revolutionists. Guerrero was unable to defend himself, and fled to his southern mountains, while the rebellious troops entered Mexico City, and Congress again began to seek for procedure to legalize the elevation of Bustamante to the Presidency of the Republic.

Bustamante was a strong, capable and energetic man, but his rise to power had been even more defective than Guerrero's and furthermore he had all the popular element against him.

V

BEGINNINGS OF LIBERAL REFORM

1

Representative men at this time are Valentin Gomez Farias and Doctor José Luis Mora.

Doctor Mora, on the subject of politics in his time, divides parties into two classes, and calls one of them the party of progress and the other the party of retrogression.

"To avoid arguments on words, I must, before going any further, say that by political march of progress I mean that which tends to take place more or less swiftly; the secularization of the property of the clergy, the abolition of its privileges and of those of the army, the diffusion of public education among the people, absolutely independently of the clergy, the suppression of monasteries, absolute freedom of opinion, equality of aliens with natives as regards civil rights, and the establishment of trial by jury in criminal cases."

In 1833 the movement for reform in Mexico began, and Valentin Gomez Farias is for that reason called the Patriarch of Reform.

It may be said that as pioneers of liberal reform, Gomez Farias and Doctor Mora were even as hand and brain working together.

2

When one has chronicled the events that took place during the first thirty years after independence, it may be said that one has presented the actors and the argument of a drama with many acts, repeated over and over again, and which continued to be repeated for many years.

Valentin Gomez Farias.

The two great parties, after calling themselves centralists and federalists, began to recognize each other as liberals and conservatives.

The latter called the former demagogues or *chinacos*, and at the same time described themselves as the party of decent people, upholders of law and order, respectful of peace, religion, discipline, law and order, and God; their fundamental power lay in the clergy, the army and big merchants.

In turn, the liberals and federalists looked upon themselves as the party of progress, reform, new ideas, social transformation, and after calling themselves federalists they became reformists, pure liberals and patriots.

3

The separation between these parties is affected by the personal character of political contests, due to motives of expediency or lack of sound doctrines, or to the compelling force of war with other nations that shake all classes of society and in part make internal conflicts disappear or mingle the various groups confusedly.

Bustamante, despite his energy as a soldier, and harsh repressive measures that went as far as the murder of Guerrero, who fell a victim

Military Uprisings.

to betrayal, was in turn overthown by Santa Anna, and after the provisional governments of Muzquiz and Gomez Pedraza, who like so many others, merely passed hurriedly through presidential office like shadows, a new victory for the popular party was registered in 1833, with Santa Anna as President, and the old federalist, Valentin Gomez Farias, who had, as we stated above, undertaken a vast movement for reform, as acting Vice-President.

4

The liberals by then had a much more extensive program than the old federalists, which is explicable by the difficulties of centralized administration in a country of enormous distances and traditional sectionalism. The struggle had made them grow in strength and pretentions.

The essential principles of reform were, separation of Church and State, suppression of civil action for payment of tithes, suppression of the University, still impregnated with a colonial atmosphere and with a profound churchly spirit; primary education to be laical and gratuitous, and secularization of property frozen in the hands of ecclesiastical corporations. In substance. liberal reform is the continuation of the program of the progressive or federalists.

The Parian or Bazar; grew up after the Conquest, was several times burnt down, and finally demolished in 1843. All kinds of European and Oriental goods were there sold.

VI

THE WAR WITH TEXAS

1

The principles of reform also meant radicalism and defied the power of the Church.

The conservatives answered with their program of Religion and Privileges, that is privileges and stagnation, and won over the army, with Santa Anna himself at the head.

Gomez Farias was overthrown and exiled, and Santa Anna returned to centralization, having thereby provoked seccessionist feeling in Texas, which thus found a pretext for throwing off a political commitment that did not suit its local development. Colonists of Anglo-Saxon origin were the actual dominant element in Texas, and their natural tendency was to draw closer to the United States and separate from Mexico, mainly on account of expediencies of trade, industry and the agrarian and social problems of slavery.

Santa Anna not only afforded them the pretext for this segregation, but laid the foundation for a future war that was to prove more costly still.

Squandering the resources and blood of the people, he led a military expeditionary force through the provinces about to secede, and after a few victories he was defeated and taken prisoner. To save his own life, he allowed the disaster to be consummated, and signed an agreement with the enemy; Texas was lost for ever.

2

In the year 1836 a centralist constitution was enacted, which meant a step backward, not because the centralized form of government is in itself inferior to the federalist, but because these changes which did not in reality modify the real constitution of the nation, served as fuel to inflame the spirit of the people, which had pinned to federation their simple and generous faith.

By mean of the formality of new elections, Bustamante returned to the Presidency, and Santa Anna, as was his wont, lay low awaiting a new opportunity to rise to power.

3

The position with regard to Texas had not been decided, and preparations for a new expedition served as a reason for expending further precious resources. The situation was one of instability due to frequent federalist pronunciamentos, the constant struggle between liberal action and conservative reaction, still complicated by commercial and clerical hispanicism, and by the menace of war with France, which at last did break out in the humiliating form of a claim for inflated indemnities, the occupation of Vera Cruz by irresistible forces, and a costly agreement under which we were compelled to pay sums we did not owe.

4

The country continued this kind of existence, now under Santa Anna, now under Bustamante, corroded by pronunciamentos and poverty.

Nothing was built, nothing was organized, nothing was learnt and nothing was taught. Colonial isolation had been succeeded by anarchical isolation. During this troubled period, the nation sank to the lowest depths of its decline.

Besides, during those years of absolutism and industrial depression, two tremendous disasters that all but put an end to its existence as a free country, were brewing; the war with the United States and the War of Reform, with French Intervention and the Empire.

5

Antonio Lopez de Santa Anna, after a painting by Margarita Torres Martinez.

Santa Anna clumsily laid the foundation for the war with the United States, due to his obstinacy in leaving the problem of Texas unsolved. To this he resorted to cope with enemies at home; to keep up the army, to invent new taxes and divert the attention of the people. The only sensible course to pursue would have been to fortify, pacify and settle. California, New Mexico and the regions adjacent might thus perhaps have been saved.

But Santa Anna continued to mislead the people and to inflame their patriotism, supported by the conservatives, who endeavored to unite, or combine the political interests of the older classes, known as aristocrats, great landowners, clericals, pro-Spanish, absolutists or centralists.

VII

THE AMERICAN INVASION

1

The selfsame causes that had contributed to the loss of control over Texas, continued to work for war with the United States and invasion by that country. The main reason was undoubtedly the expansion of the United States, whither European emigrants flocked, driven by poverty and war in the Old World, and drawn by the great open spaces of the virgin lands of America. This movement of population increased due to new methods of transport and production of things required by daily existence (steam engines.)

But that same movement of expansion, in so far as Mexico was concerned, was not merely a drive for invasion and penetration. It was complicated by the fact that there were other and opposing forces on either side. On ours, the depression engendered by severance and by the elimination of the colonial Government of Spain, and after that, internal warfare in the midst of an economic crisis affecting mining and agriculture, accompanied by social and political disturbances.

2

On the American side expansión pushed its way south, first the farming communities of England's old colonies, who introduced negro slavery in the country where the staple crop was cotton. New machinery, especially that for ginning cotton, and the advances in manufacturing industry in the northern states, began to create a rift between North and South, federals and confederates, republicans and democrats, advocates of slavery and abolitionists, and protectionists and free traders, in foreign commerce.

This split in the United States was of great importance to Mexico, as we shall see farther on. But we here point it out in so far as it affected the war of 1847-8. The slaveholders of the South availed themselves of the situation of the earliest American colonies in Texas, and stimulated the tendency to make of Texas and Coahuila a Mexican federal State, to preserve its sovereignty and dwell with the utmost freedom possible within the central Government of Mexico. In this regard the problem was complicated by the breach between Mexican federalists and centralists.

3

Later, the move for secession was carried farther, due to the conflicts that arose in the internal political contests in our country, which joined with that economic weakness that had prevented settlement and government of those remote northern regions. Advocates of slavery, and Texas, then sought the erection of a Federal State of Texas, apart from Coahuila; after that a Texan Republic as a buffer state between

Mexico and the United States, and lastly full annexation of Texas to the United States, but as an integral portion of the Southern or slave-holding States.

4

Northern abolitionists opposed the increase of slave-holding territory to the south, so as not to be swamped in the elections and in the commercial and industrial contest. But at last the forces of expansion triumphed, and the Southern States succeeded in seizing Texas by means of commercial penetration and the establishment of agricultural settlements. Mexico attempted to assert her rights and to resist. Hence, first the war with Texas and the loss of all the country north of the Rio Grande. The war of 1847-8 was waged to complete the work of spoliation; as the Northern States opposed the growth of the Southern Slave States, once engaged in the war, and since the slave States had extended their area by the entry of Texas into the Union, they extended invasion to New Mexico, Colorado, Arizona and California.

And just as in internal politics, international procedure clothed these happenings with diplomatic trappings, calling them boundary disputes, and claims for debts and indemnities. Reality asserted itself, first by the military occupation of the northern regions, after that by the war of invasion and underlying all this, the force of industrial and economic expansion.

5

In the war with the United States, and in the military operations incidental thereto, we are unable to find a single outstanding figure to represent the defense of Mexico, in the form of a hero or military leader. Invasion first of all took place from the north, and the American troops defeated our armies, not beneath them in courage, but due to inferior organization, armaments and high command. The classes that controlled material resources and the groups at the head of the political situation failed to rise to the occasion in that desperate situation.

6

A chronicle of the march of invasion makes painful reading. Our soldiers were defeated at Matamoros, at Resaca de Guerrero and Monterrey, in spite of the sacrifices of the troops.

Santa Anna again occupied the Presidential chair, availing himself of the national danger, and raised an army which he himself led against the invaders, whom he encountered at La Angostura, near Saltillo. There the efforts of the Mexicans made victory almost theirs, and in the first stages of the battle success was on the side of the defenders of their own land. But the mistakes of their commanders and the lack of material elements and supplies once more bestowed victory on the invaders.

The same thing happened with the American troops that entered the country by way of Vera Cruz. The population of that seaport heroically withstood a destructive bombardment, but their bullets were unable to reach the enemy and the Mexican garrison was forced to surrender.

7

Santa Anna once more led ill-armed and equipped recruits to defeat at Cerro Gordo. Puebla fell without resistance. In the city of Mexico, the Vice-President, Gomez Farias, attempted to undertake at one and the same time, the work of defense and of liberal reform, and the complications of internal politics reached such a pitch that the battalions of volunteers themselves, known by the name of "*polkos*," raised to defend the soil of their country, wasted their strength on base attempts at rebellion, and the funds needed for expenses of war had to be raised by levying special taxes. And yet, in spite of all this, the frozen wealth of the clergy and ruling classes was not contributed, though urgently required for equipment and support of troops.

8

When one follows, event by event, the military operations and the political happenings of this period, one's feelings are harrowed by the details.

In this swift historical sketch, we shall be content to mention, if no great captain representative of defense, the youthful heroes who saved the honor of Mexico; the cadets of the Military College, who fell on September 13, 1847, when the school was stormed by the invading troops, then on the point of occupying the capital of the Republic.

The glorious death of Francisco Marquez, Agustin Melgar, Juan Escutia, Fernando Montes de Oca, Vicente Suarez and Juan de la Barrera, in an unequal contest, without hope, crushed by an overwhelming force, are as it were a symbol and image of this unrighteous war.

The Boy Heroes.

9

To Mexico, the American invasion contains a terrible lesson. In this war we saw that right and justice count but little in contests between one people and another, when material force, and organization, are wanting.

A great portion of Mexico's territory was lost because she had been unable to administer and settle those regions, and handed them over to alien colonization.

There is no principle nor law that can sanction spoliation. Only by force was it carried out, and only by force or adroit negotiation could it have been avoided. That which Spain had been unable to colonize, and the Republic to settle, was occupied by the stream of Anglo-American expansion.

10

The war of 1847 is not, so far as Mexico is concerned, offset by anything but the courage of her soldiers. At Matamoros, at Resaca de

Chapultepec.—September 13, 1847.

Guerrero, at La Angostura, at Veracruz, at Cerro Gordo, at Padierna, at Churubusco, and at Chapultepec, victory was won by a well organized and instructed General Staff; by longer range rifles and cannon, better fed soldiers, abundance of money and ammunition, and of horses and wagons.

History must record, if not all names, at least the collective appellations that earned for their country a ray of glory in that period of gloom; the people at Vera Cruz, the soldiers at La Angostura, the disorganized crowd mowed down by cannon at Cerro Gordo, the San Blas Battalion, and the National Guards of Mexico. And above all, the Boy Heroes of Chapultepec.

11

May that generous blood serve to efface the shame of those traitors who turned their backs to the enemy, like Paredes Arrillaga, of the fanatical and base who started a riot while the invaders advanced from Vera Cruz and Puebla; of those mistaken individuals who declared a shameful neutrality in the Peninsula of Yucatan; of those selfish persons who showed fear, avarice or indifference; of those who after defeat, aggravated it by their misdeeds.

And above all, may that lesson not have been given in vain, and may it, through the years, help us to forestall other and similar dangers, under the disguises of economic conquest and dominating capitalism.

Map of Mexico, showing territory lost in war with the United States.

VIII

WAR OF REFORM

1

The American invasion cost Mexico the total loss of Texas, whose boundaries were, without the slightest right, brought down to the Rio Grande; the Province of New Mexico and Upper California, and an outpouring of blood, energy and wealth, offset only by material compensation in the amount of fifteen million pesos, by way of indemnity. Santa Anna then lost, if only momentarily, that unbelievable prestige that the people had bestowed on him, and was once more forced into exile.

And at the same time as calamitous defeat extended all over the Republic, filling it with mourning, sadness, rage and gloom, a terrible race war broke out in the Peninsula of Yucatan. The creoles had armed the Indians and incited them to disorder in connection with factional politics, and after that the Indians revolted against the whites, and engaged in a war of destruction.

2

When the peace treaty of Guadalupe Hidalgo, forced on Mexico, and more like a surrender than a treaty, was signed, the Republic had hardly more than the shadow of a Government, whose seat was at Queretaro. Then great self-sacrifice was required to accept the post of President.

Manuel de la Peña y Peña had courage sufficient to become the chief of Mexico's executive, and to face the invaders, in an endeavor to salvage what was left. When the decision was adopted to sign the treaty of Guadalupe Hidalgo, the Mexican Government did everything in its power to avoid total annexation and the final disappearance of our country's sovereignty.

3

The saddest chapter of the tale is the fact that those same pronunciamentos that paved the way for the entry of the invader, served to escort him when he left.

Paredes Arrillaga again revolted; there were Indian uprisings in Jalisco; Leonardo Marquez rose in arms and the tragic situation in Yucatan reached its culmination.

The Government of Mexico, organized in accordance with legal forms, with Jose Joaquin de Herrera as President, did nothing more than make desperate efforts to check anarchy, until General Arista was inaugurated in 1851.

General Arista's administration was marked by order and moderation. But all was in vain, so long as the main causes still persisted: economic destitution and pronunciamentos. As always, lack of funds interfered with restoration of order. Hence military coups and disorder, with accompanying stagnation of industry, almost nothing done for education, extinction of credit and constant growth of the foreign debt.

4

However, the Conservative party that had remained out of office, especially in the provinces, where liberal elements abounded, though less radical, again thought of Santa Anna's return.

Rebellious attempts succeeded one another ever more frequently, until Arista gave up the struggle and withdrew. And then the inevitable Santa Anna again occupied the presidential chair, surrounded by the centralist, conservative and reactionary group.

Santa Anna had now come back more eager than ever for command, honors and injustice. He returned refined by dictatorship. This was when he had himself addressed as Your Serene Highness, the period of persecution of freedom of thought, of exiled citizens, of unrestrained military leadership and of wilful and shameless extravagance; of the Gadsden purchase, another tract of land surrendered to the United States, and of the decrees establishing life and hereditary dictatorship.

That being so, the Plan de Ayutla framed in 1854, could not but be looked upon by the whole nation as an urgent remedy, not only on account of its liberal tendencies, but because it was aimed at the Dictator himself.

5

And then began the cruellest and longest civil war in the history of Mexico. Up till then, it may be asserted that there had been nothing except pronunciamentos, riots and military coups. Quarrels between the military, riots that flared up and were soon over, and purely political conflicts, had not exhibited that violent aspect of hand to hand fighting, of combat without quarter, shown by the revolutions of the people against military dictatorship.

The Plan of Ayutla, that paved the way for the great revolution of Reform, was another uprising of the people, led by liberal groups against the privileged classes, which upheld dictatorship and flourished under its shade; and more especially against the two most conspicuous and powerful elements, the clergy and the army. Or rather against clericalism mixed with politics and militarism in the form of a corrupt army.

6

The aims of the Plan de Ayutla were at the beginning confined to disavowing Santa Anna's authority and to convening a Constituent Congress, that is, the revival of federalism, and from the moment that hostilities broke out in the region of Acapulco, in 1855, all activities were purely military in character.

Military leaders and reformist groups began to arise, and the names of Juan Alvarez, Ignacio Comonfort, Santos Degollado and Jesus Gonzalez Ortega, began to be distinguished above the rest.

In the conservative camp distinguished officers also arose; Miramon noted for his courage and soldierly ability, Felix Zuloaga, Osollo and Leonardo Marquez.

IX

THE PRINCIPLES AND THE MEN OF THE PERIOD OF REFORM

1

The triumph of the Revolution of Ayutla raised Ignacio Comonfort to the Presidency of the Republic, after a short provisional term filled by the southern leader, Juan Alvarez.

On taking office, Comonfort began to comply with the desires of his party, by re-establishing the federal system, and he ordered the suppression of the Society of Jesus. Through his ministers, Miguel Lerdo de Tejada, Benito Juarez and Melchor Ocampo, he took the first active steps towards an economic and social transformation of Mexico, as planned by liberals many years before, beginning with the secularization of property held in mortmain, that is, the throwing back into circulation and movement of the property of religious communities and the doing away with fossilized and routine administration of such property.

2

There probably has not been in our whole history as an independent people, a more transcendent decision. To understand how bold it was, one must imagine the state of the public mind in the middle of the nineteenth century, when the specter of dogma, that confused the Church and priesthood with religion itself, and the property of monasteries, convents and bishops with the essence of divinity, had not yet disappeared.

Secularization of the property of the clergy marked the beginning of Mexico's economic redemption, and if the initiators thereof only reached the period of destruction and did not enjoy the fruits, it is hard to say to what extent the consequences that flowed from this far-reaching measure, once the struggle had died down, served later on to create the industrial and commercial prosperity of Mexico in the closing years of the last century and the first decade of this.

3

The Constituent Congress, called by Comonfort, enacted the Constitution of 1857, which ratified the formulas of liberal federalism and sanctioned the declaration as to the rights of man.

Valentin Gomez Farias takes the oath to uphold the Constitution.

The Constitution of 1857 is throughout a declaration of principles that were in its time looked upon as advanced and bold. But a writ-

ten Constitution could not alter the actual organization to the country, and the conservative party, counting more than ever on the support of Santa Anna's army and of the clergy, incensed at the proceedings of the liberals, continued to foster revolt.

The Constitution, and the attitude of the most prominent members of the Congress, and of the intellectual element of the new régime, had perforce to clash with a cultured and conservative minority, used to managing public opinion.

Military opposition was overcome at Puebla and San Luis Potosí, but the opposition persisted in its work, from the pulpit, in plots and conspiracies, secret propaganda and preparations for fresh uprisings.

Ignacio Ramirez.

4

But on this occasion the old culture, as represented by the most select members of the conservative group, was faced by a new culture, that had not come from Universities of colonial type nor from theological seminaries. It was a disordered and incomplete culture, full or romantic illusions, but also abounding in strength. It had not been formed in the ancient University, but in provincial Institutes, which were the ones that molded the intellectual and ruling element of Reform. Its outstanding representatives were Ignacio Ramirez, Altamirano, Riva Palacio and Vallarta. Its poet was Guillermo Prieto.

Melchor Ocampo.

5

The intelligentsia of 1857 undoubtedly were richer in enthusiasm than in knowledge and experience, but they did not, when they clashed with the former rulers of Mexican society, allow themselves be crushed as on previous occasions. The times were more favorable, and good fortune endowed them with an aggregation of men that rose above

their environment, due to strong will, ability and honesty. They boasted no great military leaders, for though Degollado was brave and a clever organizer, he was invariably defeated. Gonzalez Ortega was a soldier by good fortune and intuition. But on the other hand, the liberals found their best representative in Juarez.

Ignacio M. Altamirano.

6

Just as Hidalgo and Morelos, being the first and greatest, represented the liberating movement of 1810, and Guerrero stood for consummation of independence; just as Iturbide stands for the transition between the colonial period and that of independence; just as Santa Anna is the outstanding figure of the alternating periods of military dictatorship and anarchy that went on until the middle of the nineteenth century, so Juarez is Mexico's representative personality during the period of Reform, the Intervention and the Empire.

When **Comonfort** lost faith in his own cause and consented to compro-

mise with the conservative party, so as to render null and void, by

Vicente Riva Palacio.

means of the Plan of Tacubaya, all that had been achieved after a formidable struggle that had lasted for three years, one of the very few men who did not lose his firmness, persistence and calmness, was the President of the Supreme Court of Justice, Benito Juarez, entitled to succeed to the office of President, by provision and operation of law.

Guillermo Prieto.

7

Comonfort withdrew in discouragement and departed into exile, a defeated man. The Republic had two Presidents; Zuloaga in the Capital, supported by the Army and by the opinion of the ruling classes; Juarez, wherever he happened to be, followed by the greatest, most sincere and most loyal men of his party.

Defeat and poverty attended them. Their forces were annihilated at Salamanca, they were captured and very nearly executed at Guadalajara; fugitives and wanderers, the reformist leaders were on the point of falling for all time.

Juarez proceeded to Vera Cruz via Manzanillo and Panama, and on arrival firmly installed himself as a sort of wedge. Meanwhile, the ever defeated General Degollado, fought obstinately against Miramon, who had, unfortunately for himself and for his country, thrown in his lot with the foes of liberty.

The men of Reform.

8

Degollado got together an army despite disastrous defeats, and Juarez crowned his political work by legislating from his Vera Cruz stronghold. There he enacted the Reform Laws, which completed the work begun by Gomez Farias in 1833, and continued in 1856 and 1857, to achieve supremacy of the State over the Church. Degollado forged the tools of victory, which was consummated by Gónzalez Ortega at the battle of Calpulalpan, and Juarez consolidated the fruits of triumph, by carrying his revolutionary task farther still; he confirmed secularization, decreed the nationalization of church property and achieved separation of Church and State.

When the liberal troops at last, after their victory at Calpulalpan, occupied the capital, no one was better fitted than Juarez to take charge of the country's destinies, as danger still threatened.

The office of President of the Republic, in 1862, was still an honor with a terrible responsibility attached. Miramon had left the country, but there were yet in the field guerrilla leaders like Leonardo Marquez, Manuel Lozada, Cajiga and others who fought like wild beasts at bay. Melchor Ocampo was murdered. Degollado fell in an obscure encounter.

9

At this period of the Revolution of Reform the name of Juarez stands out in the first place. We have also mentioned Ocampo, Ignacio Ramirez and Degollado.

And after mentioning Degollado, we should also say something about Leandro Valle.

Leandro Valle, killed at the age of twenty eight, was an elder brother of the Chapultepec cadets.

In the confused march of Mexican politics during almost the whole of the last century, it is almost a marvel to have lived a glorious career without ever having left the straight and narrow path and always beneath the same flag. A lawful son of the Military College, a second lieutenant at the age of fourteen, when his country was invaded in 1847, he at once volunteered for active service and defended the post entrusted to him against the uprising of the "polkos." He served through the war with the United States and when it was over resumed his studies, to be at last rewarded with the rank of Lieutenant of Engineers. He brilliantly aided the Revolution of Ayutla and specially distinguished himself at the siege of Puebla in 1868; he went to Europe to perfect himself in the study of his career.

10

When Comonfort allowed himself to be dragged into the coup d'état, Captain Leandro Valle at once decided to uphold the cause of Reform, and in the company of his own father, joined the liberal army, and in the fighting at Salamanca qualified for promotion to the rank of Lieutenant-Colonel.

From that time on, until the battle of Calpulalpan was fought, in which Leandro Valle took part as Quarter-master General, he was in the liberal army a soldier without fear and without reproach. He personally took a fort at Guadalajara and Degollado promoted him to the rank of colonel; he took part in the fierce fighting in the Valley of Mexico, where the Reform troops came very close to victory, and made their way almost right up to the Capital, and was promoted to Brigadier General. When the victorious troops finally did enter the City of Mexico, there was no military leader more popular or more applauded, after Gonzalez Ortega and Degollado.

11

Leandro Valle.

He left on an expedition to punish Melchor Ocampo's murderers. Surrounded by bandits commanded by Leonardo Marquez, the "Tiger of Tacubaya," he insisted on fighting like a soldier by profession and training. He drew up his scanty troops, first in a square and then in triangular formation, and finally attempted to retreat as calmly as if he had been in command of a training squad.

Overwhelmed by weight of numbers, he was taken prisoner and prepared for death. He wrote a few last letters with boyish frankness, bidding his parents good-bye, and became indignant because he was to be shot in the back, he who had ever served the cause of freedom. And finally he threw his arms round a tree to await death, and was found with a faint smile on his mutilated face.

X

THE FRENCH INTERVENTION AND THE ARCHDUKE MAXIMILIAN

1

Juarez strengthened his political situation by means of an election, but felt that his government was menaced by internal revolt, and more than anything by the penury of the Treasury. The foreign debt had been swollen by accrued interest, indemnities, claims for funds confiscated, credits of money-lenders and merchants who supplied arms, ammunition and uniforms, and the claims of France, England and Spain.

Payment of the Public Debt had to be suspended, and as the American Civil War had paralyzed the effects of the Monroe Doctrine, it was in Europe deemed expedient to revive attempts at monarchy in Mexico.

England wished to collect, Spain also wished to collect and to seat a Bourbon on the Mexican throne. France likewise desired to collect, and to instal a monarch to the taste of Napoleon III, of the Empress Eugénie and of court favorites. England and Spain withdrew from the adventure in good time, and Napoleon III was left by himself to force Maximilian, Archduke of Austria, on to the throne.

French intervention in Mexico had the character of a military and political adventure, undertaken by the Emperor of the French, Napoleon III, though he had not at his disposal, fortunately for Mexico, sufficient elements for a war of conquest.

2

England had espoused claims for debts and sought commercial advantages. Spain's pretensions were a medley of attempts at re-conquest and protection to Mexican conservatives.

Napoleon attempted to assist the Confederacy, in the Civil War of the United States; he wished to embark on a military expedition that would achieve for him glory in his own country, in order to check and divert the attention of the French people; he wished to make a political combination to attack Austrian influence in Italy and to bestow a throne upon the Archduke Maximilian of Austria. There were also at work influences of courtiers and merchants, the ambition to extend France's power by possible colonies in Sonora and the intention of creating in Mexico a field for expansion of French trade and industry.

All this complicated web of intentions was founded on premises that proved to be false. It was believed that Mexico would welcome the invaders, to put an end to the disturbances inherent in civil war, and that the wealth for which our country was famous would more than repay the expenses of the war and the maintenance of an Empire with a court composed of Frenchmen, Austrians and Belgians.

It was hoped swiftly to subdue the Republic of Mexico, in alliance with the conservatives, to crush the liberals, and at the same time to threaten the Federals of the Northern United States, by lending assistance to the slave-holding confederates of the South.

3

But all these hopes failed, one by one. The military expedition did not prove to be a pleasure trip, nor did it succeed in occupying the country with the desired rapidity. England withdrew from the adventure, because it did not suit her to be mixed up in an enterprise fraught with danger, when her commercial claims could be satisfied at much less trouble to herself. Spain's designs could not be carried out without clashing with French plans, so that she also withdrew.

4

The invaders counted on the assistance of the leaders of the conservative party—military officers, politicians and churchmen—but not with the sympathy, nor even the resignation of a people supposed to have been bled white, to be worn out and lacking in means to put up a fight. After diplomatic negotiations in which a stain was put upon France's honor by her representatives, who failed to keep their promises and their word, the invading troops from France sustained a defeat of far-reaching consequences.

5

To Mexico, the war of French intervention is symbolized by the battle of May 5, 1862. The military exploit in itself was not of such very great importance, if one takes into account the number of men engaged and the immediate results. But to us its moral significance was enormous. On the 5th May the French troops appeared before Puebla, and the Mexican Army, commanded by General Ignacio Zaragoza, repulsed them with heavy losses, after three fierce attacks. General Zaragoza reported to President Juarez as follows:

"The national arms have covered themselves with glory. The French troops behaved with courage and their commander blunderingly."

6

Napoleon III found himself compelled to send out more troops and better commanders. The invading army eventually occupied the most important cities in the country. But the Mexican troops were yet destined to live glorious days in the siege of Puebla, which only surrendered after a valiant and vigorous defense. More effective still was the work of guerrilla troops, and the steady opposition of the great mass of the people. The French were never able to control more than the ground under their feet, speaking literally. Their thirty thousand men could not cover the whole country, and the natural defenses of the latter, its mountains, climate, deserts and enormous area, supplemented the work of the liberal Government's soldiers.

Battle of the 5th of May.

7

This being so, the Archduke Maximilian was never able to establish his Empire on a firm foundation. The conservatives helped him enthusiastically at the start, but much less so later on, because the Archduke, as Emperor of Mexico, attempted to follow a conciliatory and moderate policy, without allowing the clergy to control him in a reactionary sense, nor repealing the Reform Laws.

Through this policy of compromise, Maximilian forfeited considerable conservative support, without gaining that of the liberals, who mostly stood firm on the side of Juarez' Government, despite the fact that he was compelled to withdraw to the northern border.

But above all, neither the Emperor of the French nor Maximilian realized the economic advantages they had hoped for. Mexico's wealth, undeveloped due to lack of industrial resources and internal disturban-ces, could not be made to pay the expenses of the expedition, nor afford profits to speculators, nor support the Imperial Government on the lavish scale of a European Court.

The other combination, consisting in a possible alliance with the American Slave States, also fell through, because the Civil War was won by the Northern or abolitionist States. The American Union thus came out stronger than ever, with an available surplus of arms and ammunition. American interests were contrary to Maximilian's Empire which they looked upon as European interference in America, while they considered that the schemes of Napoleon III, aimed at blocking American expansion.

8

Lastly, political complications in Europe itself, the weight of liberal opinion in France contrary to Napoleon's Government and the menace of Germany, strengthening her military power, made Napoleon order the withdrawal of his troops, and leave Maximilian without any support other than his Austrian and Belgian soldiers and the military forces of the conservative and clerical party.

That same support kept on diminishing, because the so-called Emperor of Mexico did not show sufficient capacity for the situation in which he was placed. Maximilian was merely an ornamental figure, lacking in firmness of character, wavering, insincere and entirely out of his element in an aggressive and turbulent American country, with enormous problems of a racial and geographical nature. The Empress Carlotta, his consort, exercised undue influence over the Archduke's will, and insisted on pursuing the adventure to the end. She herself went to Europe to pray and demand of the Emperor Napoleon that he continue to assist Maximilian, but she failed and lost her reason on the trip.

9

Maximilian was left more than ever alone in Mexico. He continued his hesitating policy, while the liberal armies gained in strength and oc-cupied all the cities as they were evacuated by the French troops. The unfortunate Emperor was unable to hold out in the City of Mexico and with the best troops at his command, he shut himself up in Queretaro, where he hoped to be able to resist, while the so-called Lieutenant of the Empire, the sanguinary Leonardo Marquez, took over the command in the Capital.

The Archduke Maximilian.

But the Republican General Porfirio Diaz defeated Marquez at Puebla and even invested that imperialist officer in the City of Mexico, while General Escobedo besieged Maximilian at Queretaro. The Archduke was acompanied by two Mexican generals, Miguel Miramon and Tomas Mejia, who staid with him to the very end and behaved with courage and loyalty.

Finally the defenders of Queretaro were no longer able to resist and the town fell into the hands of the soldiers of the Republic. Maximilian, Miramon and Mejia were tried by Court-Martial and sentenced to death. Despite petitions of foreign Governments, the United States included, Juarez Government remained steadfast, and the Archduke was executed, with his two generals.

10

We should, from a study of the period just outlined, learn two important lessons. The first is closely connected with one of the problems which our country has had to face, due to the fatality of its geographical situation, and from its very first steps as an independent nation: our relations with the United States.

French Intervention and the American Civil War developed along parallel lines. The apparently generous intention of the Emperor of the French, which served as an instrument for other and darker schemes, was that of checking and combating Anglo-Saxon expansion in America.

The action of England and France, and afterwards of the Emperor of the French only, was directed at Mexico as a preliminary victim, and with a desire to protect if tutelage were admitted; but it was also aimed at the American Union.

If Mexico had offered no resistance, the slave-holding States of the South would have recived open and timely French support; when General Zaragoza triumphed at Puebla on May 5, 1862, he remotely contributed to Abraham Lincoln's victory over the advocates of slavery.

If at the end of the war of French Intervention, the United States did give some help to our country, out of natural interest, in the defense of its own institutions and of plans of expansion, that assistance had been paid for in advance, not only by diplomatic notes and good intentions, but with blood and honor.

11

The second lesson is a more direct one. During the war of Intervention Juarez was the outward and visible head of nationality menaced by extinction. His name was joined to that of Zaragoza in Puebla, and to that of Escobedo at Queretaro.

Invaders and imperialists caught us, as so often before, disunited, torn by civil war, the public weal and spirit at a low ebb; and only a faith as deep as that of Juarez could have faced the challenge of adversity. He resisted the dangers to which he was subjected, from the landing of the French troops at Vera Cruz, until the "Novara" frigate bore away the body of the Archduke executed at Queretaro. And final and decisive victory may only, in addition to outside factors that brought pressure to bear, such as the policy of the United States and the German menace, be ascribed to the united front presented by the liberal elements within the Republic.

The name of Juarez has the honor of heading the roll of honor whereon are written other names, Zaragoza, Gonzalez Ortega, Porfirio Diaz, Escobedo, Negrete and the serried ranks of humble heroes, Lancers of Oaxaca, Chasseurs of Morelia, San Luis Riflemen, Puebla National Guards, Acultzingo irregulars, nameless and fearless guerrilla fighters, Indians from the eastern sierras, Mixtec cavalrymen, officers from the Border, infantry from the heart of the country, all the cannon fodder recruited among the proletarian masses and led by the leaders of liberal Revolution.

XI

RESTORATION OF THE REPUBLIC

1

The liberals again occupied the capital of the Republic in triumph and the Government of Benito Juarez once more took up the slow work of reorganization, by proclaiming the constitutional amendments of 1857 and the radical Reform Laws; it again faced the economic problem and endeavored to suppress the remnants of reaction, still very tenacious.

Santa Anna made one last effort to return to power, but his star had by then definitely set and his attempt at rebellion failed. Pronunciamentos were, one by one, defeated and conspiracies nipped in the bud.

Industrial progress came to the country gradually, in the form of the railway to Vera Cruz, a plan postponed for many years; attempts at reorganization of public education, the enactment of new civil laws, tranquillity of people's minds by amnesty and restoration of political federal institutions.

2

After the restoration of Juarez' Government, the country continued, notwithstanding, to tread the old path of political disturbance and economic destitution. The serious damage caused by an uninterrupted series of civil wars and foreign invasions, and by the unbalance inherent in a crisis of social, industrial and spiritual transformation of the world, in Mexico realized in the midst of great obstacles and complications, could not all at once be remedied.

The introduction of new methods of production, with increasingly efficient machinery, for mining, agriculture and transports, and the investment of capital, with new commercial, banking and financial methods to facilitate the movement of money and credit, had taken place very slowly and tardily in Mexico.

Due to natural obstacles and internal disturbances, and also to rivalries and excessive greed of foreign Governments, manufacturers and traders, the country ceased to be a field for exploitation of the colonial type and became a restless and dangerous market, of extractive industries and speculative adventure, It was, above all, very difficult to take over the sierras, the lines of railway that were to replace slow and heavy stage coaches, wagons and mule trains.

3

Immigration was but scanty due to the unhealthiness of a great part of Mexico's territory and difficulties of communication. Wars of invasion or interventionist combinations in favor of one party or another had made contact with other races and cultures harder, due to rancor and differences of language, religion and habits.

Foreign capital and commerce were unable to find sound investments that would enable persons and interests to become firmly settled, but only the inducement of quick profits, usurious loans, smuggling and speculative ventures.

All this retarded the benefits of social and industrial reform. It is true that the legislative rules that had served as a slogan in the civil wars for emancipation and reform were consolidated, but modification of the written law was not in itself sufficient.

4

Besides, the political program of reform, which was not only radical enough, but exceedingly so, for the beginning of the century, had ceased to be in accord with the transformations of new world ideology or the needs of the country.

The existence of the Federal Constitution as the supreme law was assured, with all its accompaniments of separation of Church and State, secularization and nationalization of Church property and suppression of the privileges of the clergy.

But agriculture continued to be weighed down by the age-old defects of backward methods, poor communications and faulty distribution of property, great estates and the truck system. In the heat of warfare, to assail agrarian Indian corporations, and to combat the accumulation of collective property by the clergy, the collective property of village common lands and communities was attacked. The old slaves and serfs continued to be oppressed by peonage.

Exalted individualism, the romantic forms of jacobin politics and confidence in the formulas of liberty and equality, did not allow the realities of the social and economic problem to become visible; unbalance among the various classes continued; a situation exacerbated by penury and want of proportion between needs and resources; the burden of the foreign public debt and the pressure of alien expansive forces that continued to push against frontiers to open up markets and spheres of influence.

5

Benito Juarez might have continued to direct the onward march of the country during the work of reconstruction. But the rise of new political personalities, destined to profit by the changed conditions, was beginning. The greatness and the ambition of Benito Juarez had to be limited to serving the country in its hour of need. Other men were to rise as the representatives of a period of peace and material progress, and the work of reformative education was to be continued along different paths, with difficulty begun by the foundation of the Preparatory School and the courses of study planned by Gabino Barreda.

When Juarez succeeded in having himself re-elected in 1871, his adversaries in the election were Sebastian Lerdo de Tejada and General Porfirio Diaz.

6

General Porfirio Diaz aspired to the office of President, and when he lost the election attempted to resort to the usual procedure, by revolting and proclaiming the *Plan de la Noria*. But this first attempt ended in failure.

Death removed Juarez from the presidency and Sebastian Lerdo de Tejada succeeded him in office, Mexico had not, since the days of Gomez Pedraza, been ruled by a President of such great mental attainments; clever, distinguished, a great orator, a great student, polished and well educated.

Lerdo de Tejada wanted to go on being President, and after holding office provisionally, to remain at his post by popular election.

General Diaz had, on the other hand, his military prestige, having served honorably in the front rank, in the War of Reform and against Intervention and the Empire; he had the reputation of being a good administrator; an advocate of civilization, railways, foreign capital, colonization, authority, conciliation and order. He was a man of action and promised the reign of peace and order.

General Porfirio Diaz.

The fundamental difference between Lerdo's policy and that of Diaz, lay in their attitude towards foreign capital. Lerdo feared the expansive force of American capital, as though he foresaw danger in railroad tracks.

The nation was terribly tired and worn out; the drive of European and American industrialism sought new fields of action; railways, electricity, the cyanide process for the reduction of metals, pneumatic air drills and dynamite in mines, brought about a revolution in methods of work.

Economic reform as effected by the liberals, which Maximilian's Empire had neither been able nor desired to check, had stimulated the public wealth, by clearing away obstacles in the way of progress, consisting in property held in mortmain; now was the time to consolidate the nation's gains.

7

After Benito Juarez, General Diaz was presented by his followers as the Man for Mexico. By political stratagems and rebellious acts, Porfirio Diaz finally attained the longed-for Presidency.

The civil Government of Sebastian Lerdo de Tejada was overthrown, and General Manuel Gonzalez only filled the office to bridge the gap between two of Diaz' terms. The latter had in his rebel Plan of Tuxtepec upheld the principle of no re-election. But the Presidency once attained, for thirty years General Diaz ruled the country like a big boss; he made friends with the Church; he established relations with all the rulers of the earth, by protecting capital; he bettered the nation's finances by measures for orden and administrative moderation and the increase of public and private wealth. The population of the country augmented more rapidly than ever.

On the other hand, he suppressed the working of political life. The Constitution was merely a written word, and the whole of law was condensed in the President's words.

8

Under cover of material progress, a knowledge and manifestations of the arts were promoted, and future history, which will the better be able to judge, the farther it is removed from our generation, may perhaps some day mention as one of the greatest benefits of this time, the creation of a modern and progressive culture, which produced on the plains, the growth of a middle class, and on the summits, as a supreme manifestation of national life, personalities worthy to figure among the most famous men produced by Graeco-Latin civilization in the Americas. Mexico can, at the turn of the cen-

Justo Sierra.

Jesus Urueta.

tury, point with pride to the names of Justo Sierra, Amado Nervo, Manuel Jose Othon, Jacinto Pallares, Jesus Urueta and Salvador Diaz Miron.

According to another standard of judgment, more obvious from its practical significance, Mexico, in exchange for the loss of political liberties, was left with great material works of public utility, palatial buildings, railways, port works, the refunding of the public debt, the drainage of the Valley of Mexico, the paving and sanitation of her cities, works for water supply, lighting

Salvador Diaz Miron.

and electricity; Chapultepec Park; schools and libraries, the re-establishment of the National University, brought up to date.

9

But we must seek to penetrate to the bottom of reality. "It is a proven fact," said Francisco Bulnes, "that when the political work of a statesman does not survive him, it is a failure. General Diaz has displayed great respect for the outward form of institutions, and has wielded power with a minimum of terror and a maximum of benevolence. What the country wants is that General Diaz' successor shall be the law... The Nation desires political parties, institutions, laws actually enforced; it desires contests of ideas, interests and passions..."

What the Nation did want, more than anything, without knowing it, was a social revolution to adjust itself to industrial and economic upheaval.

From Ox Cart to Airplane.

PART FOUR
THE REVOLUTION

I

1

The slogans of the Diaz régime were: peace, order and progress. But this was only for the benefit of the privileged class, and almost entirely on the surface. Advances in education, railways, and culture generally, did not reach the immense majority of the population.

The ruling classes of past years, the clergy and the great landowners were favored by the so-called policy of conciliation. Instead of strengthening and continuing the work of Reform, a retrograde policy was pursued, and the Catholic clergy, and families owning great haciendas, money, credits, city real estate and revenues, to a great extent recovered their old position and their advantages. The Laws of Reform were in fact nullified, and were evaded with the benevolent consent of the Government.

On the other hand, laws that should have been repealed were enforced, the property of Indian communities having thus been wiped out. To the old privileged classes were added new groups of favorites, such as politicians and soldiers of fortune who were rewarded with governorships, concessions and favors, and built up provinces and feudal estates and were added to the number of great landowners with large revenues. Decided protection for foreign capitalists gave rise to yet another favored class, injuring the proletariat by a system of exploitation, which was aggravated by the circumstance that capital continued to be alien, while labor was never other than Mexican.

2

Even industrial progress itself was rendered of less use by its own defects and by the work of time. The increase in population, and the apparent increase of wealth, were due to the construction of railroads, and to improved methods of working mines. Machinery, which formerly it had not been possible to take up to the high table-lands of Mexico, evolved in accordance with the needs of industry; the investment of capital, the cyanide process for silver ores, and new means of transport rapidly increased the public revenues and benefited agriculture.

But just as colonial towns had been founded to serve the needs of mining, railways were laid out with the same end in view, and not so as to serve the national interests, but only those of the alien capital used on their construction. On such a foundation, the remainder of the structure could not but be lacking in soundness and permanence.

And more than anything, this progress and this culture did not reach the Indian population, nor the workers and humbler classes, and their actual salary, as expressed in corn and foodstuffs and the standards of living of a majority of Mexicans, did not show any real improvement. These fundamental facts could not but be aggravated as time went by, due to the increasing concentration of wealth in the hands of the few, and the disintegration of a Government that daily grew more antiquated both as regards its staff and its methods. That absolute and dictatorial Government, that had in the early days been tolerated, became ever more unbearable.

3

General Diaz' methods of government were copied in almost all the States of the Republic, on a smaller scale. Governors remained in office indefinitely; they rallied round them their relatives, friends and favorites, and protected the owners of great estates and foreign merchants. Constant endeavors were made to increase railways, telegraphs, and public works, while at the same time authority was applied in the form of the so-called iron hand, that is to say, unremitting and at times brutal repression of anything against order or the government. Such repression was during the Diaz régime a ground for irritation, the most notable examples, on account of their notorious injustice and serious results, having been outrages on the freedom of the press, by means of the suppression of newspapers and even the murder of journalists; the impressment of offenders into the army, criminals being placed in the company of minor offenders or victims of injust persecution, and lastly, the sanguinary throttling of early attemps at labor organization, which coincided with the first definite stirrings of the Revolution. The workers at the Orizaba cotton mills, who began to organize a union and to point the way to proletarian betterment, were attacked by force of arms, with loss of life and serious consequences in the way of excited public opinion.

4

To justify or offset the defects and the errors of the Diaz Government, two main conditions were, in its time, alleged in its behalf; first, that peace established at the cost of such great sacrifice was lasting and would continue indefinitely, as genuine progress fully achieved; and secondly, that the material advantages obtained were due to the direct and personal action of the Government.

Lapse of time has not established the truth of either of these conditions. Peace was destroyed by the effects of the system itself which got out of order as it was indefinitely prolonged, and became more antiquated and less efficient, by concentrating wealth and power and barring the way to evolution, to reform and to changes in proceedings, social doctrines and men. And experience, together with new methods of historical study, shows that the increase of the public wealth and of population and the growth of material resources, was due to improvements in systems of production, and to new industrial, transport and operating methods.

5

In order clearly to point out the features of this evolution, we should, rather than vague formulas of abstract principles or personalities of rulers, take the actual data relating to the transport industry, which lies at the bottom of production. So that we might say that the Diaz régime was typically the epoch of railways, which had been preceded by that of stage coaches and wagons; while this in turn had been preceded by the colonial era of mule trains and Indian carriers.

After the railroads came the automobile, truck and tractor, and after them the airplane.

Twentieth century machinery uses petroleum and its derivatives for motive power. New routes over land, air and sea are opened, by new methods employing electricity (cinema, radio, etc.), and the vital political technique of which is economic, scientific, artistic and philosophical.

All this marks a new cycle in the history of Mexico and of the world.

II

THE ECONOMIC ASPECT

1

The following examples reveal the actual and deep-seated causes of Revolution in its essentially economic aspect, by showing the want of balance between the forces of production and political forms.

According to reliable data, in colonial times and in good years a fanega (Spanish bushel) of corn sold for six reales ("bits,") which meant that one hectoliter was worth seventy five cents. As the Indian's wage was then twenty-five cents, his actual wage in corn was equal to thirty three and a third liters.

Round about 1910 the mean price of corn, if the year were good, and on the spot where grown, was three pesos and fifty cents per hectoliter. A majority of the peons earned thirty to thirty seven and a half cents for one day's work, which made their wage really eight liters and fifty seven hundredths of a liter.

Almost one fourth of what it was in colonial times.

2

Mexican mine operators exported large quantities of lead ores to be treated at the great American smelters. American mine operators producing lead succeeded in having a prohibitive duty placed en Mexican ores, which brought about the stoppage of several smelters fed by such ores.

American smelting enterprises realized that the completion of the railways from Tampico to San Luis Potosi and Monterrey enabled English or American coal to be taken to those cities at reasonable rates, and that they could open smelters under more favorable conditions, because the saving in freight enabled them to treat poorer grade ores than those usually exported to the United States.

So that in 1890 they applied for concessions, to build at Monterrey and San Luis Potosi, those great smelting works that contributed to the recovery of the silver mining industry, notwithstanding the heavy drop in the price of this metal.

Those concessions were granted in 1890. The concessionnaires in 1891 started construction of their great buildings, furnaces, offices and railroad branches. This explains the industrial progress of sections like the Monterrey district.

In the first year's working the smelters turned out over thirty five million pesos' worth of silver, and due to them the output of this metal rose from thirty nine million to seventy four million pesos.

3

By far the greatest part of Mexico's silver output was produced by very costly methods of amalgamation. Treatment of lead ores by fire is the cheapest and most scientific process, provided fuel be available.

A metallurgist had reasoned that if non-lead silver ores were artificially leaded by the addition of lead or lead carbonate, the same advantages would be obtained as in the case of treatment of natural lead ores. His process was successful and was applied in Mexico.

4

In 1891 the inventors of the cyanide process for reduction of low grade gold ores applied for a patent from the Mexican Government, and obtained it. Before that the annual output of gold from Mexico had not exceeded three million pesos; on the introduction of the new process production of the yellow metal gradually rose, until in 1906 it reached fifty million pesos.

5

Railroad construction, though it brought down the price of foreign coal, was not sufficiently extensive to stimulate copper mining operations in Mexico. When electric lighting for public and private purposes began to be extensively applied, the price of copper went up and development of non-paying deposits in Mexico became possible. Electric lighting all over the world called for large quantities of copper, which sent up the price of this metal considerably.

After that came another great development, the utilization of electric power from waterfalls, and its transport to great distance over copper wires, which caused a still greater demand for this metal, its price having risen until it allowed of the working of low grade deposits in Mexico.

6

The drop in the price of silver, mining operations at great depths due to exhaustion of upper levels and ever lower assays of ores as workings went down deeper, should have brought about the ruin of silver mining in Mexico and limited operations to small scale mining of gold, copper and lead ores, if the year 1893 had not witnessed improvements in technical methods that made gross production of precious and industrial metals rise from forty million pesos in that year, to one hundred and seventy millions in 1906.

7

Furthermore, in 1896 there was a rebellion against the Spanish power in the Philippine Islands, and the crop of Manila hemp, that competed with sisal from the Mexican State of Yucatan, suffered considerably, thus causing a tremendous rise in the value of the Yucatan fiber, which flooded the State with gold and doubled the proceeds from the Customs House at Progreso, and greatly contributed to the prosperity of the Federal revenues.

The spread of the use of rubber tires, first on carriages and then on automobiles, sent up the price of India-rubber and stimulated operations therein. Mexico, which had exported one million pesos' worth in 1893, exported as much as ten million pesos' worth in 1908.

The disparity between the growth of the population of the United States and that of its cattle industry, as far back as 1897 brought about a reduction of import duties on foreign cattle, and four Mexican cattle states, Chihuahua, Coahuila, Sonora and Tamaulipas, found a better market for their product.

Lastly, due to collective effort, social action and improved methods of production, exportation of Mexican goods went up up as follows:

1893 .... Pesos	84.000,000.00
1910 .... ,,	300.000,000.00

8

That great savant, Humboldt, with information supplied to him by the clergy in·regard to births, marriages and deaths, found that the Indian race was one of the most prolific of the world, in healthy climates.

By 1650 *encomiendas* or grants of Indians had in New Spain been abolished, the Indians were free men, living in villages, endowed with arable lands, which they could utilize individually.

After the massacres of the Conquest were over, and when the Colonial Government began to govern peacefully, without either civil or foreign wars, the total population of New Spain cannot have been less than two millions. Assuming that by the middle of the seventeenth century, in 1650, the population were only one million, its increase should, given the conditions of its physical environment, have been the following:

In 1650	1.000,000	inhabitants
In 1700	5.000,000	,,
In 1750	20.000,000	,,
In 1800	30.000,000	,,

Now, the population of the country in 1910 was about fifteen millions.

9

What were the decisive causes that kept back the increase of Mexico's population?

Humboldt said: These causes are small-pox, that cruel disease by the Indians called *matlazahuatl*, and more than anything, famine, the effects of which are deep-seated and lasting.

Nowdays we would say unhealthful conditions and starvation or malnutrition.

Among the causes of lack of foodstuffs are, firstly, the irregularity of the rains, which makes crops unreliable, and agriculture a speculative venture in which the life and future of a large population are at stake. The second reason is continued exhaustion of lands by widespread cultivation of a single cereal like maize.

From which it may be inferred that in order to prevent starvation in Mexico crops must be placed on a secure footing, which can only be done by means of irrigation works.

Irrigation of the country should have been the economic, scientific and fundamental work of the Diaz dictatorship, as it has been that of the Revolution. And round irrigation cluster all those problems connected with production and distribution of the staples required for the existence of the people.

III

THE REVOLUTION, ITS HISTORY, MEN AND PRINCIPLES

1

A study of the Revolution of 1910, from an historical standpoint, is by no means easy, for three main reasons:

I. It is a quite recent event, which is still unfolding divers phases of its evolution in our own day.

II. The men who took part in it, who started it, carried it through, resisted it or deflected it, not having yet entered the realm of history may not be finally judged, because they are too close to us, and the atmosphere in which they lived and moved is still agitated by heated passions and personal and political contests.

III.   And lastly, historical events due to their very recency, have
not yet been calmly studied, documents and testimony are not yet fully
known, and the time for dispassionate and ample judgment has not yet
come.

However, taking these limitations into account, the task of broadly
outlining the revolutionary movement of 1910, as an historical event,
should be undertaken.

2

Before going any further, we must point out its connection or direct
relation with all the previous events of Mexico's historical evolution,
and especially the similarity and affinity of the Revolution of 1910
with the revolutions of Independence and Reform.

We must likewise distinguish between the political or outward form
of the Revolution, that is, express declarations and written or concrete
formulas, revolutionary ideology and the actual substance of social
needs and impulses.

In the outward appearance itself of political forms, the transformation of ideology, which develops, grows and adapts itself to reality
and to the needs of new doctrines, must also be studied.

IV

MADERO

1

The Mexican people had changed in a sense contrary to the personal
conditions of its President, who seemed to have become a fixture. General Diaz, and all his governmental staff with him, grew old.

The nation needed other hands to guide its destinies.

General Diaz insisted on designating his heir, but Mexico desired
and hoped to complete material by political progress. The elimination
of General Bernardo Reyes and the nomination of Ramon Corral to
the Vice-Presidency of the Republic, were the immediate political antecedents of the new Revolution. Francisco I. Madero prepared the
minds of the people by an intense and bold electioneering campaign.
He was not the cause, because the true original motives lay much
deeper, but the danger signal.

On November 20, 1910, the Revolution began its military and political phase.

There was no lack of pioneers and martyrs: Camilo Arriaga, Enrique and Ricardo Flores Magon, Juan Sarabia, and nameless heroes, workers of Orizaba, miners of Cananea, peasants, railway workers. Closer up, Aquiles Serdan, at Puebla. After this, new ideas and proposals were little by little incorporated into the Plan of San Luis.

Round Madero rallied not only political rebels, but the champions of integral redemption, who advanced or expressed tendencies towards agrarian, labor or anti-capitalist socialism, that is to say, a rebellion of the proletariat.

Death of Aquiles Serdan.

The Revolutionaries of 1910.

3

The provisional presidency of Francisco L. de la Barra was merely a transition period, representative rather of the autocracy then declining, than of the democracy about to triumph.

Once in the presidency, in virtue of popular elections, Madero continued to rule as a revolutionary, and allowed himself to be carried along by his own inspiration and by the impulse acquired from the proletarian uprising. Francisco I. Madero was the spokesman of the exasperation of the oppressed populace; he had the prestige of his immense popularity; he was unfortunate as a statesman and passed into the realm of history anointed by betrayal and martyrdom.

4

In the early days the revolutionary movement as started by Francisco I. Madero purported to be an effort for democratic regeneration, to consummate the work of the Revolution for Reform and to enforce the provisions of the Constitution of 1857.

Outwardly, all that was desired was to establish the principle of popular suffrage and purify the electioneering system, by overthrowing the continuity of a personal and dictatorial régime.

The substance of the social movement was as it were latent and almost concealed in the promise to distribute lands contained in the Plan of San Luis. The success so swiftly achieved in the first stage of the revolution, was due to the disintegration and wearing out of the preceding régime, which had reached extreme senility as regards men, institutions and doctrines, and to the sudden upheaval of proletarian and popular forces that had lain dormant, but not extinguished nor satisfied.

5

These same factors made themselves felt in the Government that emanated from the Revolution. The fall of General Diaz and the rise to power of Francisco I. Madero, in compliance with legal and democratic forms, consisting in the resignation of General Diaz, the provisional Presidency of Francisco de la Barra and presidential elections won by Madero, are as the crowning and triumph of constitutional democracy in Mexico.

But at the same time they are an indication of a new political and social epoch.

6

Madero's Government was faced by the problem of its own impulse, carried to extremes by the more radical elements, who insisted on following the path of agrarian recovery (Vazquez Gomez, Molina Enriquez, Cabrera, Zapata), and by the resistance of conservative or reactionary elements. The outstanding representative of agrarian reform was the Chief of the Revolution in the South, Emiliano Zapata, who set down in the Plan of Ayala the proletarian basis of the distribution of land.

The reactionaries were at the beginning supported by the combinations of diplomacy and international policy, and although the Madero Government adopted a system of compromise and endeavored to avoid either radical extremes or open retrogression, it was unable to consolidate itself finally, or to open the way to socialistic reform by purely democratic methods. It was combated at one and the same time by the agrarians, socialists, and workers, and by the remains of the old régime and reactionary, clerical, conservative and aristocratic elements.

This hostility assisted the movement which at last brought about the fall of Madero, and which General Huerta attempted to direct into channels favorable to himself, by means of military sedition, *coups de main,* crime and violence. But far less could Huerta's Government satisfy the radical elements of the Revolution, nor the moderate liberals who upheld the political necessity of respecting the Constitution. The murder of Madero, lack of legality and capacity, and above all, the agitation of the Nation's spirit, which had penetrated down to the proletarian masses, caused Huerta to be overthrown by the growing force of the Revolution.

V

CARRANZA

1

This stage of the Revolution took the name of Constitutionalist and its outstanding political director was Venustiano Carranza. Military action was realized mainly by popular effort, with improvised armies recruited from the peasant and working classes.

Venustiano Carranza.

Francisco Villa and Emiliano Zapata headed campaigns marked by great destructive effects. Furthermore, Zapata, as a tenacious guerrilla fighter and rebel, succeeded in making distribution of land an actual fact. And in another sense, the military leader who succeeded at one and the same time in being a victor, organizer and politician, was General Alvaro Obregon.

The Revolution finally defeated the old régime in the military phase, when the Federal troops, under the Agreement of Teoloyucan, in August, 1914, were disbanded and dispersed.

2

The fight against Huerta gave rise to international difficulties, complicated by great capitalistic interests. The European War of 1914-

Emiliano Zapata.

1918 made the industrial and financial competition of big world business more acute. For the purpose of controlling oil fields and assuring sea communications, especially through the Panama Canal, vast manoeuvers of international politics were resorted to, more particularly between the United States, on the one side, and capitalistic Governments and companies of Europe, on the other. In this complicated interaction of interests and rivalries, Mexico's oil fields played a leading part, in the midst of financial and diplomatic manoeuvers, sales of arms, contracts for loans, concessions for working, etc. And things went so as far as an unjust and useless military intervention, consisting in the occupation of the Port of Vera Cruz, on April 21, 1914, by American forces. The defense of Vera Cruz, was brightened by the heroic acts of the Vera Cruz townspeople and the cadets of the Naval School, among them Jose Azueta and Virgilio Uribe, who fell gloriously.

Agrarian troops

Those who succumbed in the defense of Vera Cruz in 1914 take their place in history alongside the Boy Heroes of Chapultepec, of 1847.

3

Venustiano Carranza, as duly elected President, began to organize a government that would satisfy aspirations for social renovation.

The reactionary tendency was definitively controlled, and the anarchical tendency was also conquered.

In another line of activities, the government of Venustiano Carranza succeeded, at great cost, in introducing into Mexico the most advanced methods of modern science and industry, by installing workshop and schools of aviation and radio telegraph stations.

Nationalism served to awaken new currents of thought in the study of historical science, of archaeology and ethnology, and in artistic manifestations stimulated a tendency to seek inspiration in Indian and creole founts.

4

The driving force of the Revolution was no longer purely in defense of the cause of constitutionalism and democracy. Venustiano Carranza stood for an inheritance from Madero, but among other leaders and intellectual directors of the campaign, new tendencies of a deeper character had by then appeared, which were eventually crystallized in the Law of January 6, 1915, enacted at Vera Cruz, that clothed with the forms of law the Zapatista tendency to agrarian reform by means of grants of lands to peasants, and in articles 27, 28, 123 and 130 of the Constitution as amended at Queretaro. To the body of law of the democratic, individualistic, bourgeois and classically liberal system, was added a principle of socialistic reform, marking the appearance of a new ideology.

This may be condensed in the following fundamental points:

Portion of a mural by Diego Rivera, showing a number of contemporaries.

I. A general tendency to progressive reform in a revolutionary sense.

The remains of the old feudal classes and the wealthy middle class, on the strength of their social, political and economic privileges, lorded it over the proletarian classes. The principles of the Mexican Revolution sought to level up the working class or at least to better its condition. (Art. 123.)

II. The former economic régime upheld the principles of free industrial or commercial competition, with no limits other than private agreements between companies or firms.

The formula of transition was intervention by the State in economic production, and as a controlling, supervising and balancing agency (managed economy.) (Art. 28.)

III. The bourgeois system recognized private ownership of all property, without limitations and as an absolute and personal right. The Mexican constitutional system recognizes private property, but with limitations in the public interest and considering it as a social function; it endeavors to promote small holdings, small industries, the pro-

One of the New Farmers' Banks.

perty of Indian agrarian communities and cooperative forms of production and consumption, and the utilization of credit and technical methods for the cultivation of the soil (farming schools and banks, Art. 27.)

IV. The bourgeois régime did not permit the organization of labor organizations nor their taking part in the managing functions of industry. The Constitution recognized the standing of workers' organizations in the form of unions, grants to them a moderate intervention in production and works for community of interest between workers, peasants, and soldiers. (Art. 123.)

Other changes in the different sections of spiritual and material activity unfold along parallel lines, and cross and combine by exercising mutual influences, actions and reactions. The most notable, besides those above set down, are:

A tendency to complete separation of the Church and the State and curtailment of church action in educational functions. (Art. 130);

Emancipation of woman by making the bonds of family organization ampler and less rigorous;

Stricter State control over charities, education, and public health;

A struggle against clerical fanaticism and any remaining interference by the Roman Catholic Church in education, politics and ownership of property in mortmain;

And lastly, a strong nationalistic tendency, in the sense of promoting the development of a strictly Mexican culture, but connected with creole or Spanish-American, Iberian and European cultures, and with all those that have contributed to form the heritage of present-day humanity.

Adolfo de la Huerta.

5

The conflict between the divergent tendencies of the Revolution, and internal struggles for the consolidation of power, weakened Venustiano Carranza's Government and precipitated his downfall and death. The Presidency was occupied, *pro tempore*, by Adolfo de la Huerta, in order finally to transmit office to the group that had carried through the movement against Carranza, the leaders of which were Generals Alvaro Obregon and Plutarco Elias Calles.

VI

OBREGON AND CALLES

1

Government action, by that time, had to consist preferentially in reconstruction, along the following lines:

Consolidation of revolutionary conquests by means of labor and agrarian laws;

Administrative, educational, judicial and financial house cleaning;

Revision of antiquated laws;

Purification of the army by elimination of the elements less amenable to military discipline; transformation of the army into an organ recruited neither by compulsory service, nor gnawed by a mingled disregard of discipline and love of disorder;

Defense of national honor and integrity against foreign pressure, and, lastly;

Defense of economic integrity in the midst of a world-wide crisis and more especially in view of the depression in the mining industry;

Adaptation of revolutionary ideology to reality, by endeavoring to gather and concretely express principles and doctrines, and after that to write them into the laws;

And, lastly, their crystallization into political action, with the inevitable distortions, delays and violent efforts inseparable from the resistance offered by the medium, vested interests and compromises with or deviations due to militant politics and human shortcomings.

2

One must, to draw closer to reality, specially stress tendencies towards nationalism, Indianism and agrarian reform. Nationalism aims at promoting economic independence, protecting national industries and remedying that conflict that has so long existed between capital, mostly foreign, and labor, which is Mexican. Hence the extraordinary importance of the labor problem.

Indianism demonstrates the recognition of a fact, for a long time almost entirely overlooked, that is, that the great mass of the Indian population constitutes the main part of the culture maintained and upheld in the land of Mexico, and that contributions from outside cultures have not been fully incorporated into the culture of the Mexican land. This being so, the endeavor should be made, rather than to "incorporate the Indian into civilization," to "incorporate civilization into the Indian," that is to say, into the land itself.

As an immediate and practical realization of nationalism, there has always been found, avowedly or otherwise, the dominant note of labor and agrarian reform. The subject of the distribution of land had already been brought up, as far back as the Plan of San Luis. The agitation in favor of Francisco Madero, and afterwards that which arose under his government, at bottom meant a great drive of the peasant masses, due to aspirations of an agrarian character. The Zapatista movement was mainly agrarian. The triumph of Constitutionalism headed by Venustiano Carranza was hastened by promises of distribution of land and restoration of village common lands. Among the mandates of the Constitution of 1917, article 27, which deals with agrarian problems, and article 123 which is the basis of the whole of labor legislation, are looked upon as the most essential. The solution of the agrarian problem must mainly be credited to the Obregon-Calles period, and may perhaps be the secret of their political success.

This importance of the economic and social problem in the program of the Revolution is not in any way a matter of external or superficial policy, but is in response to the most urgent need.

Nationalism, laborism, Indianism and agrarian reform, are paths leading to the summit marked out since the origins of historical evolution in Mexico. It is that same situation of economic unbalance, lack of resources essential to existence, in the way of popular diet, means of subsistence, rations, salaries, clothing and housing. The same causes that provoked the disturbances registered in early history, in the colonial period, in the wars for independence and reform, reappear outwardly modified, but identical at bottom.

3

This is why in programs and efforts for achievement we find, besides the general principles of labor and agrarian reform, the following points aiming progressively at actual consummation:

I. To pass from theoretically equal rights, or equality on paper, to actual, that is, economic equality; and in the field of labor to begin with unionism, so as later to achieve socialization.

II. To establish actual equality as regards distribution of land, by means of increased salaries, restoration of village common lands, grants of land, laws on cultivation of land lying idle, taxation, subdivision of great estates or haciendas, creation of small holdings, and generally any provisions modifying the old system of exclusive individual property, so as to create property limited by the interests of society.

III. After improving the system of land tenure, to promote reclamation and utilization of the land itself, by making available water rights, farming implements, acquisition of agricultural knowledge, credits and financing, and all resources necessary for improved methods of cultivation.

IV. By combining intensive education of the masses with their economic betterment, to determine and achieve the essential points of an agrarian policy, as follows:

To free agriculture from absolute dependence on extractive industries like mining and petroleum, and to work for industrial independence of the country;

To reclaim new regions for cultivation, to extend irrigation systems, and

To foster communications in agricultural and industrial districts;

To advance the technics of agricultural production, in combination with industrial production and the commercial movement of the Republic.

To foster the cultivation of tropical products and the introduction of new crops and national industries.

To promote more especially such activities as cattle breeding, poultry farming, fisheries and such auxiliary industries as refrigeration, packing plants, fuel, electric and hydro-electric power, etc.

To work for health and sanitation of urban proletarian districts and farming communities, by combating more especially the diseases that affect the rural population, such as malaria, tuberculosis, etc., and professional diseases affecting workers.

And by all the above methods to labor efficiently for social transformation, by combating all forms of exploitation of the work of man, considered as a commodity, and class inequalities.

4

The transmission of office when General Obregon finished his term, and Calles took over the Presidency, and also the presidential campaign when Calles finished his term, did not take place altogether peacefully, Both before and after the elections, uprisings took place that were severely repressed by the Government. In these agitations, besides political action for ascent to power, there mingled the personal ambition of military men and politicians, remnants of banditry and in some cases passions wearing a religious apect. These latter movements meant a prolongation of the revolutions for In-

General Alvaro Obregon.

General Plutarco Elias Calles.

dependence and Reform in the effort of the State to throw off the connection formerly existing between it and the Church and to deprive the clergy of its economic and social power, based on accumulation of wealth and monopoly of education

According to the new forms of political activity, the State, ever stronger and more expansive, and the growing energies of new classes of society that contend for conquest of power, meet in their development with a number of obstacles left over from former structures, remains of feudalism, of retrograde fanaticism, of ariscracies and privileges, in alliance with bourgeois and capitalistic institutions. In these contests,

present-day active forces in their drive for expansion, attack every obstacle in their way and overthrow whatever comes first and is most
worn out by economic and political decline.

5

In any event, those elements that count on the support of the
peasant and working masses have succeeded in gaining the mastery

Transformation of the Army.

as also those in the best position to assure the Nation's individuality as an international entity. And tendencies towards reaction and anarchy have been overcome, although among them, unfortunately, there have at times been sincerely democratic aims.

We should point out as of greatest importance and decisive force at this time, the enormous and profound transformation of urban labor systems, and of ownership and exploitation of the land, by restoration and grants of village common lands, laws on idle lands, family homesteads, etc.

To this movement corresponds a great cultural effort, by reforming and extending education through revolutionary schools imbued with a new educational spirit.

Furthermore, the reforms introduced into the National Army, by creating an institution more modern and better equipped, morally and materially, may be looked upon as yet another element that ensured consolidation of the governments of the Obregon-Calles régime.

6

In the midst of all this agitation, with the additional complication of economic and financial problems of a world-wide character, due to the crisis involved by the European War and the disturbances and contradictions of imperialistic capitalism and proletarian disquiet, the integration of new economic forms on top of the complicated Mexican structure was continued.

During a new electioneering campaign, General Obregon was murdered by a Catholic fanatic, and General Calles, by then nearing the end of his presidential term, in his Message of September 1, 1928, drew up the bases of a new system of government, for the purpose of limiting dictatorial methods and substituting a government by institutions, for government by men exclusively. Political control and the dignity of Chief of the Revolution continued to be vested in General Calles, with modifications consisting in a presidential system and a State political party, which at the same time constitute limitations upon and amendments to the old procedure of theoretical democracy and actual dictatorship.

7

This system was consolidated during the provisional presidency of Licenciado Emilio Portes Gil, under whose government the agrarian policy of land distribution and strengthening of the peasant class was prosecuted with still greater intensity; an autonomous National University was established, the National Revolutionary Party was placed in active operation as a State institution; the rebellion provoked by the electioneering problem was put down, and also the religious conflict which seemed to have been settled by submission of the clergy to laws and regulations, and the task of putting into legal form the social conquests of the Revolution, especially by drafts of labor and

Licenciado Emilio Portes Gil.

agrarian laws and amendments to civil and criminal legislation, was continued.

8

After Pascual Ortiz Rubio became President, and on his resignation in september, 1933, General Abelardo L. Rodriguez was appointed Provisional President; he persevered in revolutionary policies and especially aimed at betterment of the working classes by means of legislation on minimum salaries. He was succeeded, on November 30, 1934, by General Lazaro Cardenas.

Pascual Ortiz Rubio, C. E.

General Abelardo L. Rodriguez.

As the basis of political and social reform, new industrial, agricultural and commercial methods, instruments and procedure should be studied. Automobiles, tractors, trucks, irrigation systems, highways, new construction materials and methods; progress in social medicine and sanitation, are also bringing about a revolution in methods of cultivation, clothing, traffic, diet, teaching, organization of the family, art and religion.

And so the country marches onward through the stages of the rise of new classes with their own ideology, directing groups, economy and spirit, and at the same time constantly working for reform and consolidation of political, social ,educational and economic institutions.

9

The program of General Lazaro Cardenas' Government is marked by the framing of a definite plan of political and administrative action, to be carried into effect during the six years of the presidential term.

This Six Year Plan includes the whole of the tendencies previously adopted by former revolutionary governments, in an advanced onward march, in a radical direction. It may be said that the Revolution continues its cycle of evolution, and advances at varying speeds along its different stages, as and when resistance or inertia, allow.

General Lazaro Cardenas.

VII

THE NEW IDEOLOGY

1

The ideas of a radical tendency in the Mexican Revolution may be stated as follows:

I. Civilization and culture are the result of the work of man to bring Nature under control.

II. Labor is the fundamental cause and the closest measure of the value of useful things.

III. The structure of society is based on the organization of labor, that is the technique of production.

IV. The main historical factor is class war.

Symbols of new Ideology. (Diego Rivera.)

V. Classes of society arise according to their position and functions in the organized work of economic production.

VI. The struggle or conflict is usually for control of means or instruments of production and utilization of surplus value, and is consequently directed against exploitation of man by man.

VII. Direct action in this struggle is aimed at all wealth withdrawn from circulation by concentration and absorption, such as property in mortmain held by religious corporations, owners of great states and exploiting capitalism.

2

By means of science and method we arrive at a rule of life, that is, its technics, the postulates of which may be condensed as follows:

1. Modern systems of production create relations of a capitalistic character, by evolving from the middle class world to higher capitalism. In this cycle the social classes engaged in conflict or contest, are on one side, the proletariat and the other the capitalistic bourgeoisie.

2. The fight or conflict for control of instruments of production chiefly centers round the land and machines, and especially round "machines for making machines," with all their appurtenances: (communicatons, fuel, raw materials, etc.)

This division by classes is chiefly disturbed by subdivisions into sub-classes and intermediate classes, or formless and unclassified mobs. And also by remnants of classes surviving from former structures. In our country, these factors of alteration and disturbance compel us to take into account two fundamental problems in the alignment of classes, and consequent tactics:

The need for nationalism, which shows itself by:

A defensive attitude to resist the pressure of other nationalisms and imperialistic capitalism.
A policy of seeking relations with countries whose historical, racial and social affinities are similar. (Spanish-Americanism.)
Tendency to preserve own culture rooted in the soil. (Indianism.)
Destruction of ancient race or class privileges.
These complications of nationalism, the defense of national interests and national culture, compel the adoption of special procedure in poli-

tical action, by limiting the international character of the Revolution, and by suiting it to the conditions of our own medium and our international complications.

Alignment of classes once recognized, the fundamental points of the program, according to the technics of the Revolution, are:

1. Insurgency of the proletarian classes seeking economic and actual equality.

2. Creation of a new State to realize progressive socialization of means of production.

But above all, as a supreme rule and objetive, this criterion or standard: Mexican reality. That is to say, the progress of the Revolution as rooted in the soil and opening out to the future.

Monument to the Revolution

BIBLIOGRAPHY

GENERAL HISTORY

HERRERA, A. DE. *Historia General de los Hechos de los Castellanos.*

CASAS, BARTOLOMÉ DE LAS. *Historia de las Indias.*

TORQUEMADA, J. DE. *Los Veintiún Libros Rituales y Monarquía Indiana.*

———*Anales de la Sociedad de Geografía y Estadística.*

———*Anales de la Sociedad Científica "Antonio Alʒate."*

———*Anales del Museo Nacional de México.*

ALAMÁN, LUCAS. *Disertaciones Sobre la Historia de la República Mexicana Hasta la Independencia.*

———*Historia de la Conquista de México.*

———*Historia de México Desde los Primeros Movimientos que Prepararon su Independencia.*

CAVO, ANDRÉS. *Los Tres Siglos de México.*

———*México y su Evolución Social.*

ZAMACOIS, NICETO DE. *Historia de México Desde sus Tiempos más Remotos.*

———*México a Través de los Siglos*, editada por Vicente Riva Palacio.

RABASA, EMILIO. *La Evolución Histórica de México.*

LEÓN, NICOLÁS. *Compendio de la Historia Mexicana.*

PÉREZ VERDÍA, LUIS. *Compendio de la Historia Mexicana.*

PEREYRA, CARLOS. *Obras.*

SIERRA, JUSTO. *Compendio de Historia de México. Obras.*

TORO, ALFONSO. *Historia de México.*

CHÁVEZ OROZCO, LUIS. *Obras.*

GENERAL HISTORY

Primitive Culture

HUMBOLDT, ALEJANDRO DE. *Ensayo Político Sobre la Nueva España.*

BANCROFT, H. H. *Recursos y Desarrollo de México.*

CHEVALIER, M. *México Antiguo y Moderno.*

FARNHAM, J. T. *México, su Geografía, su Pueblo, sus Instituciones.*

PRIESTLEY, I. H. *José de Gálvez, Visitor General of New Spain.*

OROZCO Y BERRA, MANUEL. *Apuntes para la Historia de la Geografía de México.*

BANDELIER, A. *Organización Social y Gobierno de los Antiguos Mexicanos.* (Peabody Museum, "Twelfth Annual Report," II Nº 3.)

BIART, L. *Los Aztecas, su Historia, sus Costumbres.* Boletín Núm. 28 de la Oficina de Etnología Americana.

CLAVIJERO, FRANCISCO JAVIER. *Historia de México.*

CASTILLO, BERNAL DÍAZ DEL. *Verdadera Historia de los Sucesos de la Conquista de la Nueva España.*

JOYCE, T. A. *Arqueología Mexicana.*

KINGSBOROUGH, G. H. *Mexican Antiquities.*

NUTTALL, ZELIA. *Los Principios Fundamentales de la Civilización en el Antiguo y en el Nuevo Mundo.*

De Acosta, J. *Historia Natural y Moral de las Indias.*

Boturini Benaducci, Lorenzo. *Idea de una Nueva Historia General de la América Septentrional.*

Brasseur de Bourbourg, E. C. *Historia de las Naciones Civilizadas de México y de la América Central.*

Durán, Diego. *Historia de las Indias de Nueva España.*

De Sahagún, Fray Bernardino. *Historia de las Cosas de Nueva España.*

Orozco y Berra, Manuel. *Historia Antigua de la Conquista de México.*

Genet, Jean. *Histoire des Peuples Shoshone-Azteques.*

Spinden, H. *Ancient Civilizations of Mexico.*

Mendizábal, Miguel O. de. Obras.

THE DISCOVERY

Columbus' Diary and Letters

Colón, Fernando. *Historia del Almirante.*

Ruge, Sophus. *La Epoca de los Descubrimientos Geográficos.* (Historia Universal, de Oncken. Tomo 19.)

Fernández de Navarrete, Martín. *Colección de Viajes y Descubrimientos que Hicieron los Españoles desde Fines del Siglo XV.*

Harrisse, Henry. *Cristobal Colón.*

Vignaud, Henry. *Estudios Críticos Sobre la Vida de Colón.*

Pereyra, Carlos. *La Conquista de las Rutas Oceánicas.*

Andre, Marius. *La Verídica Aventura de Cristobal Colón.*

THE CONQUEST

CORTÉS, HERNÁN. *Relaciones y Documentos.*

DÍAZ DEL CASTILLO, BERNAL. *Historia de la Conquista de México.*

DE AGUILAR, FRANCISCO. *Relación de la Conquista de México.*

DORANTES DE CARRANZA, BALTAZAR. *Sumaria Relación.*

LÓPEZ DE GOMARA, FRANCISCO. *Historia de las Conquistas de Hernán Cortés.*

PRESCOTT, W. H. *The Conquest of Mexico.*

SUÁREZ DE PERALTA, JUAN. *Noticias Históricas de la Nueva España.*

FERNÁNDEZ DEL CASTILLO, FRANCISCO. *Doña Catalina Juárez Marcayda.*

PEREYRA, CARLOS. *Hernán Cortés.*

TORO, ALFONSO. *Un Crimen de Hernán Cortés.*

TEJA ZABRE, ALFONSO. *Historia y Tragedia de Cuauhtemoc.*

THE COLONIAL REGIME

RIVERA, AGUSTÍN. *Principios Críticos Sobre el Virreinato de la Nueva España.*

MOTOLINÍA. *Historia de los Indios de la Nueva España.*

ALEGRE, F. J. *Historia de la Compañía de Jesús en Nueva España.*

MENDIETA, G. *Historia Eclesiástica Indiana.*

GONZÁLEZ OBREGÓN, LUIS. *México Viejo.*

ANTÚNEZ Y ACEVEDO. *Memorias Históricas Sobre la Legislación y Gobierno del Comercio de los Españoles.*

CLAVIJERO, F. J. *Historia de la Antigua o Baja California.*

García, Genaro. *Don Juan de Palafox y Mendoza.*

Navarrete, M. de. *Instroducción de la Relación del Viaje Hecho por las Goletas "Sutil" y "Mexicana."*

Solórzano Pereira, J. de. *Política Indiana.*

Sosa, Francisco. *El Episcopado Mexicano.*

Priestley, H. I. *The Coming of the White Man.*

Mariscal, Federico. *La Patria y la Arquitectura Nacional.*

Mariscal, Nicolás. *Monografías Mexicanas de Arte.*

Pimentel, Francisco. *Historia Crítica de la Literatura en México.*

González Peña, Carlos. *Historia de la Literatura Mexicana.*

Revilla, M. G. *El Arte en México en la Epoca Antigua y Durante el Gobierno Virreinal*

Romero de Terreros, Manuel. *Arte Colonial.*

Urbina, Luis G. *La Vida Literaria de México. Antología del Centenario.*

Acevedo, Jesús T. *Disertaciones de un Arquitecto.*

Tablada, José Juan. *El Arte en México.*

De Valle Arizpe, Artemio. *Virreyes y Virreinas.*

Zepeda, Tomás. *La Instrucción Pública en la Nueva España.*

INDEPENDENCE

Revillagigedo, Conde de. *Instrucción Reservada que dió a su Sucesor.*

Torres Quintero, G. *México Hacia el fin del Virreinato Español.*

García, Genaro. *El Plan de la Independencia de la Nueva España, en 1808.*

GONZÁLEZ OBREGÓN, LUIS. *Los Precursores de la Independencia.*

TERESA DE MIER, FRAY SERVANDO. *Historia de la Revolución de Nueva España.*

MORA, J. L. *México y sus Revoluciones.*

BUSTAMANTE, CARLOS MARÍA DE. *Cuadro Histórico de la Revolución Mexicana.*

FUENTES, J. M. *Apuntes y Documentos Sobre las Familias Hidalgo y Costilla.*

ZERECERO, A. *Memoria para la Historia de las Revoluciones en México.*

ARRANGOIZ, F. DE P. *México Desde 1808 Hasta 1867.*

ARRONIZ, MARCOS. *Biografía del Iniciador de la Independencia.*

ZÁRATE, JULIO. *Biografía de Morelos.*

TEJA ZABRE, ALFONSO. *Morelos, Caudillo de la Independencia.*

CHÁVEZ OROZCO, LUIS. *Sitio de Cuautla.*

RODRÍGUEZ, PELAGIO A. Y GARCÍA, RUBÉN. *Campañas de Morlos Sobre Acapulco (1810-1831.)*

AGUIRRE COLORADO, RAFAEL, GARCÍA, RUBÉN Y RODRÍGUEZ PELAGIO, A. *Ataque y Sitio de Cuautla.*

GUZMÁN, MARTÍN LUIS. *Mina el Mozo.*

BULNES, FRANCISCO. *La Guerra de Independencia, Hidalgo, Iturbide. Memorias de don Agustín de Iturbide.*

HELIODORO VALLE, RAFAEL. *Cómo era Iturbide.*

———*Correspondencia y Diario Militar de Iturbide.*

EARLY YEARS OF MEXICAN INDEPENDENCE

BOCANEGRA, J. M. *Memorias para la Historia de México Independiente.*

BULNES, FRANCISCO. *Las Grandes Mentiras de Nuestra Historia.*

IGLESIAS CALDERÓN, FERNANDO. *Tres Campañas Nacionales.*

PRIETO, GUILLERMO. *Memorias de mis Tiempos.*

SALADO ALVAREZ, VICTORIANO. *De Santa Anna a la Reforma.*

————*Vida Azarosa de don Carlos Bustamante.*

SECESSION OF TEXAS AND AMERICAN WAR

FILISOLA, VICENTE. *Memorias para la Historia de la Guerra de Tejas.*

PEREYRA, CARLOS. *Tejas, la Primera Desmembración de la República Mexicana.*

LÓPEZ DE SANTA ANNA, ANTONIO. *Manifiesto de sus Operaciones en la Campaña de Tejas.*

TORNEL, J. M. *México y los Estados Unidos.*

ALCARAZ, R. *Apuntes para la Historia de la Guerra Entre México y los Estados Unidos.*

BUSTAMANTE, CARLOS MARÍA DE. *El Nuevo Bernal Díaz del Castillo.*

————*Las Guerras de México con Tejas y los Estados Unidos.*—Edición Genaro García.

FERNANDO RAMÍREZ, JOSÉ. *México, Durante la Guerra con los Estados Unidos.*

ROA BÁRCENA, J. M. *Recuerdos de la Invasión Norteamericana.*

GRANT, ULYSSES. *Memories.*

REVOLUTION OF AYUTLA AND WAR OF REFORM
INTERVENTION AND EMPIRE

BULNES, FRANCISCO. *Juárez y las Revoluciones de Ayutla y de Reforma.*

GARCÍA, GENARO. *Los Gobiernos de Alvarez y Comonfort.*

————*La Revolución de Ayutla, Según el Archivo del General Doblado.*

CUEVAS, LUIS G. *El Porvenir de México.*

LAFRAGUA, J. M. *Historia de la Revolución de México Contra la Dictadura del General Santa Anna.*

BAZ, GUSTAVO. *Vida de Benito Juárez.*

GALINDO Y GALINDO, M. *La Gran Década Nacional.*

GARCÍA, GENARO. *Juárez, Refutación a Bulnes.*

IGLESIAS CALDERÓN, FERNANDO. *Las Supuestas Traiciones de Juárez.*

MOLINA ENRÍQUEZ, ANDRÉS. *La Reforma y Juárez.*

DE LA PORTILLA, ANSELMO. *México en 1856 y 1857.*

OCAMPO, MELCHOR. Obras completas.

RABASA, EMILIO. *La Organización Política de México.*

SIERRA, JUSTO. *Juárez, su Obra y su Tiempo.*

ZARCO, FRANCISCO. *Historia del Congreso Constituyente.*

DE ZAYAS ENRÍQUEZ, RAFAEL. *Benito Juárez, su Vida y su Obra.*

ZERECERO, A. *Biografía de Benito Juárez.* (En las Memorias para la Historia de las Revoluciones en México.)

PUIG CASAURANG, J. M. *Juárez, su Interpretación Humana.*

PÉREZ MARTÍNEZ, HÉCTOR. *Juárez el Impasible.*

INTERVENTION AND EMPIRE

BULNES, F. *El Verdadero Juárez y la Verdad Sobre la Intervención y el Imperio.*

SALADO ALVAREZ, V. *La Intervención y el Imperio.*

GAULOT, PAUL. *Sueño de Imperio.*

NIOX, G. *La Expedición de México.*

IGLESIAS CALDERÓN, FERNANDO. *Rectificaciones Históricas.*

———*El Egoísmo Norteamericano Durante la Intervención Francesa.*

———*La Traición de Maximiliano.*

SALM, SALM. *El Príncipe.* Diario.

———*La Princesa.* Diario.

BASCH, S. *Recuerdos de México.*

LUIS BLASIO, JOSE. *Recuerdos del Emperador Maximiliano.*

DÍAZ, PORFIRIO. *Memorias.*

THE DIAZ ERA

RIVA PALACIO, V. *Historia de la Administración de Lerdo de Tejada.*

GARCÍA GRANADOS, RICARDO. *Historia de México Desde la Restauración de la República en 1867, Hasta la Caída de Porfirio Díaz.*

VELASCO, EMILIO. *Planes de Tuxtepec y Palo Blanco.*

H. H. BANCROFT. *Biografía de Porfirio Díaz.*

HERNÁNDEZ, F. *Un Pueblo, un Siglo y un Hombre.*

B. CEBALLOS, CIRO. *Aurora y Ocaso.*

DE FORNARO, CARLO. *Díaz, Czar de México.*

CREELMAN, J. *Díaz, Master of Mexico.*

TURNER, J. K. *Barbarous Mexico.*

DÍAZ DUFOO, CARLOS. *Limantour.*

BEALS, CARLTON. *Porfirio Díaz.*

THE REVOLUTION OF 1910

AGUIRRE BERLANGA, MANUEL. *Revolución y Reforma.*
———*Génesis Legal de la Revolución Constitucionalista.*

ALVARADO, SALVADOR. *La Reconstrucción de México.*
———*Un Mensaje a los Pueblos de América.* México. Ballescá y Cía., Sucs. 1919.

BOJÓRQUEZ, JUAN DE DIOS. *Figuras de México. Calles.*

OBREGÓN. *Apuntes Biográficos,* Djed Bórquez.

BONILLA, MANUEL. *Diez Años de Guerra. Sinopsis de la Historia Verdadera de la Revolución Mexicana.*

BRECEDA, ALFREDO. *Don Venustiano Carranza. Rasgos Biográficos Escritos en 1912.*

CABRERA, LUIS. Obras.

CREELMAN, JAMES. *Díaz, Master of Mexico.*

DÍAZ DUFOO, CARLOS. *Limantour.*

ESTRADA, ROQUE. *La Revolución y Francisco I. Madero.*

FABELA, ISIDRO. *Los Estados Unidos Contra la Libertad.*

FLORES MAGÓN, RICARDO. *Epistolario Revolucionario e Intimo.*

FORNARO, CARLO DE. *México tal cual es.*

GAMIO, MANUEL. *Forjando Patria.*

GARCÍA GRANADOS, RICARDO. *Historia de México Desde la Restauración de la República en 1867, Hasta la Caída de Porfirio Díaz.*

GARCÍA NARANJO, NEMESIO. *Porfirio Díaz.*

GONZÁLEZ ROA, FERNANDO. *El Aspecto Agrario de la Revolución Mexicana.*

GRUENING, ERNEST. *Mexico and its Heritage.*

INMAN SAMUEL, GUY. *Church and State in Mexico.*

LARA PARDO, LUIS. *De Porfirio Díaz a Francisco Madero. La Sucesión Dictatorial de 1911.*

LOMBARDO TOLEDANO, VICENTE. *La Libertad Sindical en México. El Sentido Humanista de la Revolución Mexicana.*

LÓPEZ PORTILLO Y ROJAS, JOSÉ. *Elevación y Caída de Porfirio Díaz.*

MADERO, FRANCISCO I. *La Sucesión Presidencial en 1910.*

MANERO, ANTONIO. *El Antiguo Régimen y la Revolución.*

MANJARREZ, FROYLÁN C. *La Jornada Institucional.*

MÁRQUEZ STERLING, MANUEL. *Los Ultimos Días de Madero. (Mi Gestión Diplomática en México.)* Habana.

MENDIETA Y NÚÑEZ, LUCIO. *El Problema Agrario de México.*

MOLINA ENRÍQUEZ, ANDRÉS. *Los Grandes Problemas Nacionales.*

NEARING, SCOTT Y FREEMAN, JR. *Dollar Diplomacy.*

OBREGÓN, ALVARO. *Ocho Mil Kilómetros en Campaña.*

PALAVICINI, FÉLIX F. *El Primer Jefe.* Obras.

PANI, ALBERTO J. *La Política Hacendaria y la Revolución.*

PRIDA, RAMÓN. *De la Dictadura a la Anarquía.*

PUENTE, RAMÓN. *Pascual Orozco y la Revuelta de Chihuahua. Calles.*

RABASA, EMILIO. *La Evolución Histórica de México.*

REED, JOHN. *Insurgent Mexico.*

ROJAS, LUIS MANUEL. *La Culpa de Henry Lane Wilson en el Gran Desastre de México.*

TORO, ALFONSO. *La Iglesia y el Estado en México.*

VASCONCELOS, JOSÉ. Obras.